A REAL FOOTBALL LIFE

GRANT HOLT

MY AUTOBIOGRAPHY

twocan

© Norwich City Football Club 2019

ISBN: 978-1-912692-36-1

AUTHOR: Grant Holt with Daniel Brigham

FOREWORD: Jake Humphrey

PICTURES: Norwich City FC, Reuters, Grant Holt, Workington AFC.

CONTENTS

FOREWORD
BY JAKE HUMPHREY

You are going to love this book.

Whether you've picked it up because (like me), Grant Holt gave you some golden days in the famous green and yellow of Norwich City. Perhaps you support one of the 17 – yes, 17 – teams he played for! Or maybe you are intrigued by the rare mix of talent, determination, belief, and graft that takes someone from a non-league player and tyre-fitter, to the Premier League, banging in goal after goal along the way.

As a Norwich fan, it's the four years he spent with us that will live long in my memory. As a football presenter I've had some tough times being a Canary. Back when I was hosting *Final Score* on the BBC, I dreaded the producer saying, "OK, Jake, there has been a goal at Carrow Road... hand to the reporter." I was hosting that show back when goals at Carrow Road weren't usually being scored by us. More recently I was the host on BT Sport when Norwich lost 5-4 to a late, late Adam Lallana goal for Liverpool as we hurtled towards Premier League relegation. I literally had to pick myself up off the studio floor and be as impartial as possible, moments later.

However, I do have one glorious memory of doing my job while supporting my team. It was also one of Grant Holt's greatest days. Back in 2010 the BBC had the rights to show Championship games, and I was the host for the local derby against Ipswich that November.

The atmosphere that day was red hot... even hotter when Holty wiped out Jack Colback right at the start. It set the tone.

Ten minutes later. Holt, 1-0.

Back to 1-1, then Grant again, 2-1.

FOREWORD BY JAKE HUMPHREY

Moments later it was a foul on Grant that saw Damien Delaney sent off, and I was out of my seat waving the Ipswich player down the tunnel. Hardly professional, but even I was getting carried away.

Fifteen minutes from the end, a Holt hattrick, a 4-1 Norwich win. Ask any Norwich fan about Grant, and those goals against Ipswich are usually the first thing they mention.

He was a big character for the big occasions. A villain to our opponents, a hero for us. However, we all knew every other team would much rather have him in their corner, than ours.

Those were the very public, headline-grabbing, season-defining moments that Grant Holt offered us, but this book will reveal so much more.

From how his ankle nearly stopped him from ever pulling on the famous Norwich shirt (until he gave the manager and owners a very clear ultimatum), to how he was out with the weekend revellers in Norwich city centre the night before Paul Lambert's first home game, to how his teammate Adam Drury couldn't handle his drink (no shock there).

Above all else, however, this book will reveal Grant's modesty, his love of hard work, and his pride when he reflects on a career where he absolutely fulfilled his potential.

I'm proud to call Grant a friend, and now a colleague at BT Sport. I'm so pleased Norwich City have been smart enough to keep him involved at Colney. I just hope he gets through his wrestling career unscathed!

Grant, on behalf of us all, thanks for those great times you gave us and, without wanting to embarrass you, I want to end this foreword by making it clear what you mean to us. Take a look on the next page at a selection of messages I've gathered from my fellow Norwich fans, and remember, you are forever one of us.

Jake Humphrey, 2019.

'He played for the badge on the front of the shirt,
so we'd never forget the name on the back.'

Ashley Howell

'At our lowest ebb, a hero for the ages who led
a spellbinding surge 52 places up the divisions.'

Mick Dennis

'He was bought by the fans, and he's repaid the fans many
times over.'

Bryan Gunn

'He took us from one of our lowest lows to our highest
highs, all whilst looking like he should be repairing my car.'

Chris Sharman

'Thought he was the new groundsman.'

Paul McVeigh

'From the flatlands of Norfolk stood a mountain that no
team wanted to take on.'

DC Kim Taylor

'Legend is an overused word, but never is it more
applicable.'

Ibiza Jack

'He was a bastard to play against, but he was our bastard.'

Graham Morrell

PROLOGUE
LET ME INTRODUCE MYSELF

I am on the edge of the penalty area, facing the famous Kop at Anfield. I'd been on the pitch for three minutes, sent on to help Norwich City, 1-0 down, get back into the match against Kenny Dalglish's Liverpool. For almost an hour I'd been warming up at one of the most iconic football grounds in the world, itching to get out there.

With the game being broadcast in hundreds of countries, this is my chance, at the age of 30, to show the world what I can do.

Anthony Pilkington receives the ball wide right. He always whips balls into the box early, so I get on the move into the area. In the corner of my eye I spot the Liverpool 'keeper, Pepe Reina, coming out. I immediately know that's given me a chance. He's never getting there. With the ball hurtling into the box I tell myself: win the header, get it on target. The only thing that matters is the ball. Don't get in a grapple, don't get in a fight; just watch the white ball.

From the ninth tier of English football on some shocking waterlogged pitches, to the pristine surface at Anfield, it's what I always told myself: just watch the white ball. Don't worry about the defenders, just worry about the ball.

There's a space between the centre-back Jamie Carragher and the right-back Glen Johnson. England internationals, but it doesn't matter to me. I know I have the advantage because they're both static. It's a perfect cross, and I crash between Carragher and Johnson; Reina isn't close enough to it, and I win the header. Bang! As soon as I've connected I know it's in. Goal. In front of the Kop.

I run off, with 50,000 fans stunned. The beautiful sound of silencing a huge crowd. The first thing I think of is my father-in-law, who's in the stands. He's a Liverpool fan, and he's going to be properly pissed off. A kiss on my wrist, where my wife and daughters' names are tattooed; a knee slide. Pandemonium in the away end. Beautiful.

I'll never forget scoring at Anfield, like I'll never forget scoring at Stamford Bridge, the Emirates and the Etihad, or at home to Manchester United. For someone who never expected to play in the Premier League, it's a decent collection of goals to remember.

You play football for much more than just those memories, though. Approaching 40 years old, I often get asked why I still turn out in Sunday football. "You've scored at Anfield, why are you still bothering with non-league?" But I don't think people get that there's a very simple reason: I love football, and always have. I've been playing since I was five; it's all I've ever known. Whatever the level, whatever the age, the thrill of scoring doesn't change. If I score for a veterans team at the weekend, it's no different to scoring at Anfield. It's the same feeling. Honestly. It doesn't change if you're doing it in front of one person or 70,000 people.

As soon as I came off the bench at Anfield, the match became just like any other I'd played. It was 11 v 11; it could have been Sunday league, it could have been Northern Premier League, it could have been any tier in England. There were 50,000 people inside that stadium, but on the pitch it was just another game of football. Eleven blokes taking on another 11 blokes.

Throughout my whole career, although I was massively competitive and worked incredibly hard to prove myself, it was never about what league I was in. Football for me has always been about the whole culture of turning up to a match, of being around the smell of Deep Heat, of lads putting on knee bandages, others putting Vicks around their eyes; the special feeling you get before a big match at any level. The mix of nerves and anticipation; of being 90 minutes away from glory or failure.

It doesn't matter which league you're playing in, and how many people will be waiting for you when you walk out onto the pitch, the football dressing room doesn't change. The dressing room doesn't care who you are. Especially when it's me!

It's about the camaraderie and being among a group of people who are trying to achieve something as a team. That's what football is. Enjoying being among a bunch of mates sharing the same goal. Whether it's at a massive stadium or a local park is irrelevant: the grass is the same, the goals are the same, the markings are the same.

That's why I have no memorabilia up in my house. I never see the relevance of it. I've got shirts in the garage, and the trophies, but they're stored away in a box. They don't really mean anything to me. I know what I've done, what I've achieved and what I should have done better.

From the North East Counties League right up to the Premier League, via the Soccer League of Western Australia and the Singapore Premier League, through all four professional English leagues, with the likes of Norwich City, Nottingham Forest, Sheffield Wednesday, Barrow, Shrewsbury Town, Hibernian, Sengkang Marine and several other clubs, all of those memories – of celebrations, of heartbreak, of nights outs, of tin sheds, of multi-million pound stadiums – are up here in my head.

It wasn't a bad career, and it's one I'm proud of. I hope you enjoy my story.

CHAPTER 1

GETTING COMPETITIVE, HIKEY-DYKEY AND TIGER WOODS GOLF

1981-1992

I have always been competitive. Whatever it is – football, PlayStation, working in a factory, cooking, wrestling, you name it – I've always wanted to be the best at it.

With football, that ruthless streak started at a very young age. From as early as I can remember, I was always desperate to have the ball. Wherever the ball was, and whoever had it, I wanted it.

I got that streak from my dad, George. He played to a very good standard around Carlisle and in Cumbria, and me and my brother Steven would go to watch him. Whether it was sunny, freezing or tipping it down, we'd always go with him. Without knowing it at the time, going to his matches taught me a lot.

One of my earliest memories of him playing shows just how competitive he was. To this day I can clearly remember the ball coming down the line and a player from the opposition sprinting after it. My dad, a centre-half, darted across and smashed the bloke so hard in the tackle, and caught him just right, that the fella went flying over the barrier next to the pitch. Not into it, but over it. You don't forget things like that.

My dad would always come home with bruises and black eyes and dislocated shoulders, but he always loved it – and that influences you as a kid. He was just a real winner. My brother's the same, and even to this day neither of us wants to lose at two-touch. My mum, Jacqueline, and my sister, Rachael, are similar, too. The Holts are competitive people.

GETTING COMPETITIVE, HIKEY-DYKEY AND TIGER WOODS GOLF

My dad was definitely the most combative of us all, though. He hated losing so much that he once grounded my brother when Steven walked in on my dad about to take a winning putt on *Tiger Woods Golf* on the Sega Mega Drive. He messed up the putt and blamed Steven. Grounded him on the spot. Not only that, but my brother had a pal with him, Tony Roberts, and my dad grounded him too! But that's just the way my dad was – and he taught me that if I'm going to do something, then I have to put everything into doing it the very best I can. That's something that hasn't left me, and never will.

Even with something as routine as cooking, I've always wanted to win. Now, my mum's a great cook, all homemade, traditional, earthy food like shepherd's pie. Proper food. From an early age I always used to help her cook with my sister, and I remember when we were baking scones for the first time. They showed me the recipe, and I did my first-ever batch and stuck them in the oven.

While they were baking I went upstairs to my room. My mum always tells me that when I was up there they kept looking in the oven and became more and more mortified because the scones just kept getting bigger and bigger. They knew I would be gloating for the next two or three weeks about them. My mum says she was even close to opening the oven door to let all of the heat out. And let me tell you, those scones tasted great – the best you'll ever taste, and the biggest scones you'll ever see!

It just shows that when it becomes a competition something switches in my head. Even when it comes to playing a friendly five-a-side with pals. We all kick each other to bits!

My old Norwich City manager Paul Lambert always said I was the worst trainer he'd ever seen in his life, and the simple reason for that was I needed a competitive edge to be better. Some people detest it but I thrive on it – that focus, and that stress on you. It's a great motivation for me. Like my dad, I hate not winning.

I just never enjoyed the whole premise of training. My focus was always about the main event. It applies to anything: if I was asked to hit 100 tennis balls I'd be bored to death, but put me in a tennis match and I'll run around like a lunatic because I won't want to get beaten.

Maybe it's not wholly about the winning; it's also about being in combat against someone. I thrive off that.

I spoke to an actor who said that in their profession they have two heads: you're yourself one minute, but you learn to flip into your other head when you're a character. That's similar to me: when I walked into a football ground I was me, but as soon as the whistle went, it changed. My mindset changed. For example, with the wrestling that I do, I'll do the training but it won't look anything like it will in a fight because I can't replicate it: I can't go in and hit someone as I would in the ring. But once I'm actually in the fight, I wouldn't think twice about it. Boxers will tell you they don't spar to hurt, they spar to learn. But when it comes to a bout, they change. And that's always been me.

Of course it wasn't always competitive in our house. We weren't always trying to outdo each other. In fact, I had a brilliant childhood. It was a really happy time.

✳✳✳

I was born on April 12, 1981 in Harraby, Carlisle. Bucks Fizz had just won the Eurovision Song Contest for the UK with *Making Your Mind Up* (I quite like it, in case you were wondering. It's iconic, isn't it!), down south there were riots in Brixton, and Aston Villa were about to win their first Division One title in 71 years.

Harraby was a good place to grow up. It was an estate where everybody knew each other. In those days everyone played outside together and stayed in each other's houses. It had a really nice community feel and was really close-knit, and we all went to the same schools.

We had a lot of fun and they were good times.

Mum and Dad both worked full-time doing different shifts. Steven is three years older than me, and me and my sister Rachael, who is a year younger, got dragged around watching him play football. And then she'd be dragged around to watch my games too, so she had no choice but to like it!

My dad was originally a painter. He was going to sign as a professional for Workington AFC, a local side, when they were in the Football League in the mid-1970s. He was really young at the time and my mum fell pregnant with my brother and my dad decided that football wasn't the way forward to provide for the family, so he became a painter and decorator. After that he worked at Pirelli tyres until he passed away far too young in 2000.

My mum worked in a factory for a long time and then she started working at a nursing home. She left that and she's been at Tesco for a long time now – she loves to work and keep herself busy.

They both gave me a fantastic childhood. We weren't wealthy but we weren't skint. My dad worked all of the time to give us two holidays a year. That was his thing: to make sure the family always had two holidays. It might only have been a three-star hotel in Magaluf but it didn't matter. We didn't go to glamorous places but we always did things together, and any time we had off as a family was always spent well. Mum and Dad both worked hard to give us everything they could, and I'll always be massively grateful for that.

We had great Christmases, too. Mum would make a huge effort in the morning, and then do a big dinner. One of my favourite parts of the day was the way my dad showed us our presents: he'd make us walk downstairs from our rooms in the dark, and when we got to the bottom he'd tell us to walk backwards into the living room. Then he'd switch the light on, and we'd turn around to see our presents. He loved doing that.

There was nothing formal about Christmas Day. We didn't really watch the Queen's Speech, but we all loved watching sitcoms together, especially *Fawlty Towers* and *Only Fools And Horses*; they were the two favourites in the house. Us kids were basically allowed to do whatever we wanted on the day. If you got a new bike, you'd be allowed to go straight out and ride it. We were really lucky and nearly always got what we'd asked for – and it was usually football kit or boots.

The only thing I really wanted but never got was a motorbike. I wanted one from about the age of nine or 10 because I absolutely loved the BBC show *Kick Start*, which was all about motorcycle trials. Dad never let us have one, though – and he was probably right! We used to tear around on friends' motorbikes on the back fields, with mates on the back. Lads would go flying off the bike and end up with bruises all of the time, but it never happened to me, which was fortunate as I'd have been in real trouble. One day I'd like to get myself a motorbike, though, and I've always fancied a Harley.

I was adventurous as a kid, and you could get away with going around everywhere in such a close-knit community. Me and my pals would spend our time in the parks, climbing trees and not being worried about people moaning if you were making a bit of noise when playing outside.

Obviously in the '80s there were no phones, and families had one car between them if they were lucky. It meant you didn't have to worry about cars on streets so much, or your parents always calling or texting to check up on you, so you could do what you wanted. Everyone knew each other so you had to avoid getting into trouble because someone would have told your mum and dad – everything would always somehow manage to get back to them. Or, even worse, the local bobby would catch you doing something naughty and he'd stick your name in his black book.

On those rare occasions we weren't kicking a ball about we'd be playing hikey-dykey. If you're not familiar with hikey-dykey, it's a game where you jump over people's fences or hedges. The name literally comes from hiking over a dyke. I think it must be a Carlisle thing, because no one else has ever heard of it. I was all right at it because I was quick back in the day. I was tall, too, which helped with jumping. All of that leaping over hedges probably helped me become good in the air when it came to football!

It's fair to say most of my childhood was spent with a football at my feet. It certainly seemed that way, anyway. The whole street would come out to play football where we lived. We'd play up against hedges and against the walls; we'd play here, there and everywhere. Now when I go back to my mum's you see 'No Ball Games' signs, which is a real shame. If I couldn't have kicked a ball around with my mates and my brother, would I have been a footballer? Maybe not. Playing on the streets is where I got the bug for it.

Football quickly became my life. Every weekend we'd go to the games with my dad, and then after matches we'd go to the working men's clubs and have a coke in there – I was only young then, so I wasn't quite on the pints! Mum did the housework on the weekend, and me and my brother followed Dad to the football. My sister then had to decide which of those two options was more desirable, and, funnily enough, it was usually the football.

Wherever my dad was playing, me and my brother would go and kick a ball on the sidelines. When you're involved in football from such a young age, and you're in and around the dressing room, you pick up the culture quickly and become a part of that world. When my dad went anywhere in town, he'd always get asked questions about the football at the weekend. That's what it was like around Carlisle: people would be known by the team they played for and the pub they went to afterwards. If you were in football in Carlisle you seemed to know everyone and were known by everyone. It was like an extended family, and it's still like that to this day.

My dad also loved watching football. He was a Leeds United supporter, which didn't rub off on me as I've always been a massive Carlisle fan. One of my earliest memories of Dad sat in front of the TV watching the footy was the 1990 World Cup semi-final when England lost to Germany on penalties. I was nine years old.

My dad was working nights at the time, but it got to 9pm and he was still at home, watching. Quarter-past nine... still there. Half nine and extra-time... still there. Dad was supposed to be at work, and he was never late. He hated people who were late. But that night he stayed at home for the penalty shoot-out. That's when I knew the significance of what football could do to people: that it made my dad not care about being over an hour late for work.

I'll never forget the time me and my brother sneaked out to play football in the local park when I was about 12, and suddenly we saw Dad coming along the field bawling at us. He was absolutely raging that we'd not asked him to play! He'd come out with his full gear and his boots, and he hammered me for not asking him. Then he hammered my brother, and then he even hammered two of my brother's friends who were with us! The first tackle he did, he sent my brother flying in the air – all to teach him a lesson. But he just loved playing so much, and that was really infectious.

Football was all I wanted to do. It was everything. I just wanted to become a professional footballer, and it was to the detriment of my schoolwork and education. I enjoyed school, but if there was a choice between doing some footy training or doing my homework, there was no argument.

CHAPTER 2

SMITHS CRISPS, WEMBLEY GLORY AND GETTING SCOUTED

1992

I was 11 when I got my first taste of football glory, captaining Inglewood Junior School.

The school entered the 1992 Smiths Crisps Cup, which was a knockout tournament that started locally in the early rounds before expanding nationally as the tournament went on, and ending in a final at Wembley. Obviously we never dreamed of getting there; it just doesn't go through your mind when you're that age. You're just glad to be kicking a ball about with your mates.

We nearly went out at the first hurdle. Our first match was against local Carlisle school Petteril Bank. We usually battered them but we were too cocky that day, and a pal of mine who played for them, Wayne, still says to me, "We should have put you out!" We managed to fluke a win, and we went on to another game in Carlisle which we won. That moved us on to the county-wide round, which was a tournament with other Cumbrian teams, and we won that too. We then played a tournament against teams from the North-West – including sides from Liverpool and Manchester – and ended up winning that. Win, win, win. The momentum just kept us going, and it was great fun, especially as we were the first team from Carlisle to ever get that far.

Winning the North-West tournament meant we got the ultimate prize: playing at Wembley.

We got the train down the day before the final with our teacher Alasdair Robertson and his assistant Dave Ruddick, who was also a friend of my family. We stayed in a hotel that night, and even though it was exciting being away from home with a group of mates, we must all have been taking it seriously because we went to bed early.

The next morning we did a little bit of training in a park near Wembley, and then we were off to the famous stadium.

✳ ✳ ✳

It was the first time I'd been to Wembley, and seeing the Twin Towers was amazing. They looked absolutely enormous. I walked out onto the pitch and stood in the centre circle at what is now the old Wembley, with the running track around it, taking it all in. It felt like the biggest place I'd ever been to.

We were drawn against the South-West winners, while the North-East winners played the South-East winners. There was this weird rule where if the match was goalless it was decided by which team had won the most corners. So every time the ball looked like it was going out for a corner you had everyone sliding in to put it out for a throw or to hack it away. Because every kid loves a good slide, it ended up causing carnage on the goal line!

Luckily Jonathan Ashurst managed to get a goal to put us through to the final, and we met Ixworth School from Bury St Edmunds in the final. Brett Swift scored to make it 1-0 and then I put us 2-0 up in the second half. You probably won't be surprised to hear my finish was a thumping header from a corner. Unbelievably, that turned out to be the winning goal. From almost 10,000 teams that had entered, we'd won the Smiths Crisps Cup!

What an incredible feeling that was. To win, and then to walk up the famous steps as captain to lift the trophy, was mind-blowing. The best thing was that I'd done it with a group of friends who I'd known since we were all five years old. We all got to meet the mayor of Carlisle and do interviews for the local papers, so it was a brilliant time.

I realised that to become a professional footballer, with the chance of repeating the feeling of winning at Wembley, would be phenomenal. I stood at the new Wembley 15 years later with Shrewsbury after we'd been beaten in a playoff final, thinking, 'I never want to feel like that again.' But as an 11-year-old, I was stood there thinking, 'I really want to lift another trophy.' It was a big moment for me.

A lot of credit has to be given to Alasdair Robertson and Dave Ruddick, who really believed in us and made us think we could do well. We had a good group of players. Paul Reid was bought by Rangers, Mark Boyd went to Newcastle United and Swifty had trials at a number of clubs. Terry Brown, Ben Blair, Ryan Tulip and Ashy were all good players, too.

Bizarrely, I was at Wembley again a week later because the school had booked a trip to London. It included a tour of Wembley and I remember two things: my dad moaning he had to pay for another bloody trip to Wembley, and me being able to tell everyone when we got to the ground that I'd scored there! I may have mentioned it once or twice...

Winning at Wembley also gave me my first taste of being scouted. A few weeks later Stoke City, who were in the third tier at the time, invited myself and Brett Swift down for a trial. It went well, and we got offered a second trial. There was a problem, however: it would clash with our County Cup Final. It was against Appleby, one of our big local rivals, and it was a really big deal for us.

So we took what a lot of people might think was an odd decision to turn our back on a trial at a professional football club to play in a schools' final. But at that age you just want to play football for the fun of it with your mates, and neither me nor Brett were pressured by our parents. Besides, my competitive streak was never going to let me miss out on winning the County Cup Final.

There was also another reason to turn down Stoke: we were both confident that our hometown club Carlisle were about to come calling. To us, they were a much bigger deal than Stoke, so we were happy to pin our hopes on our dream scenario.

CHAPTER 3

LANZAROTE CELEBRATIONS, TYRE-FITTING AND MEETING THE ONE

1992-1999

Growing up, all of my pals were Carlisle fans. I had posters of the players on my wall, and all of the shirts. I was a proper fan, and still am to this day.

I used to go to games at Brunton Park with my dad and we would go into the pen. Flask of coffee, sandwiches, crisps and a Brunton Pasty – a delicious pasty with meat and potato. We always got a programme too. That was our routine.

We'd drive to away games with friends. I remember doing Wigan at Springfield Park, sitting on the old bank there when there was no stand. I saw the big games at Carlisle as well, including seeing Liverpool in the third round of the FA Cup in 1989. John Barnes, Peter Beardsley, John Aldridge and Jan Mølby were all playing. Unbelievable.

Even now, Carlisle matches are the only ones I can go to and not watch as a coach. When you get into coaching, you analyse everything. Every little detail. But at Carlisle that goes out of the window. I'll be in the stands shouting and moaning at the players, even though I'm friends with a lot of them. I can't help myself. It's your own team, and they're the only side I can truly get passionate about.

People ask if I sit in the posh seats now, but believe me there are no prawn sandwiches at Carlisle. Not a chance. The prawn sandwich brigade equivalent in Carlisle is sitting down; if you're doing that then you're in the elite section! When I go there and I'm not working for the local radio,

I still like to sing the songs with the best of them. You never lose that feeling.

I loved the Carlisle team of the mid-1990s. They won the Third Division in 1995 and the Football League Trophy in 1997 and I had posters of the players, and books signed by them. I was heartbroken when we were beaten in the Auto Windscreens Shield final by Birmingham in 1995. We lost 1-0 to a golden goal, which was the first ever scored at Wembley. I was there in the stands, my first visit to Wembley for football since the Smiths Cup final, and I was heartbroken.

Having said that, I must admit I took the opportunity to remind everyone I'd scored there! My brother kept telling me, "Yeh, we've heard ya!" "Just down there, I scored there," I'd tell him, pointing. "I walked up those steps as a winner!"

I went to a do up in Carlisle a while back in support of Tony Hopper, who sadly died far too young in October 2018. He had played at Carlisle for 10 years, and the whole team from the mid-'90s era were there. I was sat at a table and happened to look over to the bar, and my mouth dropped. I nudged Ian Arnold, who was sat next to me. "Is that Rodney Thomas who's just walked in? *The* Rodney Thomas?"

I couldn't believe it. Rodney Thomas, walking into the same room I was in! He was great at Carlisle, and should have played at a much higher level. What a player. So I started singing "Walking in a Rodney Wonderland" and I put my drink down, got up and walked straight over to him.

"Hi, I'm Grant Holt."

"Are you joking, I know you who you are!"

"Can I get a picture?"

"What? Are you taking the piss?"

"No! You're a fucking hero!"

I got my phone out, and bang! A photo with the legend that is Rodney Thomas. I was genuinely starstruck meeting him.

It's only happened one other time, and that was with George Oghani. I absolutely loved him. He still lives in Carlisle, George, and I met him at a testimonial. I couldn't believe he was playing in the match. I was in the Premier League at the time, and he also thought I was taking the piss when I asked for a photo! At the time I was coming up against some of the best players in the world, but those two people meant much more to me.

I celebrated one of the greatest moments as a Carlisle fan thousands of miles away on holiday in Lanzarote in May 1999: the day our goalkeeper Jimmy Glass famously scored in injury time against Plymouth Argyle to keep us in the Football League. What a day – and night.

I was with a couple of pals, Stephen Main and Steven Berry, and their parents, and we were all worried we were going to miss this game. We'd even contemplated not going on holiday, but we'd already paid for it. Of course in those days there was no Twitter, no live-streaming, no updates, so we didn't think we'd be able to follow it.

When we got to Lanzarote, we were told there was a Carlisle bar there. An actual Carlisle bar in Lanzarote. Miracle. It was run by a Carlisle fan who'd moved out there, so it was the ideal spot for us. There were Carlisle shirts up everywhere, and we followed the game on *Soccer Saturday*. Just a little bunch of us staring at the TV, while no one else in the bar gave a toss about what was going on.

We were bottom of the league and needed a win to stay up, and for Scarborough to not win. We were a few pints in when Plymouth took the lead after half-time, so that quickly became a few more pints. We equalised with half an hour to go, but needed the win. We were heading into injury time thinking we were down, even though Scarborough had only drawn.

It was in danger of ruining the holiday.

But then *Soccer Saturday* went over to the Carlisle game, with us having a corner in the dying seconds: "Last chance for Carlisle, and the goalkeeper's up." The corner came in from Graham Anthony – who I would play with at Barrow the following year. Scott Dobie – who I would play with at Forest – tried to get on the end of the cross. He missed it, but Jimmy Glass was in the right place and slammed it in! Oh my god!

The table went over, everyone was jumping, drinks were going everywhere, the bar owner didn't care, we were jumping up and down like lunatics, getting weird looks, the owner was shouting out, "Free drinks!". The full-time whistle went, we saw the pitch invasion, and, oh my god, we were staying up!

What a day that was. I was a bit rough the next morning, mind, what with all of those free drinks. But I didn't care at all; we were all still buzzing. Even though we were in a different country at the time, those are the moments you live for as a fan.

***

I always said if I ever played for Carlisle I wouldn't kiss the badge, I'd lick it. I thought I'd got my chance when they brought me in as a youth player when I was 12, but it turned out to be my first lesson that things don't always turn out how you expect them to in football.

It was brilliant being involved in their youth teams to start with. Who wouldn't love getting signed up by the team you supported? Obviously I had dreams of playing for them and scoring at Wembley, but if I'm honest it stopped being fun quite quickly.

I played mostly at centre-half, which I enjoyed, but I wasn't allowed to play Saturday or Sunday mornings for local teams anymore. We were travelling down to Liverpool and getting spanked 5-0 and sometimes I'd be getting just a few minutes on the pitch. What was the point? All I wanted to really do was play football as much as I could.

I spoke to my dad about it and he told me to do whatever would make me enjoy football the most. So I left Carlisle when I was 15, and with hindsight it was a fantastic decision as it meant I was free to play a lot more. It taught me to enjoy football for what it was.

I joined the Under-16s at Northbank in Carlisle and started playing central midfield, which was a great experience. I then joined Harraby, and the manager Eddie Jardine told me I needed to play up front. He was the first one to put me up there. He told me I was scoring too many goals from midfield, so I may as well play up top. Maybe he was hinting I was getting forward too much and leaving too many gaps behind me! I had a good season, scoring plenty of goals for the Under-18s in the Sunday league.

Jardine also got me a trial at Torquay. The player/coach was Steve McCall, ex Ipswich, and he knew Eddie. I wasn't offered a contract because McCall and the manager Kevin Hodges didn't think I would make it. That didn't really bother me at the time, though, because I was really enjoying my football.

I'd also been playing on a Sunday morning with a men's team called The Avenue, who my brother played for. I was at right-back for them and I was as fit as a fiddle. I could just run and run when I was younger.

I'd started playing for them when I was nearly 15, and because I was under the age of 16 I had to play under another name. The manager was Dave Milburn, who didn't really play that much, so he let me use his name a lot. I tell you what, Dave would end up with more Man of the Matches and goals than he normally would when I played under his name!

I was really comfortable in the men's team. I never felt overawed or intimidated. My mentality was if anyone was going to kick me, I'd just kick them back harder. The size of the person didn't matter! Nothing fazed me and I was fearless, probably because I'd been around dressing rooms with my dad since I was a kid. I could laugh and joke with people older than me. It was quite a relaxed atmosphere, which gave me the freedom to try new tricks, or to shoot from anywhere.

It was good to test myself against 35-year-old men who'd get stuck into me and try and flatten me at headers. But I never got into much trouble because I was on the same side as my brother and people I knew, so a lot of opponents realised that if they started something on me it would end up in a 22-man brawl!

Playing with my brother was good. He was a central midfielder, and I knew I'd get shouted at if I didn't give him the ball. I would always say that, ability-wise, he was better than me. His technique in terms of passing and vision was on a different level, but my hard work and desire made me better in the long run. He'll be the first to admit he didn't quite have that commitment to really push himself, and that he could have stuck at it a bit harder, because he was earmarked at Carlisle as really promising. But he doesn't have regrets; life just took him in a different direction.

My dad was often on the sidelines. He was always really encouraging during the match, shouting out praise. He was never one of those annoying dads, yelling at his son to do better. It was all praise with him. But after the game, he'd tell you what you could have done better. He'd tell you straight, which I appreciated. There were a few times when he wanted to run on the pitch and defend me when I was on the end of a bad tackle, but all of my teammates would beat him to it!

Life outside of football was going well. Before leaving school, I worked in a milk factory when I was 15 and 16. We were lifting massive crates of 24 pints of milk so I started to really fill out. I used to get up, meet the milkman at 6am and finish by 8am, get back home, get showered and go straight to school. I was on £20 a week, plus pocket money from doing chores around the house, so I was probably getting £25 in my pocket every week. I knew I could get a Chinese and eight cans of Foster's for £7.50 so it was a win-win situation!

Me and my pals would hang out down the park, play a bit of football, have a few cans. We also used to go to junior discos in town. I wasn't a big dancer. I preferred to sit down and have a drink. Don't get me wrong, I'd get up for a bit of a whirl sometimes, but it wasn't really for me.

Junior discos always seemed to end up in a fight. You always got groups from different areas around Carlisle and someone would always try something with another bunch of lads. I don't think I've ever started a fight in my life, but I have been involved in a few due to other people starting them. Especially when you were younger, you'd find yourself involved in a few scraps because some friends were gobby and just wouldn't back down. We've all known someone like that. Normally I'd be the peace-maker and do anything to try and calm things down, but I could handle myself if I had to.

When I got to 17 my mum and dad were OK with me going drinking in pubs. Dad said, "You'll either get caught and kicked out or you'll get away with it." Can't argue with that logic.

I'm rubbish at remembering birthdays, but there is one date I will always remember: 12/11/77. That's my brother's date of birth and I used that as my ID when I was underage. I'd show it to a bouncer, he'd ask me my date of birth, and I'd trot it out like a robot. Worked every time! I could never forget his birthday now because it's ingrained in my mind.

We had a couple of local pubs we'd go to. One was called The Inglewood, which has been turned into a nursing home. The other was The Avenue, which has been knocked down. They were what we called generation pubs. My granddad would go in and head to the lounge, my dad would go in and head to the bar. Then us teenagers would go in and head to the bar, so Dad would move to the lounge. You'd move around in groups depending on your generation.

They were the kind of pubs where there would always be the same older lads sat in the same corner. They'd have put their bets on at the bookies across the road and sat in the pub watching the telly for the day. If we came in after playing football they'd always ask, "How'd you get on today boy, score again?" And, if I hadn't, they'd just say, "You're slacking!" and turn back to their dominos. They didn't care if you'd won a match, but the day you'd lost they'd all suddenly perk up because they could give you some abuse.

Nights out would never stop me playing football the next day. Sometimes you'd look at the dew on the grass or look out of the window and see it tipping it down and just think, 'I can't be bothered today.' But I always made it. I never missed a game. I never laid in bed and skipped it, because I didn't want to let the lads down. I was the younger one so I felt I had to go. Besides, the walk from my parents' house to the ground was always enough to sober me up for the game!

Those were the days when people would smoke in the dressing room. Some would even have a quick fag at half-time. So maybe you could get away with turning up with a stinking hangover more than you might be able to today.

By this point I'd left school and, not really knowing what I wanted to do, I followed my dad into working in tyres. I started there with a great group of lads, but within two months they were still doing the basics and I was running the inside of the yard. It just clicked; I got on with it, asked questions and learned quickly. It was pretty similar to football in that way: the more you ask and the more opinions you get, the better you do.

Within five months I'd passed my tyre-fitting course for truck tyres, and I'd gone from £50 to £150 a week. Once again it was like a competition for me. As I've said, I always want to be the best I possibly can when I do things. Well, the same applied to fitting tyres.

The bosses were great. They looked after me and kept pushing me to play football, which was really helpful when I signed for Workington AFC for the 1998-99 season.

***

Workington had recently been taken over by a businessman called Bill Wilson and he had invested a good amount of money into the first team. As a subsequence they started to need a reserve side and an Under-18s team, and that's where I lucked out. Harraby played Workington's Under-18s and we beat them 5-0 and I scored a hattrick. So Workington ended up pinching me and around four of my teammates.

I'd also started playing Saturday afternoon football for Gillford Park. This meant I was playing men's for them on a Saturday, playing Sunday morning for The Avenue, and Under-18s on the Sunday afternoon for Workington. It was a great time.

Workington were once a Football League side, and had even been managed by the legendary Bill Shankly. Now, though, they were in the North West Counties League, which was the ninth tier of the English pyramid. It wasn't that big a jump in quality. I was just happy getting the £50 for playing, and a lot of my friends had gone there so it was a perfect fit for me. I was just having fun and enjoying playing football. Good times, no pressure. I went to work, played football, went out drinking. Just the usual 17-year-old lad. I wasn't thinking of a professional career at this stage at all; the plan was to go as far as I could with Workington because I wanted to test myself and see if I could break into the first team.

It was also the first time I'd been at a club with a former professional footballer. Paul Stewart, who'd had a brilliant career at the likes of Tottenham Hotspur and Manchester City, finished at Workington. I think his accountant was the brother of our manager, Peter Hampton, so he ended up with us.

Paul was a really good guy. He was the first big player I'd been around, and there was definitely a pinch-yourself moment when I ended up playing for the first XI because he was injured.

I'd been suspended for the reserves, and when I returned I couldn't get back in up front. So I was moved to right-back. Then the first-team's right-back got injured so I had to step up for him. Then Paul Stewart got injured, and I was moved up front. Sometimes you need that luck, and I took advantage of it. I went on an incredible run of scoring in nearly every game as we won 13 matches in a row. Goal, goal, goal. I was a runner in those days; I'd run and run and run, and work so hard to put people under pressure for 90 minutes. They'd hoof it up and I'd chase everything like a dog.

That incredible run took us to the verge of promotion, and we went into the last game of the season against leaders Mossley needing a win to go up. It was at home on a red-hot day, with over 2,200 fans spilling into the old ground.

Peter Hampton called me in before the match and said he was putting me on the bench, because Paul Stewart was fit and coming back in. I was gobsmacked; absolutely raging about it. My teammates were too. I'd just scored all of those goals, but he was leaving me out. It was the first time I'd really been pissed off in football.

I knew I was better than Paul at that age. He was still good of course, and his touch was fantastic, but he wasn't moving around as much as I was. I felt I should be playing, and I told the manager, "Play me, I'll score and we'll get promoted". But his mind was made up.

The game kicked off and Paul lasted around 15 minutes before having to come off. I came on to replace him and scored the winner in a 2-1 victory. All my friends were there, the crowd went mad, and it turned into a phenomenal day.

Looking back, I can understand why Peter Hampton went with the experience of Paul, who had played at the highest level and performed in huge games. It was probably the right decision. I was just glad to be able to make a difference, and to prove to myself that I could do it. For me, it also vindicated my decision to leave Carlisle two years earlier.

After the promotion celebrations there was an end-of-season dinner, and I was chuffed to win the most improved player award.

That was also the night when my parents first met the girl I would go on to marry.

* * *

I met Fay at a football function in November 1998. I wasn't going to go, and Fay says she also wasn't going to go. But we both got dragged along by pals. Her friends knew some of my friends, and we were all from Harraby so we ended up in the same group. We sat down and chatted away. I had a girlfriend and she had a boyfriend, so nothing happened. We had a good laugh and joke, and it was a fun night.

After that, I was thinking about her quite a bit, and I ended up splitting up with my girlfriend a couple of weeks later. Me and Fay bumped into each other a little while later and by that time she'd split up with her boyfriend. I ended up chasing her a bit (well, quite a lot actually!), and by then we knew the same people so we frequently bumped into each other. There was just something about her I really liked.

She always tells me that just before we got together, I was riding on my bike in front of her and her friends, and someone asked me if I liked her. The story goes that I said, "Nah, course not!" as teenagers do, but then started singing, 'It's Just A Little Crush', the Jennifer Paige song that had just come out. I'm still not sure I did that, but they're adamant I did!

I didn't fancy myself as a singer, which is why I have my doubts. But then again I might have had a couple of cans of Foster's by then!

I was really chuffed we eventually got together. We'd go to the cinema a lot, go out for food. She never really came to watch me play at Workington because she hates football. Still does. Even at Norwich she'd go and sit in the players' lounge and didn't come out to watch. When I put the football on the telly now she still hates the noise in the background!

Fay's always been brilliant for me. She's made me make better choices, and I've always been lucky to lean on her when I've been struggling. You couldn't wish for a better mother for your children.

I try to be romantic. I like to book stuff without her knowing, and take her away. I always try and make an effort off the cuff. It's not the value of what you do, it's the meaning behind it. It could be as simple as walking in with a box of Maltesers so she can have a cup of tea with them.

Fay was quite shy when we first got together so it took six months until she met my parents at the end-of-season dinner. It was just a quick meeting, but they all hit it off straight away. I couldn't have been happier. Everything was going great in the summer of 1999. I was with Fay, I had a job I liked with a good wage, and I was loving playing for Workington. Then, out of nowhere, a Football League club came in to sign me.

MY TOP 5...
FAVOURITE PLAYERS

1. GEORGE OGHANI

Carlisle legend.

2. DES WALKER

A brilliant centre-half and someone I modelled myself on when I was a young centre-back.

3. ERIC CANTONA

I loved watching him play as a kid. He could just do something special out of nowhere, and you couldn't take your eyes off him.

4. STEVE BRUCE

He always looked like he was giving absolutely everything and getting every last drop of talent out of himself.

5. PAUL GASCOIGNE

I don't think you'll find anyone English around my age who wouldn't have him in their top five.

CHAPTER 4

FOOTBALL LEAGUE, TRAGEDY STRIKES AND AUSTRALIA-BOUND

1999-2001

The interest from Halifax Town came out of the blue. It was a total surprise.

I was just enjoying my football and hadn't expected a league side to come in for me. There were no trials, nothing. They just asked if I wanted to sign, and it was too good an opportunity to turn down.

To be moving from the ninth tier of English football to the Third Division felt like a big moment, and the family were proud. It was a hell of a step up, though. A jump of five tiers at the age of 18 sounded massive, and was massive. I felt miles off it in training, competing against old pros and players much fitter than I was. Even though I had been signed for the first team, I soon found myself training with the youth team, and it wasn't going as I'd expected.

Right from the first couple of weeks I'd been thinking I should have had another season at Workington to gain more experience and to work on my size and fitness. But I couldn't have turned down the opportunity of signing for a Football League side.

It was tough to be away from home. It doesn't get talked about much, but homesickness happens a lot in football, especially when you're young. I was an hour-and-a-half away from Carlisle and living in digs, and it was the first time I'd been away from home. The family I stayed with were amazing, though. Jane Grice, her husband David and their children Adam and

Lauren couldn't have been more welcoming, and really helped me feel settled even when I was homesick.

However, due to the heavy training schedule, I wasn't able to get home much. Sometimes I was going to away games and being 18th man, and I was quickly getting back into a place where I wasn't enjoying my football.

I was also missing Fay a lot. Most of my wages, which were something like £150 a week, were going on rent and on fuel to get back to see Fay, but I couldn't afford to head home all of the time. When I couldn't go back, I'd then be sat in the house bored. This wasn't what I had imagined professional football to be.

The lads at Halifax were absolutely brilliant, though, as were the manager Mark Lillis and his assistant Peter Butler. Without that group I wouldn't have lasted the first few months. It was a good bunch of old-school pros, and they looked after me. Made me feel welcome.

Chris Wilder, who'd go on to manage Sheffield United, was at the club when I joined. He was a good guy, and he hated to lose at anything. You could always see he was going to go into coaching because he had big opinions off the pitch and at the end of the games. Outside of training and on nights out he was a giggle; a real joker.

There were other leaders there too, and they demanded high standards all of the time. If there was a brawl, you were expected to roll your sleeves up and help. It was a winning mentality, and I think that rubbed off on me. Even though I wasn't enjoying being away from home and not getting on the pitch, I was still learning and soaking things up.

I made my Football League debut away at Swansea on November 5, 1999. They were a good team so I was really looking forward to it. I was sat on the bench itching to get on, and the gaffer gave me the call in the 88th minute. We were losing 3-1 but I was just buzzing to be making my debut. I nearly scored, too, but I just missed the top corner with a header two minutes after coming on. It was a proper game, with a good crowd, and I was up against familiar names. It was a completely different feeling to playing for Workington.

That didn't kick-start a run of games for me, though, and I played only four more times before Christmas. I was loaned to Barrow AFC in Cumbria to get some game time in the Northern Premier League – known as the Unibond then – as it was clear I still needed to develop. I had no arguments.

Although it hadn't gone how I had hoped in the first few months, I'm so glad I had come off the bench against Swansea, because my dad had come to watch the game. He'd driven about seven hours to see me play at Vetch Field; seven hours to see his son play about five minutes of professional football.

I'll always be eternally grateful he did, though, because sadly it was the only time he saw me play in the Football League.

My dad had started complaining about a bad back in the first half of 2000, but carried on working. Because he was always chucking around tyres and operating heavy machinery, he put it down to that and just took some painkillers. But after a holiday in Salou, Spain, he was complaining that his leg had started hurting too. He went to see a doctor and was told he had Deep Vein Thrombosis.

He got rid of it but it returned, which meant he had to go for testing. The results came back and my dad was told it was cancer. It was everywhere; they couldn't tell where it had originated. The news shook everyone; took over everything. But we were still hopeful that chemotherapy would be able to clear it.

Halifax were great for me in pre-season training. They let me get home to Carlisle as much as I wanted and I went back in July as a surprise. I turned up at my mum's house but there was no one there. My sister wasn't in, Mum wasn't in, and my dad, who was off work of course, wasn't there. So I rang Fay, and she told me my dad was in hospital, but that my parents had told her not to tell me. They hadn't wanted me to worry.

I rushed to the hospital, walked on to the ward and Mum's and Dad's faces both dropped. They hadn't been expecting me. I asked what the fuck was going on... and was told to not swear!

The cancer had spread even further than they'd thought. On top of that, the DVT had come back which meant Dad was on even more painkillers. My head was all over the place but Dad told me to get stuck into football, and I knew I had to get back to Halifax. It helped take my mind off things.

I was going back and forth from Halifax to Carlisle, which is about an hour and 20 minutes. Things had just started improving with the football, and I had been getting minutes on the pitch. I'd scored my first goal in the League Cup against Tranmere Rovers on September 6, which was an amazing feeling, but I knew the one person I wanted to see me play might not be able to anymore. It was a horrible realisation.

Just a week after that match against Tranmere, things took a turn for the worse. Dad had had a stroke, caused by the DVT, and was back in hospital. I set off straight away, but there was a problem: the country was in the middle of a fuel crisis, and I couldn't get petrol anywhere for love nor money.

I thought, sod it, I'll head off anyway and see how far it took me. I jumped in the Clio and sat doing 50mph for as far as I could. My head was scrambled and all over the place, trying to think about what might happen when I got there. It felt like the longest drive in the world.

The fuel gauge had gone into the red when someone rang to tell me Kendal Services had just got petrol in, and I got there just in time. I filled the car up to maximum and absolutely bombed it home. I just had to get back.

I pulled up outside the hospital, but didn't want to get out of the car. Seeing Dad would make it real, and I couldn't face it. I got the courage, took a deep breath, prepared myself, and walked in.

My mum was in the corridor. I cuddled her, she broke down, and that set me off; the tears just hit me. I knew I had to go in and see Dad; it couldn't be put off any longer. As I walked in, with only me and him in the room, he started crying.

Seeing him absolutely killed me. I'd never seen him so weak. He was sitting there, so frail, and I looked at him and thought, 'You know you're dead'. That was the worst thing: he knew he was dying. He'd seen my nana in that state after she'd had a stroke and he would have been thinking that she'd died soon after.

Nothing prepares you for seeing your dad like that, and every time I think about him that day it sets me off.

Before that moment, we all thought he might be all right. You think the chemo will help him, it will make him better and everything could be OK and he'll still have a long life. Everyone was thinking positively, but then the stroke happened and you knew his ability to fight that horrible disease had gone.

He'd already mentally moved on. All they could do was make him as comfortable as possible, but everyone knew what was coming.

Mark Lillis told me that the best thing for me was to see my family and not drive back and forth from Halifax. He arranged a loan back at Workington, and told me once I was ready I could come back to Halifax. I was very grateful to him for that.

I was staying with Fay's parents while I was back from Halifax, and I remember their landline ringing at 3am. And I just knew.

I got up, went downstairs and answered the phone. My brother was on the other end, and told me our dad had gone. I put the phone down, walked upstairs and had the best sleep I'd had in three months. It was a weird sensation; it was relief. Of course I hadn't wanted Dad to die, but I'd mentally prepared for it and I knew his suffering was at an end.

I'm very similar to my dad. Both quick-tempered, both competitive, both devoted to our families. I'm so glad he got to see me play in the Football League, but the only thing I regret not ever doing is signing for Leeds United. He was a massive fan. I used to freak the Leeds fans out whenever I played against them by singing *Marching On Together* before games. I wasn't a fan, I just did it for my dad. He'd have loved to have been at Elland Road to watch me play, and I knew he'd be looking down with a smile on his face, laughing at me singing *Marching On Together*.

Initially I was devastated that he wasn't there to watch my progress in football, but I soon started to see my achievements as something he'd have loved. I'd always have a smile thinking about him looking down at what I was doing.

I wore shin pads with the date of my dad's passing on them and for my whole career I said a prayer to him in the shower before every game: keep me safe, take care of yourself. That was always my routine. Just a moment in my head to be with Dad.

✳ ✳ ✳

I would go out most weekends after my dad passed. It's not like I was getting shitfaced, but I just wasn't looking after myself well. I decided the best way to sort myself out was to cancel the loan at Workington and return to Halifax. They'd really looked after me during everything with my dad, and I was also keen to return to the family I was staying with as they had been so supportive. Jane was absolutely fantastic. A great woman. She lives in Australia now, and I've been to visit her a couple of times.

Mark Lillis and Peter Butler had been sacked in October before I got back to Halifax. They'd been brilliant to me, so I was really disappointed. Paul Bracewell came in as manager, and he was obviously a big name after his playing career. He'd won a few caps for England and was a legend at Everton, so I was excited to have the chance to work for him. It didn't work out as I'd hoped, though.

I'd been back at Halifax for about a week when Bracewell pulled me into his office for a conversation. He told me I wasn't going to play, and that he didn't think I was good enough. He understood what had happened with my dad and was really sympathetic, but he just didn't think I was the right fit.

That conversation was completely unexpected. To be fair, he'd probably not seen me at my best, so I can understand why he came to the decision. Everything I'd been through meant I'd come back from Workington a bit overweight and not as fit as I should have been. But to get that rejection just after Dad had died was a bit of poison down my throat. It hurt.

Bracewell told me my choice was that I could go out on loan or leave permanently. A few clubs had come in to take me on loan, but I didn't fancy that as there wasn't a way back for me at Halifax. So I chose to leave permanently.

I called Kenny Lowe, the manager at Barrow. I'd enjoyed my month on loan there at the back end of the 1999-2000 season, and I felt it would do me good to return to the Northern League knowing I'd play week in, week out. I'd also be back in Cumbria, and closer to the family and Fay.

Kenny wanted me back, and thought it was a disgrace how I'd been treated straight after my dad had died. He told me the signing was done, to get my gear, and he'd see me at the weekend. Deal done.

In the end, it was a big relief to leave Halifax. The only thing that was difficult was leaving Jane's family. They'd been a part of my life for over a year and knew everything that had gone on, and I had really good bonds with them. So it was quite emotional when I headed away in my Clio for the final time.

But I concentrated on the positive side of things. I was going to see Fay every day, I could see my mum, sister and brother more and I'd actually be on more money playing for Barrow than for Halifax.

Now that I knew exactly what was happening, it was up to me to show everyone how good I was: score goals in non-league and put a smile back on my face.

The lads at Barrow were brilliant and it was great to be playing and scoring again. I felt at home in the sixth tier, and it was a nice step up from Workington. The coaching team, especially Kenny Lowe and Lee Turnbull, looked after me and knew what had happened with my dad, but they would also be ruthless with me if things weren't going right on the pitch. That's exactly what I needed.

What a lot of people don't realise about non-league football is that people are desperate to win for each other because of the win bonuses. They could sort out your kids' Christmas, or a family holiday. That money is needed.

But I was feeling no pressure. I was young and I was doing what I wanted to do: go out on a Saturday, go out on a Sunday; I had no kids, no house, no nothing. I could do what I wanted, but I knew it meant a lot to those with families and mortgages to get the extra money so I would always give 100% for them.

✴ ✴ ✴

Life took an unexpected turn at the end of the season. I got a call from my old assistant manager at Halifax, Peter Butler, who was moving out to Australia. He asked if I fancied going out there to play for a team called Sorrento for a month during the English pre-season. They were semi-professional, based in Perth, and played in the Professional Soccer League of Western Australia, which was the highest league in the state. Peter told me if I did well I might get a shot at Perth Glory, who play at the top level in the A League.

So I booked the flights.

It was a great little club and the people were absolutely fantastic. They had a really small ground and the standard probably compared to reserve level at Workington, but it was just a bit more fun and chilled out. Everyone at the club couldn't do enough for you. Just a really great bunch of people.

I stayed in a house with a couple of lads, got a bit of money for playing football, and headed down to the beach every day. I was embracing the lifestyle, doing a bit of bodyboarding. We got a cheap car to rent and run around in and we'd go for drives down the west coast of Australia. I also went to see the British & Irish Lions give Western Australia a battering at the famous WACA stadium in Perth, which was an amazing experience.

I was 20 years old, scoring a few goals and really enjoying it. There was one big problem, however: I wasn't with Fay. We did have a plan that if it went well and Perth Glory came in for me, Fay would then come over on a year's travel visa. But it got towards the end of the month and there was something niggling at me, telling me that although the lifestyle was brilliant this wasn't what I wanted to do. I had unfinished business at home.

CHAPTER 5

SINGAPORE STAR, GETTING ENGAGED AND GIVING UP ON FOOTBALL

2001-2002

There won't be too many British Premier League footballers who had spells playing football in Australia and Singapore before the age of 22, let alone started their careers in the non-league. My route to the best league in the world was far from conventional.

Less than a year after my spell with Sorrento, I headed off to Southeast Asia for my next footballing adventure. It was at the tail end of the 2001-02 season, in which I'd not only carried on my goalscoring form for Barrow but had taken a step closer to returning to playing in the Football League (or so I thought...).

When I returned from Australia, I contacted a friend of mine called Billy Barr. We'd been teammates at Workington, and he was now the academy coach at Carlisle. He said I could train with their youth team while I was playing for Barrow in order to help keep up my fitness.

This progressed to occasionally training with Carlisle's first team, and in February they were a bit short for a reserve game so they asked me to play as a trialist. Kenny Lowe at Barrow told me it was OK because we didn't have a midweek game, but more likely it was because he was hoping Carlisle might sign me and they'd get a bit of money for it!

I scored in the game and played really well. I was asked to train with the first team a little bit more, and play in more reserve matches as a trialist. Things were looking promising.

SINGAPORE STAR, GETTING ENGAGED AND GIVING UP ON FOOTBALL

Carlisle were under a transfer embargo, but I was told that when they came out of it they would be really keen to sign me. Even though I'd left them when I was 15, there was no way I would turn down the chance to play for my hometown club in the Football League.

At the same time I got a call from my old Sorrento manager, Trevor Morgan, who was now manager of Singapore side Sengkang Marine. Trevor wanted to know if I fancied heading out there to play for him for three months at the end of the season. I'd be lying if I said I knew anything about Singaporean football, but it sounded like an amazing opportunity. A new culture, a new group of lads and a new experience. It was a no-brainer.

Carlisle were fine with me going. After all, playing football through the summer would mean I'd come back as fit as a fiddle. Trevor was also aware of the situation, and knew I'd be off if Carlisle came in for me.

A year after packing my bags to fly to Australia, I was packing my bags to fly to Singapore. There was a key difference this time, however: Fay was coming with me.

There was a little matter to clear up before we could set off, however. Because Fay was 18, Sengkang dropped a bombshell: we might have to get married if Fay was to come too. Well, that was a shock!

But it got me thinking. We'd been together two years and if I had to marry her I would, and she said the same thing. We started going through the process, but before we got too far we got a call to say there'd been a mix-up and Fay could get a visa without us being married. The news was both a shame and a relief! If I'm honest, it was mostly relief because we couldn't really afford to get married and didn't fancy a shotgun wedding; when the time came, we wanted to do it properly. I think we knew from then that we were destined to be with each other.

Panic over, we jumped on the plane not knowing how the adventure was going to go, what to expect or how long we'd be out there for. I thought it would be something different, and the chance to try a new lifestyle. What an experience it could be. In my head I was already thinking I could go every year during the summer if I didn't find a Football League side.

We got picked up at the airport, and went straight to the condo the club had arranged for us. We'd be sharing with a pal called Danny Hill, who I'd played with at Sorrento. It was right in the middle of Singapore and we had a pool and gym. From the condo I could walk to the training ground and walk to the matches, so it was perfect.

I was surprised to find that Singapore didn't seem that big, and we settled really quickly. The most interesting things to get used to were the different culture and learning how to conduct yourself differently. No person was ever late when I was there. Not one person. It's a culture of respect, which I liked.

We absolutely embraced living out there. We went everywhere. They had beaches, the city centre was brilliant, we loved the food – who doesn't love a bit of curried fish head – and we went on night safaris. I remember bricking myself that a hyena was about to jump on me!

We led a really relaxed lifestyle. At times it might have been a bit boring for Fay, because I was at training a lot and she was left by herself, but she still had a fantastic time.

The weather was red hot out there. Once, I was walking down the road to training and suddenly it absolutely pissed it down. It was like a flash flood, and I was soaked to the bone. By the time I got to training, my clothes were completely dry because of the heat. It was certainly a different experience to training under damp, grey skies in Cumbria.

The football was a bit sluggish and the standard was up and down. We did really well, though, especially for a team little was expected of. We got to the quarter-finals of the cup, and we were doing well in the league. The ground was small, with a running track around the pitch and one stand. We'd started with about 700 fans turning up, and then as we did better, that crept up to around 1,400.

We had a couple of Brits, Simon Harland and James Morgan, and an Aussie in the team but it was mainly a mix of Chinese and Malaysian. We had a really good group, and the locals enjoyed us being around them. We were perhaps a little more demanding, and I think they liked having people who came from a football background which was a bit more professional.

The football was pretty relaxed, but you had to have your wits about you whenever you got a taxi from the ground because there's a big betting culture in Singapore. We were always told not to say anything about the games to taxi drivers. Just smile and say you don't know anything, they'd tell us. If you said to them, "We've got a good chance at the weekend" then they'd stick everything on you winning. Or they'd ask about injuries, to see what the team news might be. But the fans were brilliant, and they'd sing songs at games and turn it into a good atmosphere.

Tiger Beer held an outdoor event for the World Cup final between Germany and Brazil. They invited one player and the manager from each side, so myself and Trevor headed down there, and he brought his wife and son. Fay didn't fancy it because she didn't like watching football. Fair enough.

When I got there it was like a carnival atmosphere. They'd put up a massive screen in front of a huge shopping centre, and there were 5,000 people there. The drink was free, which you're especially grateful for when beer is normally £7 a pint! It was just a really good vibe. So I called Fay from a pay phone – we didn't have mobiles out there – and she changed her mind and got a taxi down. We'd meet on the corner of the street near the bar.

I came back out 20 minutes later to wait at the meeting point, but we were on the corner of an L-bend and it was absolutely mobbed because the event was so busy. I was waiting on one corner, craning my neck to try and see her, but the taxi driver had dropped her off on the other corner. We couldn't ring each other, and she'd used all of her money on the taxi. We were both walking around the corners, battling our way through the huge crowd, and passing each other without knowing it.

She was starting to worry about how she'd get back home, and I was thinking about her on her own; a good-looking girl with blonde hair in the middle of a big city! But luckily I finally spotted her from the other side of the road, and she ran over. We had a little fall-out because we'd both been papping ourselves that we'd lost each other! But we were soon having a good laugh about it, and enjoyed watching the game in such an amazing atmosphere.

We took full advantage of the free alcohol, got absolutely hammered and had a great time. You knew we were a bit worse for wear when, on our way home, Trevor's wife buggered over and fell through a hedge! We were crying with laughter as we pulled her out of the bush. It was basically Brits abroad embarrassing ourselves, but it was a really fun night. If you ask most England fans what they remember of the 2002 World Cup, they'll probably say beating Argentina or Ronaldinho's free-kick that sailed over David Seaman for Brazil. For me, the first two things that pop into my head are crapping myself thinking I'd lost Fay, and Trevor's wife poleaxing into a hedge.

Going to Singapore really opened my eyes to the world. Australia was very much like England, but my time in Singapore made me want to do more travelling. I want my kids to explore the world and to experience different cultures. It taught me a lot and, even though I was only there for a few months, it made me grow up quicker.

Things were going great in Singapore. I'd been approached by Geylang, one of the biggest clubs out there, and they'd offered me a two-year contract and to double my wages. That was incredibly tempting, but it went out of the window when Carlisle finally called to say they wanted to sign me.

I rang a few people connected with Carlisle who said the embargo was definitely being lifted, so that was my mind made up. The chance to sign for Carlisle outshone anything, so there was no hesitation on my part about leaving, and Fay knew how much it meant to me. Plus it was only £1.15 for a beer in my local pub back home!

There was a lot of chatter about me joining, and things were going well in training at Carlisle. But the weeks started to go by, and I kept being told by Roddy Collins, who'd just been brought back in as manager, that the contract was coming. Another week went by, and then another, and I was getting really frustrated.

The season had started, and I still hadn't been signed. I played in friendlies against Celtic and Newcastle on consecutive days at the start of September, and scored in both games. I knew I was impressing, but still nothing was getting sorted.

Roddy was telling me the chairman was trying his best, but there was another boy they wanted to bring in and they were going to do him first. Then I'd be next.

I'd been back four or five weeks now and I couldn't play, and it was becoming ridiculous. I had Kenny Lowe ringing me because he wanted me back at Barrow and in the end I went to Carlisle and said, "Are you giving me the contract or not? I want to sign tomorrow or I'll leave." They told me to wait another week, but after those seven days the inevitable happened: they said they could no longer make it work and wouldn't be signing me. So I said, "OK, good luck," and re-joined Barrow the next day.

What a waste of time it had all been. I was absolutely gutted. Fuming. I've learned since that these things happen in football. You never quite know what's going on, but most of the time everyone is trying their best to get things over the line, and sometimes it just doesn't work.

At the time, though, I was feeling bitter towards Carlisle. They told me I could carry on training with them while I played at Barrow, but I told them where to stick their offer.

Despite the rejection, I was still interested in pursuing football as a career. When the chance came up to play in a trial match for Exeter City in October I jumped at it. I had a game for Barrow at Hyde on the Monday, and after the match me and Fay jumped into the Peugeot 307 – a bit more glamorous than the Clio – and went all of the way down to Exeter. Well, I say it was glamorous, but the radio wasn't working. So for the whole five-hour drive we had no music or radio to listen to. Fay had a sleep, which was preferable to listening to me boring on.

We got to the hotel at 3am. Time for a quick sleep, and then up for training at 9am. After that I came back to the hotel to pick Fay up, before heading to St James Park for my chance to impress. It was freezing, so Fay sat in the car for the whole 90 minutes.

I scored and felt I'd done really well. The manager, Eamonn Dolan, thought I'd been excellent and said he'd be in touch. We drove back up to Carlisle and got home around 8pm, got to bed, got up and went to work at 6am. Ridiculously long day.

After work, I got home, slumped down on the sofa and turned on Sky Sports News. On the ticker-tape it said that Exeter had appointed a new manager. Unbelievable! I sat bolt upright and just thought, 'Are you having a laugh!' I'd gone all of the way down there for a trial, and the manager goes and gets replaced the next day!

I never heard anything back off them. It's impossible to say how things would have been if the Exeter manager had stayed and I'd signed for them. They went down that season, so maybe it was for the best. Maybe I'd have played and kept them up; maybe we'd have got relegated and I'd never have kicked a ball. You just don't know. My nana had a saying: "What's for you, won't pass you by."

* * *

I was getting paid by Barrow and had started working at food manufacturers Cavaghan & Gray in Carlisle, so I told Kenny Lowe I was done with going on trials. I just didn't want to do that anymore. I was getting £200 at Barrow a week and £350 a week at work, and I was happy. I was living with my mum and seeing Fay all of the time, so I was in a good place. After what had happened at Halifax, and getting messed around by Carlisle, I turned my back on my football ambitions. That was me done with professional football.

Of course I'd always wanted to be a footballer, but I got into the mindset that I was done with it. That was one of the best decisions I'd ever made because I relaxed. It stopped me being desperate and took the pressure off. I was playing at Barrow and enjoying my football. The weight of chasing a dream had gone.

Work was great. I was basically a storeman, which was brilliant for me. I was lifting all of the time, which kept me fit. On an evening I'd go to the gym or for a run. I was playing Tuesday, Saturday for Barrow, and playing five-a-side with my friends.

I also started playing for The Avenue on a Sunday morning again. People knew who I was, and that I'd played a bit of league football. But we had a hard group, so no one was ever going to really target me because we'd always have a bunch of lads on our side who were over six feet tall and about 18 stone!

Without wanting to sound big-headed I'd got to the point where I was too good for that level. I always gave my all and it was good fun, but I found it easy. Even on Saturday afternoons I knew I was getting better for Barrow. I was stronger, and my game was changing. I was more powerful, I was faster, I held the ball up better. I was able to knock people out of the way and win the majority of headers. Playing at Halifax had taught me a lot, as had training at Carlisle. At 21, I was a wiser footballer.

I was just happy scoring goals, playing non-league, earning decent money and being around family. I was in such a good place that on Christmas Day 2002, I asked Fay to marry me.

There weren't too many nerves about her saying yes, but you do still have your doubts of course. We'd obviously already discussed it ahead of going to Singapore, and I hadn't done anything since then to make me think she might have changed her mind!

On Christmas morning I put a card with the message 'Will you marry me?' in a box, and when she opened it I had the ring in my pocket and pulled it out. Thankfully she did say yes, and I was ecstatic. I may have given up on my dream of being a professional footballer, but I was engaged to the love of my life.

CHAPTER 6

RIGHT PLACE, RIGHT TIME AND WEDNESDAY CALLING

2003

You always worry when the manager unexpectedly asks for a word. What have I done wrong? Have I been dropped? Am I going to be told I'm not working hard enough? It's not usually good news, so the walk down a corridor and into the office always feels like you're heading into trouble.

I'd turned up for a Tuesday night game at Barrow at the beginning of March 2003. I'd been scoring goals and was on fire, so I was surprised when I got a message saying Kenny Lowe wanted to see me. Something didn't feel right.

I walked into the gaffer's office, and Kenny says to me, "You're not playing tonight."

I just started laughing. "Are you joking?"

"No. You've got a trial tomorrow, so you're not playing tonight."

A trial? That annoyed me even more. "I'm not going anywhere. I've told you I don't want to piss about with trials. I'm not doing that anymore. Who is it this time? Is it Third Division again?"

"No Grant, it's Sheffield Wednesday."

That stopped me in my tracks. "Well, they're all right aren't they!"

That was the last thing I was expecting. I'd been more than happy with my decision to give up on a professional career, and I'd turned down trials at lower league clubs. It had got to the point where Kenny wasn't even telling me about offers. But this was very different. Wednesday were a massive club, in the First Division at the time. It didn't feel real that they were interested in someone who was playing in the Unibond League, four tiers below, but Kenny said they were keen to see what I could offer.

He told me, "You're definitely going," and I certainly wasn't arguing this time! In fact, Kenny had already spoken to my boss at work to tell him I wasn't going to be in the following afternoon, as that's when the trial was.

After collecting my thoughts and getting over the initial shock, I went to the bar to tell everyone I wasn't playing. I couldn't tell them the truth, so put it down to an injury. I stuck around to watch the game, and afterwards my mum asked why I hadn't played.

It felt good to tell her: "I've got a trial at Sheffield Wednesday tomorrow!"

Mum started laughing. She was properly stunned. Couldn't believe it. Then she told me she was coming with me! Straight away she was on the phone to work saying she wasn't going in the next day. I phoned Fay to tell her I had a trial at Wednesday, but, Fay being Fay, she didn't know who they were or what league they were in.

It was all a bit surreal, and it was only when I got to Hillsborough that it really sunk in.

The biggest club I'd been at before was Carlisle, and Hillsborough is four times the size of Brunton Park, and the club is four times the stature. It was on a whole different level to anything I'd experienced before. I knew they were struggling in a relegation battle, but you could tell as soon as you saw the stadium how massive they were.

I met the manager Chris Turner, did the formalities, got changed for the reserve game and walked out into this 40,000 stadium with only a handful of people there. We were a mix of first-team players and some of the younger boys, and I did OK. I didn't score but played well. Wednesday said they'd be in touch.

RIGHT PLACE, RIGHT TIME AND WEDNESDAY CALLING

I played for Barrow at the weekend and had an inkling that someone was probably watching the game for Wednesday, and I did well and scored.

Wednesday called me on the Sunday asking if I could play in another reserve fixture at Newcastle on Tuesday. I got the day off work – which meant I would lose money – but Wednesday called me on Monday afternoon asking if I could play in a game at Hillsborough on Friday instead. I told them I couldn't. I'd already changed my shift, had lost £80, and would have to drive over which would be another £50. I just couldn't afford it, and I thought my chance had slipped away.

Luckily, they agreed to stick to the original plan and let me come down for the Newcastle game. It was the best thing I ever did.

Newcastle had former Spain defender Marcelino at centre-half, they had both Steve and Gary Caldwell at the back too. Lomana LuaLua was on the wing and Shola Ameobi was up front. It was a really good group of players they had, while we were playing kids. Jon Shaw, a striker who went on to have a good career, and Richard Wood, a centre-half who would play almost 200 games for Wednesday, were in our side that day.

Our assistant manager Colin West told us Newcastle had a great team, and he just wanted to see hard work from us. It was me and Shaw up front and we both ran our nuts off and harried, and the match finished 0-0. It was the highest quality I'd played against, but back then I knew I could press people for 90 minutes and be a nuisance, and me and Jon did just that. It didn't faze me at all. I just kept grafting.

Off the back of that I got a phone call telling me Wednesday were coming to watch me on Tuesday night at Hucknall Town, and Chris Turner would also be there. There was pressure now. The expectancy had shifted. Should I be scoring against Premier League Newcastle? Probably not. But now I'm in my zone, in my domain where I've scored goals, they'll be expecting me to get on the scoresheet.

Within six minutes of the match starting, a long ball went over the top, I chased it, the goalkeeper came out and went to clear it as hard as he could. Thwack! The clearance hit me square in the face. I was down and blinking with my nose bleeding and suddenly everyone jumped on top of me, celebrating. I hadn't realised the ball had hit me so hard it had flown off me and into the net!

Scoring that goal took all of the pressure away. My nose was hanging off, so I was pissed off about that, and it made me put even more effort in to winning the game. I scored again in the second half – I think it was off my shoulder – and felt I had a really good match.

On Thursday morning I was at work, and I got a call from Wednesday's club secretary. He told me they'd spoken to Barrow, had sorted the money and wanted to sign me. "What do you want to do?"

I was in shock. I'd just had a fry-up and was sitting on my stacker in the warehouse, with a big jacket on because I was working in the chiller on my own, and I was on the phone with Sheffield Wednesday, who were telling me they wanted to sign me. What did I want to do? Well, yes, I did want to sign for them actually!

I got off the phone, and sat there for a little bit. I looked around at the warehouse, at these massive boxes of food I'd been stacking, and thought, "Well, I won't be doing this for a little while."

It still gives me a lump in the throat thinking about it. To go from where I was then, to the First Division, just doesn't happen. It changed everything, and it had come from nowhere.

* * *

Sometimes you need a bit of luck to get your first big break. For a second tier side to come in for a 21-year-old playing four rungs below them often means somewhere along the line things have had to fall into place.

RIGHT PLACE, RIGHT TIME AND WEDNESDAY CALLING

My bit of luck was Bill Green being in the right place at the right time. Bill, who sadly died in 2017, was a fantastic defender for Carlisle in the '70s. He'd had spells at other sides, including West Ham, and went on to become a scout for a few clubs after a bit of management. At the time he was doing some work for Sheffield Wednesday.

Bill was from around Newcastle, and was back up in the North-East for a christening. Barrow had been playing at Bishop Auckland, and Bill had decided to catch the game while he was up there.

I scored for Barrow that day and had worked really hard. Bill was sat watching the game and took a little note of my performance. He knew Kenny Lowe – they were both from the North-East – so Bill had a chat with him to find out about me. We had another game near Sheffield, so, unknown to me, Bill came to watch again. Over the month he did a bit of groundwork on me, talking to people at Halifax and Workington. Once that was done, he recommended me to Chris Turner.

All of that was going on in the background and I had absolutely no idea. It was probably for the best I was oblivious, because I had the mindset that I was no longer bothered about pursuing a professional career. That meant I was playing football with no pressure and just enjoying it, and that was probably reflected in my performances.

Now I'm coaching, I always say to the young lads that you never know who's watching when you're playing. You never know who's going to be willing to take a chance on you. If Bill hadn't been up for a christening that weekend, I may never have got my second chance in the Football League.

* * *

The day after I'd got the phone call from Sheffield Wednesday, I was due to play for Cavaghan & Gray in a work match that just happened to be against a team in Sheffield. They didn't think I'd play as I wouldn't want to risk an injury but, being daft and loyal, I said of course I'd be there.

We won something like 7-2 and I scored four and set up a couple. I had an unbelievable game, and during the match I heard a few people saying, "He's a bloody good player isn't he", and someone saying, "He's signing for Sheffield Wednesday next week", which got a, "Fuck off is he!" No one believed it.

After the game some Wednesday fans asked me if it was true, but they still didn't believe it when I said yes. There were also a couple of Sheffield United fans there, and when they heard about me they started giving me a bit of abuse! That gave me a little insight into what living in Sheffield would be like.

The following week I signed forms with Wednesday and headed back to Barrow to say my goodbyes and to thank everyone. They were really pleased for me. Everyone there had been brilliant and had looked after me. They'd given me a kick when I needed it; kept me grounded. Every single one of them played a part in me getting to where I had. Without those boys I wouldn't have done it.

It was tough leaving Fay, but Sheffield wasn't too far and we'd still see each other most weeks. We were engaged, and knew at some point in the near future we'd move in together. But at the time we were just excited that I had this opportunity, and the bit of extra money I'd be on meant I could drive back and forth as much as I wanted.

Although I was delighted to get the chance, I was under no illusion that Wednesday had given me a contract to basically have a look at me. Could this rough-and-ready striker from the non-leagues cut it at their level?

I made my debut off the bench at home to Watford on Saturday March 29, 2003, coming on in the 71st minute for Lloyd Owusu. We were in a relegation fight at the time, and we got an injury time equaliser, so it was a brilliant feeling to be on the pitch for that.

I was getting a few minutes here and there, and loving being in training.

The quality was much higher than I'd experienced, but I didn't feel out of place. I was just a sponge, soaking everything up.

In April we went to Portsmouth on my 22nd birthday. Top v bottom. They were just about to lift the First Division trophy under Harry Redknapp, and Fratton Park was absolutely bouncing. It was a great team, with the likes of Tim Sherwood, Steve Stone and Paul Merson outfield, and Shaka Hislop in goal.

I'd come from Barrow where I'd play in front of 1,500, and now I was playing in front of over 25,000 people in one of the best atmospheres in the country. I was on the bench thinking, 'Is this actually happening?' But that feeling went as soon as I came on. It was just another game of football, 11 v 11. It became normal again as soon as I was out there.

We'd been 1-0 down when the manager put me and Michael Reddy on in the 73rd minute, replacing Owusu and Shefki Kuqi up top. Three minutes later Ashley Westwood scored a header, and me and Reddy worked really hard and helped the team get a winner, with Reddy scoring. Redknapp was fuming, but we were loving it. We'd given ourselves a chance of staying up.

There was another crunch match the following week. We were second bottom, and were facing the only team below us: Grimsby Town. I came on in the 70th minute, but we were out of luck that day and drew 0-0. It left us five points off safety with only three matches remaining.

We went to Brighton two days later, and the match was bittersweet for me. I got my first start, and latched on to a knockdown from Paul McLaren to give us the lead in the 16th minute. It felt brilliant to score my first goal in the First Division, but we knew we needed to win the game so I didn't really have time to let it sink it. It was all about keeping concentrated and focused on the match.

After half-time, Bobby Zamora equalised through a penalty. Unfortunately for me, I'd given the pen away – although it was a terrible decision! I got shoved in the area, which made me accidentally handball it and the ref pointed to the spot. It should have been a free-kick for the foul on me, but Zamora scored, the match ended 1-1, and we were down.

I'd gone from my first start, to the exhilaration of scoring, to giving away a penalty, to relegation. All in 90 minutes. The mood afterwards was awful in the dressing room, but there was a small part of me that was proud of scoring in the second tier of English football just three weeks after I'd been scoring in the Unibond.

I started the final two matches of the season, including a ridiculous 7-2 win at Burnley. Despite relegation, things were going well personally. Chris Turner was pleased with how I'd got on, the local press were raving about me a bit, and I was really looking forward to coming back for pre-season, even though we'd been relegated.

I hadn't felt out of my depth at all, so I was looking forward to having a real crack at the third tier. As I said before, though, things don't always turn out as you expect them.

MY TOP 5...
KIDS' TV SHOWS FROM THE 1980S

1. GOING LIVE!

Loved that show. Phillip Schofield was great,
and my dad loved Trevor and Simon on there.
I always had that on every Saturday morning.

2. THUNDERCATS

The best cartoon ever.

3. THE A-TEAM

I had the A-Team truck as a kid. Great themetune, too.
I used to hum that around the house all week.

4. THE DUKES OF HAZZARD

Great car, great action. Always made me laugh as a kid.

5. FUN HOUSE

What a mullet the presenter Pat Sharp had!
It's a miracle I never decided to grow one.

CHAPTER 7

BUBBLE BATHS, HAVE A LITTLE RESPECT AND DISCONNECT

2003-04

Respect is a big thing in football. You learn that from an early age. You respect your seniors, and those who've been there and done it all. Even if you don't particularly like someone, it's possible to respect them for their achievements and for what they do on a football pitch.

In any dressing room there is always a hierarchy, usually based on seniority. When you're a young lad, you quickly earn approval if you stick to that.

At Sheffield Wednesday there were quite a lot of big characters. It was a brilliant group, full of people who really looked after you. One of the biggest characters was our goalkeeper Kevin Pressman. How could you not respect the big man? He'd been at his boyhood club since 1985, had played a countless number of Premier League matches and had been involved in England squads. He was a Wednesday legend, and quite rightly so.

So if Kev wanted something, Kev got something.

After a heavy training session, I was aching all over. I ran a bath at the training ground, put the radox in and couldn't wait for a soak. I really, really needed it. I was just about to climb in when Kev walked through the door.

"Holty, what you doing?"

'I'm just getting in my bath."

"No, that's my bath! I need a bath, and I'm older than you!"

"But Kev, I've just run it."

"Thanks for putting the bubbles in for me!"

BUBBLE BATHS, HAVE A LITTLE RESPECT AND DISCONNECT

I could have argued with Kevin Pressman, legend of Sheffield Wednesday, but I knew there'd be only one winner. I was 22, had achieved sod all, and Kev was 35 and had achieved it all. I showed him the respect and let him take my bubble bath, and boy did he let me know how relaxing it was in there!

Now, he wouldn't have done anything if I'd said no. He wouldn't have had a problem at all, but I'd learned, almost without realising it, that there's a level of respect in the dressing room for senior players. I think letting him take my bath, as daft as this sounds, helped me achieve the respect of my senior teammates.

✳✳✳

I don't think that level of respect exists in football anymore. Not to the extent it used to, anyway. I heard a story from a former teammate that an old pro, a legend at a club, asked a young lad to do him a favour and wash his boots. The kid turned to him and said, "I'm not washing your boots, wash them yourself." He walked off, leaving the senior player open-mouthed.

Now, you might not see anything wrong with that. Maybe the senior pro should have washed his own boots. Maybe Kevin Pressman should have let me have the bath. But I think respect goes a long way in a dressing room, or in any similar environment. It shows you can be trusted, and it shows a bit of humility, and both of those things are important for groups to get along together.

That's not the only story like that I've heard, which makes me think I retired at the right time.

Of course, it won't be like that everywhere. The majority of young players will still be happy to muck in, and will be respectful of senior players. But when younger teammates aren't respectful, I think it stems from the increasing lack of respect some fans and the media have for players.

I don't want to go on a rant, because no one really wants to hear a former footballer have a moan about how they're treated. But I really believe it's impossible for players to be as close to fans as they used to, because so many people seem to want to have a pop at them. Whether that's a fan on the street, or someone on social media, or a journalist writing a column, footballers appear to be fair game to slate. Striker not scored for a while? Have a pop. Goalkeeper made an error? Have a pop. Footballer says something interesting in an interview? Have a pop. Player buys his mum a house? Have a pop.

The majority of fans are brilliant, and support their club through thick and thin. They're also entitled to have a moan if things aren't right, or if someone isn't giving their all. I have no issue with that.

What I do think is wrong is, more and more often, people are always looking to give players stick before they give them praise. That's the wrong way round. The first instinct should be to support a player, not abuse them. Players and teams get booed by their own fans way more than they used to, and that pushes the disconnect too. The media and fans are too quick to nail good players. Look at the treatment of Dele Alli and especially Raheem Sterling. Both are absolutely brilliant footballers, but most of the stuff you read about them is either nailing them for their football or nailing them for ridiculous off-field reasons. It's not good enough, and it shouldn't be acceptable, even if they are on very good money.

How much a player earns is completely irrelevant. When I was on £50 a week at Workington, and when I was on good money in the Premier League, the hurt of losing a match was still the same, and the feeling of scoring a goal was still the same. If I lost in a park on a Sunday morning, it was the same feeling as losing at Old Trafford. Honestly. I'll always say scoring a goal in front of two people is the same feeling as scoring in front of 50,000 people. How much money a player earns has nothing to do with how a player performs on a Saturday afternoon. You're still the same person.

I feel I can say that, because I've seen both sides of the coin. I've been there playing Sunday league on no money and I've played at Old Trafford on good money, and to me there's no difference. As long as a player is giving their all, that's all that matters. That applies to every level of the game.

You get paid great money at the top levels and are very fortunate, but nearly every single professional footballer would still be training all week and playing Saturday, Tuesday even if the money was crap. You don't go into football for the money, you go into it because you love kicking a ball about. Some might think that I'm talking shit, but it's absolutely true.

✳ ✳ ✳

In any job you do there are pros and cons, and I think footballers get a hard time. Because we get paid well, fans think players shouldn't complain about anything. On the flip side, players often get asked why they're laughing or smiling after they've been beaten. If you're an England player, you'll be on the back page of the tabloids if you're caught laughing the night of a loss. It's ridiculous. You can't change anything after the whistle goes. The game's gone and you can't dwell on it. It's not healthy.

I don't expect someone who works in a factory, who accidentally rips a tyre like I used to, to leave that building and worry about that tyre for the next three days. All you can do is work out that you didn't put enough soap on the tyre, so the next time you do it you'll put more soap on so it won't rip. That's all you can do. You can't be miserable about it, because it's done. You've got kids to worry about, you've got family to worry about.

That's the same with football. Once the game is done, it's done. You've got kids and family to worry about, like anyone else. Some fans don't quite understand that, yes football does matter, but you've got your own life after football. You're going to be gutted if you've lost, of course, but it doesn't mean you beat yourself up about it. You are allowed to smile afterwards, like you're allowed to smile after you've left work after a bad day. You shouldn't have to feel guilty about it.

Now that I play Sunday league, I see another side of the detachment. The same people who would abuse footballers for the amount of money they earn, then slate former pros for dropping down to non-league after retiring. There's no logic to that. Fans should be praising old pros for continuing to play. They don't need the money, they're just doing it because they love the game. That should be embraced.

That's why I still play: because I simply love kicking a ball about. Some people don't understand that. They think I shouldn't be playing football; that it's embarrassing. But I've loved playing since I was six, so why would I stop while my body still works? It's like saying to a fan, who has loved the game since they were little, "You can't support your team anymore." What reason? "Because you're 35. You're past it as a fan. And you can't go and watch a local non-league team instead, because you're over the hill. You're finished as a fan."

I think that attitude puts off former players going into non-league. Why take the stick? I still enjoy playing, and can put up with that sort of stuff, but unfortunately a lot of old pros can't be doing with that hassle. It's self-defeating, though. If more pros dropped into that level after retiring, then younger lads would learn more off them and the standard would improve. It should be win-win. A no-brainer.

Mocking former players like me for playing non-league is part of the same attitude problem that leads to fans giving a player stick before praising them, and that's creating a culture of negativity around footballers. That culture leads to some young players coming into the game without much respect for their peers, and ends up in stories like a kid refusing to clean a senior pro's boots. It's all linked.

It's easy to moan about it, like I've just done. But, like with everything, you've got to get on with it and adapt to these changes. While I think I retired at the right time, it's exciting going into coaching. How I'm learning to coach now is very different to how I was coached. Players are treated differently to when I was starting out, and some young players treat old players differently too. You have to adapt to that and move with the times.

Rant over. Back to my story. And I'm still glad I let big Kevin Pressman take that bath off me.

CHAPTER 8

MARK ROBINS' ADVICE, ROCHDALE HEROICS AND DEAD LEGS

2003-2004

Let's talk about Mark Robins. What a player, and what an all-round top man.

Sheffield Wednesday signed him in December 2003, and I will always tell everyone that I learned more training with Mark than from any coach I ever worked with. I had huge respect for him.

Mark famously, or at least allegedly, kept Alex Ferguson in the Manchester United job, scoring the winning goal in a third round FA Cup match at Nottingham Forest in 1990 when the pressure had been massively mounting on Ferguson. Robins had learned his trade playing alongside great strikers like Mark Hughes and Brian McClair at United, and then went on to have that brilliant year with Norwich when they finished third in the first-ever Premier League season in 1992-93.

Mark taught me stuff that someone who hadn't been at his level could never teach you. The timing of runs, thinking about your position before you get the ball. Moving defenders so you can concentrate on the round white thing instead. Body shape, movement.

After sessions he would come over and talk to me, and was always giving me little bits of brilliant, technical advice. I remember him scoring twice on his debut at Carlisle in the Football League Trophy, and he was absolutely brilliant. I was learning so much from him.

Like me, he wasn't naturally quick, so knew exactly how to make me a better player. Some footballers don't always listen to advice, but you'd have been a fool not to listen to a player like that. To get that sort of experience passed on to me was amazing, and I loved soaking it all in. It was golden information.

Unfortunately, I would play alongside him in only three matches.

✷ ✷ ✷

After relegation to the third tier, pre-season had gone well for me and I felt really fit. I'd done OK in the First Division so I thought I'd find the Second Division comfortable.

Out of all of our strikers, I thought I'd finished the 2002-03 season the best. Wednesday had gone and spent money on Adam Proudlock from Wolves, Robins came in from Rotherham, and we had the likes of Shefki Kuqi. Competition was tough. There was also lot of pressure on Chris Turner to get Wednesday straight back up, and it's not easy to play this young lad from Barrow when you've got some big strikers on good wages.

I started the season as a bit-part player, and you can't get any momentum like that. I played 20 minutes here and there, or some reserve football every now and again. I found myself really frustrated.

However, I wasn't doing too badly when I got a chance. I got a couple of goals in a 3-0 win at Brentford in October, and scored an injury time equaliser at Scunthorpe in December. But our form was falling away a bit, the pressure on the gaffer was rising, and the strike partners kept changing. It was hard to find any consistency.

After I'd scored at Scunny, I played 90 minutes in the win at Carlisle when Robins bagged twice. I got a whole heap of stick from the stands that day, but I was starting to feel like I was playing more of a role in the side.

The following game, in a South Yorkshire derby against Barnsley, I got sent off for a second yellow for diving. I'd got booked for a bit of a bad tackle pretty early on, and then just before half-time I went into the box and got tripped up. It should have been a penalty to us. Stonewall. But the ref carded me for diving and I had to go. I was gutted.

That killed me a little bit. After that, I struggled to get back into the side. Luckily, I had a really great group of players around me. The likes of Richard Evans, Craig Armstrong, Jon Shaw, Lewis McMahon, Jon Beswetherick and Richard Wood all lived on the same estate as me, so we were basically in one another's pockets. We'd all go to each other's houses and play Pro Evo Soccer.

They kept me going, and I still speak to them all now. It was a good group of lads, with Dean Smith as the skipper. He was brilliant, a great captain. A really nice guy. I learned a lot from him, and it's no surprise he went into management with the likes of Brentford and Aston Villa. It was playing with lads like them that made me determined to win back my place in the starting line-up.

In December 2003, less than a year after they had signed me, Turner brought me into his office and told me he wasn't going to play me anymore. Before I'd had time to process that, he then told me the club were looking to move me on in January.

I was floored. Hadn't expected that at all. I thought I'd done OK when I'd had my chances, and despite the sending off against Barnsley I felt I would be able to force my way back in.

Chris told me he had to trim the squad. I could go on loan if I wanted to, get some goals and come back and fight for a place. But I always wanted to feel settled wherever I played, so I said I wanted to leave permanently.

Maybe that was to my detriment. Maybe if I'd gone on loan from Wednesday, then I might have ended up back there when Paul Sturrock replaced Turner at the start of the following season. I knew Sturrock rated me as he'd tried to sign me for Plymouth, so perhaps I could have had a long and happy career at Wednesday.

As it was, I wanted out. Turner told me Rochdale had come in for me, and even though they were in the fourth tier, I just wanted to go and play football. Plus, Rochdale had the advantage of being closer to home and to Fay.

I met Rochdale's manager Steve Parkin in Sheffield. He'd watched me at Barrow, had seen me at Wednesday and he liked what I did. He wanted me to give Rochdale my energy and to play with a smile on my face. He offered me the chance to play all of the time, and for someone to show that belief in me was exactly what I needed.

The thought of dropping down to the Third Division didn't knock my ego at all. I just wanted to go and play football and show people everything I'd learned, especially from Mark Robins. I also liked the thought of helping a struggling team to turn their form around.

I loved what I heard from Steve, shook his hand, and it was done. I didn't even go to their ground or the training ground, I just had a good feeling. I knew, meeting him, that it was the right move. I said my goodbyes to the lads, and packed up the car for the journey to Rochdale.

When I finally saw Rochdale's ground Spotland for the first time, it was quite a shock. It felt like being back at Barrow. After Hillsborough, it was a really big change. Then I got even more of a shock with the training pitch. You got to it from the ground, walking through streets and down a hill, and you'd find it next to a cricket field and a lacrosse pitch. There was another training pitch too, on the side of a gym.

Maybe if I had seen the facilities first, I wouldn't have left Sheffield Wednesday to go to Rochdale. It was a big reality check, but in one way I quite liked being back at a club that was really down to earth, where you had to work really hard for your buck. After getting over the initial shock,

I was fine about it. Like anything, I didn't grumble and instead embraced it. I was ready for my new chapter.

Steve Parkin must have wondered what on earth he'd bought after my debut. It was at Darlington on January 31, and it was probably one of the worst performances of my whole career. I was absolutely awful. Dreadful. Terrible. I barely resembled a footballer that day.

I was trying too hard, literally working too much to try and impress. I gave the ball away all of the time, I couldn't hold anything up, I couldn't shoot properly. Everyone must have been looking at me thinking, 'Who's this useless lump we've just bought!'

If that had been a home match, I wouldn't have been able to show my face in town that night. The whole day was summed up by Fay's dad breaking his wrist while watching in the crowd. Someone had hit a shot and it was headed straight at my missus, so he'd put his arm out to protect her and, smack, it broke his wrist. It definitely wasn't one of my shots because, that day, it would have ended up sailing over the stands!

Luckily I played really well in my home debut a week later, a 3-0 win over Mansfield. I won a penalty and set up Paul Connor to score. I immediately enjoyed playing at Spotland, and it reminded me of Barrow. The crowds weren't massive but everyone who was there really wanted to be there, which created a great atmosphere.

They got behind us, and I think the fans appreciated all of the channel running I was doing for the team. It felt great to be playing 90 minutes twice a week. The only problem was that I couldn't seem to score my first goal for Rochdale to get me off and running.

It was playing on my mind a little bit, but from mid-March all of the focus was on a massive relegation battle at home against, of all teams, Carlisle.

The previous week I'd played really well when we got a draw at Huddersfield, who were in the top six. That was a massive confidence boost both for the team and for me. I knew I'd played well against a good defence and had held my own, including in a little tear-up with Efe Sodje for which we both got booked.

So I felt good, and the week leading up to the Carlisle game was the first time I'd really been in the spotlight and in the press: a Carlisle fan, rejected by the club, playing against them in a huge six-pointer at the foot of the table. But it didn't bother me. Steve Parkin pulled me in and told me to do what I do best, which was going out and enjoying my football.

It was basically a must-win match for Carlisle. If things had panned out differently then I'd probably have been in with the Carlisle fans that day, absolutely bricking it. As it turned out, however, I sent the Carlisle fans home fuming, and I still get stick for that game to this day.

Why do I still get pelters? Well, the big problem was that in the 32nd minute I got put clean through by Willo Flood, their goalkeeper Matty Glennon came out, I dinked the ball over him, and as I'd gone over him there'd been a minimal touch – but there was a touch – and the referee gave a penalty, and sent off Glennon. Our skipper Gary Jones stepped up and scored. 1-0.

All of the Carlisle fans were blaming me, saying I'd dived. I could literally see my own friends giving me absolute dog's abuse, screaming and shouting at me: "You're a disgrace", "You're a cheat", "You're a traitor", and the more simple but effective, "You're shite, Holty".

That was the first time I really got nailed. I'd be stood on the sideline for a throw-in and I'd get abuse hurled at me from people I knew. I had friends on the pitch playing for them, including Mark Boyd, who I'd played with at Wembley in the Smiths Crisps tournament. It was surreal.

I always thrived on getting stick from fans, but it's different when it's fans of the team you support. The sledging from the crowd didn't affect me that day, but for once I didn't enjoy it. I knew the reality was that at some point I'd have to go out on the town in Carlisle and I'd get even more crap for that penalty.

My brother had got a ticket for the game and was in the Carlisle end. It got to a point midway through the second half where he had to leave the ground because he would have ended up in a fight. He wasn't inclined to just sit back and hear my name being dragged through the mud, so got out of there before he got in a scrap.

It probably didn't help matters with their fans that in the second half I killed the game off with my first goal for Rochdale. I got the ball from Shaun Smith, held off a defender and tucked the shot under the 'keeper. It felt great, and Spotland was bouncing.

It was a huge win and took us three points closer to safety, but Carlisle were 10 points adrift with nine to play. It was a massive nail in the coffin for them, which was a shame, but it wasn't my fault. It was also a lesson learned for them for not signing me when they'd had their chance.

I'm still blamed to this day for their relegation, but I always tell them I can't be blamed for the other 24 matches they lost that season!

That goal gave me even more confidence, and made me fearless. It was the most I'd ever enjoyed football up to that point. You know how people talk about the pressure of a relegation battle? It wasn't like that for me. I thrived on it, I loved it, I wanted the responsibility of getting us out of it. I couldn't affect it when I was at Wednesday because I wasn't starting, but at Rochdale I was the striker they had brought in to keep them up, and I didn't see that as pressure. I enjoyed it.

Things can change quickly in football, however. We lost at Hull in the next game and the gaffer nearly killed me. Nothing was happening for me that day and Parkin kept shouting at me for no reason, so I told him to fuck off. Not clever. He would have dragged me off if we hadn't been losing.

He was properly angry with me in the dressing room after the game. The angriest man in the world at that moment. It started in silence but Parkin broke that when he turned to me and said something like, "You ever tell me to fuck off again, and not only will I take you off but I'll rip your head off your shoulders." I started to say something back, and he shut me off. "You say one more word, and that's it."

Big Gareth Griffiths was sat next to me, and I was just about to open my mouth to say something back to the gaffer when I felt Griffs' massive hand on my thigh. I looked at him and he just shook his head at me, and that made me shut my mouth. Parkin kept going on his rant, and ended it by chucking me out of the dressing room. He said to Griffs, "Grant better fucking apologise. Not today, because I don't want to hear from him today, but he has to come to me and say sorry or he's gone."

That bollocking gave me a good kick up the arse, and I'd needed it at the time. It was definitely the right thing to do. I said sorry the next day, and luckily the spat was put behind us very quickly. He knew I was emotional and raw then, and he knew how to get the best out of me.

That rawness also meant I picked up five yellow cards in 14 matches. They were all niggles, and over-exuberance. You could almost blame them on me working too hard; at least that's what I told myself back then!

I was loving my football, but in April we played Lincoln at home and big Ben Futcher – all 6ft 5in of him – gave me a dead leg early on. It had been totally innocent, but when I say a dead leg, I mean a dead leg. I had to come off after 18 minutes. I couldn't walk.

It was impossible to train all week but, with us in a relegation scrap, I found myself having to play through the pain. Within a week I was again barely able to train, and it got to the point where my leg had got so big that the physios were saying I shouldn't play at all.

We had Leyton Orient at home on April 17, and a win would be absolutely massive in our battle for survival. Parkin had been told he couldn't play me after the Orient match because of my injury, so he told me to give everything I had left in the tank and blow Orient out of the water. "Oh, and by the way, you'll be playing up top on your own." Cheers, gaffer!

Once I got going in the game I could move fine and then, on 23 minutes, bang! I headed us in front at the near post from a Neil Redfearn cross. Just before the hour mark I doubled our lead, hooking the ball over their goalie. I could barely move by this point and had to go off after 75 minutes, but I got a huge ovation, and we ended up winning the game 3-0. Even though my leg was in bits, I didn't care. This was why I'd got into football: for that feeling of scoring, of winning, of being part of a bouncing dressing room with your mates.

The win meant we'd given ourselves a chance of safety, and the lads made sure of it in the next two games as I watched from the sidelines. It was horrible not being able to play, but it was a huge relief to watch the boys doing the business to keep us up.

To give you an idea of how bad my leg was, it was still causing problems in June, two months after it had happened. I was at Alton Towers, sat on one of the rides and I still couldn't bend my leg because it was so big. I was having trouble putting it in place to get the barrier down. A girl who worked there thought I was being an idiot, came over and shoved my leg down. It was like she was pushing down a detonator! My god, I absolutely yelped and screamed. There were tears from the pain, and I think I probably swore quite loudly in front of a few startled families.

My dead leg meant I had to go into pre-season training a couple of weeks before the other lads in order to get it right. But that had the advantage of helping me to hit the ground running when the 2004-05 season kicked off. Finally, at the age of 23, I felt like a professional footballer.

CHAPTER 9

BATTERED SAUSAGES, SWAN ATTACKS AND GOALS, GOALS, GOALS

2004-05

Training well, eating right, practicing relentlessly, having a strong work ethic, looking after your body, giving 100%, making the most of your ability, playing for a manager who gets the best out of you: all of these are absolutely vital if you're going to make it as a professional footballer.

One thing that often gets overlooked, especially when you're starting out, is who you choose as your housemate. *Biiiig decision.*

Get it wrong and you could live to regret it. The bloke who seems like a good guy in the dressing room can suddenly turn out to have the kind of habits you don't want to deal with when you're at home. Noisy. Doesn't wash up. Crap taste in music. Moans. Insists on watching *EastEnders*. Doesn't like Pro Evo or FIFA. Leaves the door open when on the toilet.

I struck it lucky at Rochdale. Jamie Clarke joined in the summer of 2004, and we hit it off straight away. He was from the north and the same age as me, so we had plenty in common. We moved into a new flat together at Smithy Bridge, in the north of the town.

We got that flat for two reasons: firstly, there was a pub over the road so we could play snooker, darts and pool whenever we wanted as well as watch the football there. Secondly, there was a train station just a two-minute walk down the road so we could be in Manchester in 25 minutes, and in Leeds in an hour.

If you're thinking we chose where we lived with nights out in mind, then you'd be absolutely correct.

We got on brilliantly. We had a good laugh down the pub, never argued over the telly, entertained each other and he kept the door closed when he was in the bathroom.

Every time we speak these days, I always remind Clarkey of the time he got stood on by big Jon Parkin when we played at Macclesfield that season. Both of them had gone up for a header, and as they landed, Clarkey fell to the ground, Jon stumbled and accidentally stood right on Clarkey's chest. All 6ft 4in and 14 stone of him, right on his chest. I heard Clarkey's breath going out of him from where I was, and he had to go off.

That night we were sat watching telly and all I could hear was Clarkey trying to breathe. It was like living in a house with an octogenarian. I was chuckling to myself all night about it.

In the morning I came down and he was there with his usual bowl of cereal.

"How are you feeling this morning? Little sore are you?"

"Good laugh you had at my expense, wasn't it Holty."

"I don't know what you mean. Just concerned, pal. Wasn't funny at all!"

"Well I'll show you what's not funny."

With that, Clarkey yanked his top up to reveal every single one of Jon Parkin's studs printed across his chest. Every. Single. One. A perfect tattoo of Jon's size 12s. I've never laughed so hard in my life, and Clarkey had to stop himself from seeing the funny side because laughing made him double up in pain!

Clarkey loved his routine. When you finished your dinner he'd whip your plate away straight away to clean it. He couldn't let it rest. Last mouthful, the plate's gone from under you and it'd be cleaned and put away before you had a chance to finish chewing.

We lived close to a few other lads who'd got flats together, so there was a group of us who used to hang out around each other's digs. Rochdale wasn't the most amazing place to celebrate a win or have a night out, unfortunately, and because we were young we got bored quite easily. We always tried to keep ourselves busy after training, so we'd often get the train into Manchester and get a coffee and do a bit of shopping. There's a lot of downtime when you're a footballer, which can be quite dangerous. Boredom could too easily turn into, "Let's just go for a pint". You had to make yourself busy in order to avoid doing that all the time. Often we'd go bowling or play snooker, and maybe go out for dinner.

It was different on a Friday, though. Me and Clarkey would head back after training and stay in for the night. We had a ritual to stick to.

Initially, I'd have pasta carbonara every Friday. Clarkey always had pasta chicken arrabiata with garlic bread. Pasta was good for the night before a match, and it was an easy thing to cook after a hard day of training.

Early in the season we came home on a Friday after training and all of the gas was off. We had food in the cupboards for cooking, but nothing to cook it with. We couldn't be bothered to go out for dinner, so, being knackered and lazy, I said I was going to get a Chinese.

Now, as a man of ritual, this threw Clarkey off a bit. I told him he'd be all right, and I'd grab him a Chinese too. It was the kind of takeaway that does Chinese food and fish and chips. I hadn't had a battered sausage for ages, and as soon as I saw one behind the counter I suddenly got a hunger for it. I got myself curry fried rice, chips and a large battered sausage – not a foot-long, just a standard six-incher. I had a match the next day after all!

I took it back home, along with Clarkey's chow mein. Got it down me, played the next day and did really well in the game. So I thought, 'Well, I enjoyed that more than my carbonara, I played great, so it must have done me good.' The conclusion from that piece of logic? I ended up going to the Chinese every Friday before a home game for the rest of the season.

BATTERED SAUSAGES, SWAN ATTACKS AND GOALS, GOALS, GOALS

I scored 13 goals at home that campaign so, no matter what a nutritionist might tell you, I put it all down to my curry fried rice, chips and a large battered sausage.

* * *

Because my dead leg had forced me to come back early for pre-season, I ended up having a really good summer and felt fit and strong for 2004-05. The spirit was good in the group, and we felt we had an outside shot at the playoffs.

First, though, we had to deal with the Swan Incident.

Our first match of the season was against Scunthorpe at Glanford Park. It was a roasting hot day, and we'd started the game really well. Absolutely battering them. After 20 minutes, out of nowhere, a swan swooped down and landed on the pitch. It was a bloody beast of a bird, and it plopped down right next to our goalkeeper, Neil Edwards.

The ref stopped play and Neil, trying to be the hero, went over to get the swan. Quite what he thought he was going to do with it once he picked it up, I'm not sure. Put it in goal with him? Adopt it? Have it with some roast potatoes?

He crept up behind it and, just as he was about to lunge in to grab it, the swan turned around, stood its ground and stared at Neil. It just stood there, eyeballing him. Beak to nose. It was like it was saying, "You want some do you, mate?"

Next, the bird jerked its beak forward, grabbed Neil's glove, bit his fingers and took the glove clean off his hand!

The players were in stitches, the ref didn't know what to do, the crowd was giving Neil all sorts of abuse and I was just stood there thinking, 'Please fly off with the glove, please fly off with it!'

Sadly the swan dropped the glove, took off, circled the ground for a minute until it got high enough and then flew away to huge cheers. Unfortunately for us, after that we were absolutely dreadful and Neil ended up letting in three goals. He blamed the swan.

***

Fittingly, we had Swansea at home next. We lost but I played really well, and then did OK again in our first win of the season against Southend. I'd started the season in good form, but it nags away at you if you haven't opened your account. The gaffer said to me my goal would come, and so it did against Wycombe in our fourth match. After that I couldn't stop scoring.

Next up were Wolves in the Carling Cup at Spotland. They'd been relegated from the Premier League so had a decent squad. Manchester United legend Paul Ince was in their XI, as well as Scotland international Kenny Miller. The game was on Sky, and I loved the opportunity to test myself against a class team on a big stage.

In just the fourth minute I got myself ahead of Jody Craddock to bury a cross, and I was also involved as we went 2-0 up before the half hour. I was making my mark.

Ince scored an absolute screamer just before half-time and Wolves went on to turn the game around. But it was good to take on guys like Craddock and Rob Edwards, and to play against a player of Ince's stature was a bit surreal really. I got kicked quite a bit and had to come off in the second half, but I felt that was a mark of how well I'd played, and how much bother I'd given them. The local newspaper in Manchester gave me a good write-up, commenting, "This lad is a class act in the bread-and-butter league games, and he proved he could be a class act on the big stage. No doubt there would have been one or two managers, having watched this Sky TV game, asking the pin-stripes on Tuesday morning if they could go out and buy Holt before long."

My form carried on into a great November. I hit two against Cambridge in a 2-1 win, two against Oxford in a 2-1 win and two against Stevenage in a 2-0 win. Those last two victories had been in the FA Cup, and set us up for a third round clash with Premier League Charlton Athletic at the Valley. After the Wolves game, I had a taste for the big occasion.

Charlton put out a good side that day, with Scott Parker, Matt Holland, Danny Murphy, Francis Jeffers and Dean Kiely all starting. We lost 4-1 but played really well. They'd gone 2-0 up and I pulled a goal back with a volley. I also hit the post and Kiely made a couple of great saves from me, and we felt we'd been really unlucky to have been on the end of a harsh-looking scoreline.

By the end of January I'd hit 20 goals, scored against a Wolves side that had just been relegated from the top tier and against a Charlton team that would finish the season 11th in the Premier League. I was finding League Two, as it was now called, quite comfortable, scoring all types of goals and working hard. Those were the days I used to run the channels and pick up stupid yellow cards – I got 16 that season! None of the bookings were sinister. They were all for closing down too passionately – don't laugh – or a bit of dissent when I'd be raging at certain decisions. But it was just me being naive, and none of them were nasty, really.

I was getting quite a lot of compliments, and I knew there was interest in me. It could have gone to my head, but I was just loving playing football and scoring goals for Dale.

✳✳✳

In January, we signed an attacking midfielder from Stockport County called Rickie Lambert.

I'd be lying if I said I immediately thought he'd get to the top level: successive promotions with Southampton, signed by Liverpool, 11 England caps. I didn't look at him and think, "There's a Premier League player", but boy, was he talented. His technique was unbelievable. He could ping a ball anywhere he wanted, and his hold-up play was strong. He just got better and better, and the gaffer quickly moved him from attacking midfield to up top alongside me.

My role changed a bit when we were partnered together. When I had Paul Tait next to me, Taity did a lot of the hold-up play and my job was to hit the channels and get in behind, which meant I was really prolific. When Rickie came in, we were both doing the Taity role as well, so my goals dried up a bit. I didn't mind at all though, because we sparked off each other. Rickie's a great guy. A nice Scouser. Proper down-to-earth; jovial and jokey.

On the pitch he could do pretty much anything. We had a rule where if anyone got touched 25 or 30 yards from goal, we'd go down because Rickie's free-kick taking was out of this world. He hit the ball so sweetly, and I remember everyone applauding him after he'd scored one against Northampton Town. From the edge of the area, bent over the wall with curl and dip right into the top corner. Unbelievable.

Our partnership really blossomed, and the whole team was playing well enough to give us hope of a playoff push. Life off the pitch was good, training was fun and the football was going well. There was a new experience for me, too: I was getting recognised around Rochdale and a little bit around Manchester. Now, the public weren't exactly flocking to me for selfies or autographs. Just now and then. But it was another step towards me feeling like a proper footballer.

I scored twice away at Swansea in March, once for us and an own goal for them from a corner. I'd put us 1-0 up on the half-hour mark, but within 10 minutes both sides were down to 10 men. Lee Trundle got sent off for going in two-footed on Clarkey – there'd be no stud prints on his chest this time, thankfully – and then a minute later Taity was shown a red for a late challenge. That caused one of those almighty rucks where the ref doesn't know what's going on, the players can't remember what started it, and everyone feels a bit embarrassed when it finishes.

The draw meant we were just too far off the pace for a spot in the playoffs, and we ended the season in ninth, two places away from a crack at Wembley. We were disappointed that we hadn't given ourselves that shot, but bearing in mind we'd only just survived a relegation battle the previous season, everyone felt we'd done ourselves proud and thought we'd have a right chance the following season.

I'd scored 24 goals and was really happy. It felt good to be making a bit of a name for myself, and even though there was a lot of speculation about clubs coming in for me, I just wanted to get into the next season and keep on scoring. Once you get the taste for it, you don't want it to stop.

***

One thing I learned quickly at Rochdale was that there is often a big difference between the perception teammates can have of certain players, and what the fans think of them. A dressing room favourite can often be a crowd target, and vice versa.

Take Paul Tait. He might have scored only three goals in that 2004-05 season, and was in and out of the starting XI after Rickie Lambert came in, but he gave so much to the team. The fans grumbled about him but everyone in the squad knew what he was doing and appreciated it, especially me as I was the player who most benefited from him.

He was brilliant in the air and that took a massive weight off me because I didn't have to be the guy they hit long. I could run the channels and chase his flick-ons. He always said he didn't mind who was scoring as long as the team was winning. It's an easy thing to say, but he genuinely meant it. To have someone like that in your dressing room is absolutely massive.

Another guy who maybe didn't get the credit he should have done was Ernie Cooksey. He joined at the start of that season and just ran and ran. He never stopped running, and smashing people, and running. We called him Ernie The Fastest Milkman In The West after the Benny Hill song; we always sang that to him.

He fitted in to the group really well. Everyone absolutely loved him, and he was just a really funny guy. He lived in the same flats as I did, and he was a big kid really.

He was such a bad loser, though. We used to play cricket down the hallway and putt golf balls down the corridor, and he would get properly competitive about that – even more than me. But he would always be laughing and joking; that's how I always remember him.

It was such a massive shock when he was diagnosed with cancer in 2006. He seemed to have beaten it, but was diagnosed again in 2008. It's always shocking when someone gets diagnosed, especially when they're so young.

In May 2008, when I'd moved to Forest, there was a benefit match between Rotherham and Oldham – one of his former clubs – at Boundary Park to raise money for his treatment. I was invited along, and was on the sideline with him. He was worried about having to go on to take a penalty because he was tired after a long day. I told him to imagine he was two-footing the football like he used to two-foot the opposition and he'd be fine. I put my arm around him and I felt the frailness of him, and the reality of the situation really dawned on me. Ernie being Ernie, he went on, took the pen and scored.

After the match we had a pint like the old days and we all went to the same Indian we used to go to. Tragically, he died just a few months later. There was a huge turnout at the funeral, when it really hit you just how popular he was.

I'll always remember his infectious laugh and his love for life. He was a real team man, and a fantastic bloke. RIP, Ernie.

MY TOP 5...
WRESTLERS

1 THE UNDERTAKER

I just loved the drama of him, with his pallbearer
by his side. I loved the theatre of it all, and for a big guy
he was a bloody good wrestler as well.

2 THE ULTIMATE WARRIOR

The euphoria around him and the way he entered.
You knew he was ready for war. He was a bit different
to all of the others out there.

3 THE HITMAN

Sharp moves. Long hair. Flamboyant. And I loved
the way he wrestled, especially his finishing move
– the sharp shooter.

4 MR PERFECT

He was always the baddie, but he had the flair and good
looks. His perfect plex was renowned as being unbelievable.

5 BIG BOSS MAN

I loved the way he used to come in swinging his truncheon.

CHAPTER 10

MUDDY PITCHES, A DELIBERATE BOOKING AND A BIG MOVE

2005-06

Whenever I'm asked what the biggest difference is between playing in the Premier League and playing in the fourth tier, I think back to one game at Spotland.

It was New Year's Day, against Grimsby. The day before we'd been told the game would probably be called off, but to follow our normal routine in case it was on. Of course, we just wanted it abandoned early so we could enjoy a few beers on New Year's Eve.

No such luck. The call never came, so we all saw in 2005 stone-cold sober. Well, I say all. I can only really vouch for myself, but everyone seemed clear-headed in the dressing room the next morning! We got to Spotland, and the pitch was a right state. Despite that, we were told the game would go ahead.

The ground was frozen in places, and a bog in other areas. One minute you needed ice skates, the next minute you needed waders. I'd run in behind, and the ball would suddenly stop. That just encouraged the defenders to absolutely bury me with a tackle, and point to the surface like they were totally blameless.

At the half-hour mark it started absolutely tipping it down. Like a Singapore monsoon, but in freezing temperatures. The frozen patches turned into bogs and the bogs turned into swamps. Proper football. Or, you know, properly shit football.

Just before half-time I won a corner. The ball came in, and slapped down in the bog. Stuck. Now it became a scrap in the penalty area. A massive melee, with mud flying everywhere, legs swinging this way and that, shin pads taking a right battering. Gareth Griffiths went in, and someone booted him in the hand. The ball got cleared and Griffs, all 6ft 6in of him, rose from the ground, covered in mud from head to toe, a finger pointing out at a funny angle from his hand because it had been dislocated, and he heard the ref say, "I think I'm going to have to call this off".

So Griffs says, not so calmly, "You what?"

"It's dangerous, so it's best to call it off, but I'll let you know when we get in for half-time."

Griffs, who was already raging, turned into the Incredible Hulk. "CALL IT OFF? I'VE NEARLY BROKEN MY FINGER! WE COULD HAVE HAD A FUCKING DRINK LAST NIGHT!"

We all marched in for half-time. Both sides wanted to carry on and get it over and done with, and I was sat in the dressing room looking at Griffs, crying with laughter inside. His face was as red as anything – at least in the gaps between the mud – and he was fuming to himself. He got the physio to come over and pop his finger back in, but as soon as the finger snapped back in the ref put his head around the dressing room door and said, "Right lads, it's unplayable out there. The game's off."

Griffs exploded, and the rest of us were trying not to laugh. No way I was going to be caught laughing; in that mood he'd probably have swung a fist at me, even with a dislocated finger!

It was quite rare back then to be able to play on a pristine surface in that league. Now, pitches across the lower divisions and in non-league more often than not are really good, and very well prepared.

That's great, of course, and how it should be. Better playing surfaces mean better football, but it just shows how quickly it's changed.

However, while I reckon the standard of the top tier is probably a bit higher than when I played, despite the improvement in pitches I'd say the standard in the fourth tier isn't as good as it used to be.

When I was in League Two you had a group of players who were 18-20, and a group of older players. There weren't as many loans from the higher divisions as you see now, so every side was full of players who had already proved themselves, or young guys who were coming through the youth ranks and were rated highly.

If you go through most teams from when I played in that division, most of them will have had someone who went on to play in the Premier League or at the top of the Championship. You'd learn your trade against wily old foxes; good players who knew their football. They'd teach you the ropes. They were really tough leagues, and to get to the top, you'd have to do it the hard way. Look at Rickie Lambert. He had to keep scoring 20 goals a season for four or five years with Rochdale and Bristol Rovers until he got a move to a big side in Southampton, and even then they were only in League One at the time.

I'd scored 24 goals in 2004-05 and yet it took me another half a season of scoring consistently to get a move to League One. That shows you how hard it was. If a young lad was scoring 24 goals in that league now, they'd be getting a move up a division straight away.

***

After you've had a really good year, it's only natural to be interested in who might come in for you. You've always got an idea in your head about who you'd like to show an interest, and at what sort of club you think you could thrive. Even if you're really happy where you currently are, you want to know what sort of offers you might be attracting.

After 24 goals in a season, leading the line for a club who hadn't been fancied for a promotion push, I did expect a few sides to be sniffing around me in the summer. As it turned out, though, no clubs really picked up my scent. I was told there was a little bit of interest, and there were rumours, but nothing concrete and nothing at all that would have matched Rochdale's valuation of me.

It was a little bit dispiriting, if I'm honest. What more did I have to do to get teams on the phone? I wasn't clamouring for a move at all; I was really enjoying my time at Rochdale and believed it had been absolutely the right decision to join them from Sheffield Wednesday. There was a brilliant group of lads there, the manager was exactly what I needed and I was playing week in, week out. But I felt I could play at a higher level, and it would have been a tough decision to make if a League One side had come in for me.

I realised that the one thing I had to do to attract the attention of other clubs was quite simple: keep scoring goals. Don't worry about the future; concentrate on the here and now.

Steve Parkin told me I'd had a great year but the new season was time to prove I could get even better. That talk from him made sure I wasn't getting an ego, or thinking I was too good for Rochdale. I still had a lot to prove, and I was determined to go out and work hard for the team to show everyone I wasn't just a one-season wonder. I had to prove it to myself, too.

There was another important decision to add into the mix, too: me and Fay had spoken about moving in together. I'd said I'd like a bit more normality and stability, and I was finding the commute to Carlisle and back difficult.

If I did get a transfer, having to commute from somewhere like Swansea or a London club would negatively affect my football. Fay was on the same page as me. It just all seemed to fit at the right time. We were also arranging to get married the following summer, and Fay wanted to make sure we'd lived together first.

She came down around the middle of September to live with me and Clarkey. He wasn't bothered at all; he had a girlfriend who lived in Leeds at university, so he was there quite a lot which meant me and Fay often had the house to ourselves. He also wasn't really in a position to moan anyway because he'd bought a German Pointer dog called Pippa to live in the flat with him, who seemed to take a lot of looking after!

It was brilliant to have Fay there more often. I was eating more healthily because we'd cook together, and it gave my life more structure. I felt better in myself, like life was properly coming together.

I'd already started the season well, and had scored in our first game against Shrewsbury, putting one past a young Joe Hart to give us a 1-0 win. I scored nine goals in my first 11 games, and me and Rickie's partnership had really blossomed. So by the time Fay moved down I was in a really good place. Enjoying games, enjoying scoring, enjoying life outside football.

They used to say at Rochdale that if I picked up a yellow card I'd get a goal. They weren't far off. I got booked six times in the opening 12 games, and by the time it got to December I realised that another yellow would mean I'd be suspended for a game over Christmas.

Tempting. Very tempting.

Yes, it really does go on. If you have the chance to have Boxing Day off, then nine times out of 10 you're going to take it. You'd still have to go in for training on Christmas Day, but then you'd have the rest of the day to stuff your face with turkey, have a few beers and fall asleep in front of the telly with the family.

You tell yourself that it's a long season, so having a game off will actually benefit you and the team in the long run. To be fair to myself, I knew at some point I was going to pick up another booking anyway because I was that useless, so why not try and time it to my advantage?

MUDDY PITCHES, A DELIBERATE BOOKING AND A BIG MOVE

Against Wycombe Wanderers on December 10, I got my chance.

We were already 2-0 down, and had been given a proper chasing. Warren Goodhind had been sent off for us in the 57th minute for tugging back Sergio Torres's ponytail – fair enough really – but then 12 minutes later I did something criminal.

I didn't mean it to be as bad as it was. But it was bad. Really bad. Me and their centre-back Roger Johnson had enjoyed a running battle all game and, to be fair, he'd been having the better of me. There was a loose ball, and it suddenly popped into my head: 'Here's your chance for that yellow, Holty.' Bang! It was supposed to be one-footed but I got the timing all wrong and ended up two-footing Johnson. He'd been further away than I'd thought, so I'd just kept on going and going until I'd clattered into him.

As soon as I made contact, I knew it wasn't going to be a yellow. Out popped the red, and I thought, 'Oh my god, I'm dead!' Our skipper Gary Jones gave me an absolute bollocking as I was walking off, and it was completely deserved. I'd let the team down.

I walked back into the dressing room and Goody must have thought I'd been subbed because he apologised to me for his sending off. He perked up when I told him I'd been sent off too, because that saved him from the gaffer's main wrath. Him getting sent off was one thing; that can happen. But me also getting sent off 10 minutes later? Absolutely no excuse.

We both bricked it for the next 20 minutes, and in trooped the players. Beaten 3-0, on the back of a 4-1 loss at Grimsby four days ago, and two idiots back in the dressing room because of red cards. It's fair to say we weren't everyone's cup of tea on the way home.

On the plus side, I did end up having a lovely Christmas off. I missed three matches, including at Carlisle on New Year's Eve. We lost all three, which I felt bad about, and it made the turkey that little bit less tasty than it would have if we'd been winning.

I came back for a 1-1 draw against Northampton Town at home. Their 'keeper had a blinder, saving three or four of my shots as we searched for a winner. It wasn't to be, though. A shame, as that turned out to be the last game I played for Rochdale.

***

From the December of 2005 I'd heard a lot of people were coming in for me. Spotland isn't the biggest ground in the world, so when you're being scouted it gets around pretty quickly. I'd scored 15 in 24 matches on the back of a shed-load the previous season, so I thought there was a good chance there would be interest.

Rumours were circling that bids would come in, so I'd actually thought the sending off at Wycombe might have killed me a bit because teams wouldn't be able to watch me for three matches.

I needn't have worried, though. At the start of January I got a call from my agent telling me Nottingham Forest were going to come in for me that week. *Nottingham Forest!* I hadn't expected a big club like Forest to be the first to show their hand.

They'd just been relegated from the Championship to League One, so were a really big team in that division. They'd had a ropey start to the season, but their squad was top-notch. Of course I was interested.

A few days after the initial call from my agent, I was sat in the hairdressers waiting for Fay, and my agent's number flashed up on my phone. Forest had matched my buy-out clause at Rochdale. Wow. Things were moving quickly.

I called the gaffer from the salon and told him I'd heard Forest had bid for me. Steve confirmed it and asked if I was interested. These moments can be awkward, because you don't want to sound too excited, in case it all falls through. You try to avoid sounding desperate for the move. I said it was a really good opportunity, and I was keen to talk to them.

Steve paused and replied, "Good, because you'd be an idiot not to be!"

I waited for Fay to finish having her hair done, told her it looked lovely and said, "By the way, we're moving to Nottingham."

As ever, she didn't have a clue who Nottingham Forest were. Me banging on about European Cups, Brian Clough, John Robertson and Martin O'Neill didn't mean anything to her, but she could see how excited I was. We got some bits together and headed straight to Nottingham.

I'd not been to the City Ground before. Like Hillsborough, it was just great to walk around and take in the history of the place. I met the chairman and the manager, Gary Megson, and signed there and then. No doubts whatsoever. Done.

We headed back to Rochdale, packed up our belongings and put them in my car with the seats down; we didn't have much. I went into Rochdale's training ground, said my goodbyes and thanked the gaffer for everything. Everyone wished me luck, and off we went.

Fay was really happy to move, and the extra bit of money from the new contract meant we were more comfortable. It was a three-year deal, so we had that security too, which meant we could start planning to get a house, get the wedding sorted and maybe start trying for a baby too. Life was moving fast.

I was sad to leave Rochdale. It wasn't easy to walk out of the door.

Going there had been massive for me. It had been the perfect place to craft my trade. It was like being back at Barrow, but in the Football League: a mix of old lads and young lads all with a big desire to win and a manager with an ethos of really hard work. I loved it.

I was a far better player by the end of my time at Rochdale. I'd learned to work the channels and run in behind, as well as with different styles of strike partners. I was a more all-round player, and could make different runs because of how good Rickie Lambert was at picking passes.

I had improved physically too. I had become a stronger athlete and a more rounded centre-forward. Living with Fay had helped that, as I had stopped eating a Chinese before every home game!

I'd been to the Championship with Sheffield Wednesday and had found it comfortable, while League Two showed me I could score goals. I felt I was ready to go and prove myself in League One, and that inner belief was down to Rochdale.

I owe Steve Parkin everything. Without the confidence he had shown in me I wouldn't have been anywhere near making a move to a club like Nottingham Forest. As I said my goodbye to him, he told me, "Do me a favour. Go and fulfil your potential. Don't be worried about anything. Just go and do what you do and see where it takes you."

With that advice ringing in my ears, we headed to Nottingham.

CHAPTER 11

SACKED MANAGERS, WEDDING DAYS AND CHESNEY HAWKES

2005-06

It felt great to join Nottingham Forest. As I said, they hadn't started the 2005-06 season very well, but with their squad you knew they were capable of putting a good run together for the playoffs. They had a lot of quality players: Ian Breckin, James Perch and Wes Morgan at the back, Kris Commons, Sammy Clingan, Gary Holt and Nicky Southall in midfield, Nathan Tyson and Jack Lester up top. It was a squad that should have been too good for League One.

So it's fair to say I hadn't expected to walk in on my first day at training and find half the squad in one dressing room, and the other half in another dressing room.

Apparently Gary Megson had split the squad into those he liked, and those he didn't. I'd never seen anything like that before. Not once. I was shocked. What had I got myself into?

It was a weird scenario, and it felt like the writing was on the wall for Megson. It worried me, because I'd just signed quite a long-term deal, and the demons from my time at Halifax crept in. What if Megson was dismissed and someone came in who didn't fancy me?

My first impression of Megson had been good, so it was even more of a shock to see the dressing room like that. I'd had a meeting in his office before joining and he'd asked me to tell him one thing I could guarantee. I'd said hard work. That answer made him stand up, look me in the eye and shake my hand. He told me that everyone always answered "goals", and that you could never guarantee that; the only thing you could guarantee was hard work.

Despite that initial good impression, it was a tough start for me. It seemed he wasn't getting the best out of the team and some of the players had started to turn on him. It wasn't a healthy place to be.

Although I had my doubts, I felt a lot better after I scored on my debut against Oldham Athletic at the City Ground. I met a Kris Commons free-kick at the far post in the 25th minute and bundled it home to put us 1-0 up. It was a great feeling to get up and running in my first game, especially at home against Oldham, who are Rochdale's rivals. There was also relief that I hadn't repeated the absolute nightmare of a debut I'd had for Rochdale.

We won 3-0, I'd scored and had played a big part in the third goal, and a little weight had already been lifted. It also felt good knowing Kris was going to be supplying those sort of crosses regularly, and I could lap those up all day. Maybe things weren't going to be so bad after all.

* * *

From that match it was clear what a big club Forest are. A great crowd was in, and the boxes were full. There was a real expectancy that you'd go out there and win, and I enjoyed that pressure. I embraced it. I had wanted to really push on and to play for a club with great stature, and Forest had offered that. I was determined to repay their faith.

Everyone from my generation is aware of Forest's history. The famous red shirts, the European glory under Brian Clough. I'd grown up watching Stuart Pearce and Des Walker, who was my idol when I was younger, and watched them in the old First Division and on cup runs.

Even with all of that history you felt at the City Ground, it wasn't until you started walking around the city that you realised how much football meant to the place. The shirt is worn everywhere in town, you'd constantly get people coming up to you and saying good luck, and it seemed like everyone knew who you were. It must be a nightmare being a Notts County fan in that city. If you went for dinner, went to the shop, got your car done, everyone around you would be Forest fans and they all wanted to talk about football.

I'd come from Rochdale, where people occasionally came up to me, to Forest, where someone would recognise me everywhere I went. At first it was a little bit weird, and it took a while to get used to strangers wanting to talk to me. It's bizarre when it first happens; a bit surreal. Once I'd got used to it, I embraced it and it was fine.

It made me realise I'd gone from a nobody to a level where people were starting to know who I was. To know my name. It was another step on the journey of feeling like a proper professional footballer.

Fay and I settled into Nottingham life really quickly. We bought a house in Ruddington, a village just south of the city. Sammy Clingan was our next-door neighbour, James Perch lived over the road and Nathan Tyson lived on the corner. We all got on really well, and I still speak to the lads to this day.

Fay was pregnant, which was amazing news. We were both elated. With a new house, and plans for the wedding coming along, it felt like we knew exactly what our path was going to be. We were enjoying the ride, and we had no worries in the world.

The same couldn't be said for Gary Megson.

✶✶✶

Since my debut, we'd gone six games without a win and the pressure was really mounting on the gaffer. In February we travelled to Oldham, who we'd beaten 3-0 just a month earlier, and things went from bad to worse.

We somehow got in at half-time 0-0, but Megson took Jack Lester off, and Jack went ballistic. These things can happen in dressing rooms, but you got the sense at the time that it was a real turning point. We got done in the second half and lost 3-0. It was horrid. Our travelling fans were chanting 'Megson out', and we looked a totally different side to the one that had beaten Oldham in January. We were lost out there.

The defeat left us four points above the relegation places, which was unacceptable for a team with our squad. The next day we were informed that Megson had been let go, or rather had "left by mutual consent." None of us were surprised in the slightest.

It was the most bizarre thing, because from the next morning you went from a dressing room with 20 players to a dressing room with 30. It was an odd feeling having everyone in there for the first time since I'd joined. It felt like a fresh start for everyone. The elephant had been removed from the room, and it lifted the mood immediately. We suddenly went from worrying about relegation to looking at the league table and talking about putting a miracle run together for a shot at the top six.

You never want to see anyone losing their job, but it was probably the right thing to happen at that time. I can't really say much about what sort of manager Megson was because I didn't play for long enough under him, but I was grateful he signed me and had shown that belief in me.

It's one of the few times I'd been at a club when a manager had been let go, actually. I was away on loan when Uwe Rösler got sacked by Wigan, which was a shame as I'd have liked to have clapped him out of the door (more of that later). When Malky Mackay was sacked by Wigan I was injured, so it didn't really affect me.

While Megson leaving did release a lot of tension, I was a bit worried about who might come in and replace him. It created a bit of uncertainty, but luckily that was dealt with quickly. The board appointed Frank Barlow, who was Megson's assistant, and the reserve team manager Ian McParland as co-caretaker managers until the end of the season. I knew both of them liked me as a player, and that was a big relief. I could concentrate on trying to make my mark in League One.

The new gaffers didn't change much. Their approach was just a bit more relaxed, and they freshened things up and tweaked the training. There wasn't a massive tactical switch; it was just about getting the best out of the players in the building. They got everyone back together and playing for each other, and it felt like a cloud had been lifted.

I was up top with Tyson. They wanted me to get in the box, work hard and score goals. Keep it simple. They didn't chop and change the starting line-up as much as Megson had, and that seemed to really help our rhythm.

After that Oldham game, we went on a 10-match unbeaten run. We smashed Swindon Town 7-1 – I'm not sure how I didn't get on the scoresheet that day – and had big wins over Milton Keynes and Chesterfield. Suddenly, with three games remaining, we had a chance to get into the playoffs. It just showed the squad had always been there to challenge, and Barlow and McParland had set us free.

Unfortunately, as soon as we started believing we might creep into the playoffs, we forgot how to win. We lost 3-2 at Hartlepool, and then drew at home to Bournemouth. We went into the last game of the season with our fate out of our hands, and could only draw at Bradford. Even if we'd won, the teams above us had done enough and we finished one place and two points outside the playoffs.

It was a bitter pill to swallow. If we'd had McParland and Barlow from the start of the season, or just a month earlier, we'd have been in the playoffs comfortably. But it wasn't to be.

Although everyone was gutted not to have made it into the top six, there was a good mood among the group. We knew we had the chance to mount a serious promotion push the following season, so it was a bit of a surprise when McParland and Barlow said they didn't want the job permanently. Both of them really saw themselves as coaches, rather than managers, I think. That's fair enough.

Colin Calderwood, who'd had a great career with Tottenham Hotspur, was brought in from Northampton Town at the end of the season. It was another manager to impress, but I knew my performances since I'd come in had been good. I'd settled into League One really well, and was looking forward to hitting the ground running in 2006-07.

First though, I had the little matter of getting married to attend to.

***

Our wedding was a brilliant day, at Dalston Hall just outside Carlisle. I'm glad we'd waited because it just felt the right time: we'd bought our house and we knew we were having Evie; Fay was 13 weeks pregnant then. It was a great time. Everyone had a good laugh, everyone had a good giggle.

It was always going to be a tough day because my dad wasn't there, and I was the first one to get married. I mentioned him in my speech, and that helped my brother, who was my best man. His speech was decent, but I think he was still reeling from me coming down the aisle to Chesney Hawkes' *The One And Only*. He wasn't happy about that.

We got married in a gazebo, so I had to walk out first to get there. I hadn't told anyone apart from Fay that *The One And Only* was going to blast out, and when I was walking down the aisle my brother looked at me like, 'What an idiot'! He was right, of course. What an idiot. But everyone was laughing and that took the nerves out of the situation. Fay came down the aisle, and she looked absolutely beautiful. Everything felt right.

Most of the people there were friends and family from around Carlisle, most of whom I'd played football with. Funnily enough, we didn't get *Hello!* magazine coming along. Can't imagine why not.

Me and Fay had been through a lot since we'd got together, so this felt like the start of a new chapter. We'd just got our house, Evie was on the way, I had the safety of the contract at Forest so we were lucky to be in a good position financially. Everything had come to this moment. We were in a great place and going in the right direction.

It was a great sign off to a great year. I'd scored goals, got a move, had an amazing wedding, a great honeymoon in Dubai, and knew my little girl was on the way. Not bad for a useless lad from Carlisle.

CHAPTER 12

MANAGER FALL-OUTS, BECOMING A DAD AND PLAYOFF HURT

2006-07

It's not often you finish a season as your team's leading goalscorer and get voted Player of the Season by the fans, while also feeling like your manager doesn't rate you. But that's exactly how my second year at Forest panned out.

From the very first day of the 2006-07 campaign, my relationship with Colin Calderwood wasn't great, and it didn't get any better. I'd worked really hard in pre-season, felt in a good place and was ready to hit the ground running. We were the bookies' favourites for promotion, Calderwood had talked up our chances in the media, and I felt our squad was good enough to back it all up.

Then I found myself on the bench for the first game, at home to Bradford. That really pissed me off. Nathan Tyson got injured just six minutes into the match, so I was sent straight into the action. Nathan's injury was bad, so by default I got a run in the side. I started the season well and made myself undroppable, scoring five goals in the opening eight matches. However, I knew I wasn't Calderwood's cup of tea. I just had a feeling, and in the end I was proved right.

It had been more enjoyable playing under McParland and Barlow, and as a team we had become really inconsistent. The tag of title favourites seemed to weigh heavily on the coaching team, and that rubbed off on the players. Don't get me wrong, being a manager is a really tough job, with much more pressure than a player faces. But after I'd been left on the bench against Bradford, I just knew the relationship between me and the coaches was never going to blossom.

In November Bristol City approached Forest to ask about my availability. Even though I was scoring goals, they agreed to sell me. I knocked it back because Fay was heavily pregnant and we didn't want to move with a little one on the way. It was a weird situation: scoring goals, working hard for the team, but not wanted. Strange, right?

That was bad enough, but my relationship with Calderwood reached boiling point when we played Chelsea at Stamford Bridge in January 2007 in the FA Cup. He put me on the left of a five-man midfield, but with us 3-0 down he pulled me off at half-time. I went absolutely ballistic; hammered him at the end of the game in front of everyone. Nailed him. I told him I'd done him a fucking favour by playing on the wing against a really good side, with Didier Drogba, Andriy Shevchenko, Michael Essien, and Frank Lampard in the starting XI that day. I'd worked my nuts off and had done a job for the team and the gaffer, so to get taken off at half-time was the final straw.

Even though I was at Forest for another 18 months, I knew me and Calderwood were done. It's funny, because even though I was the club's leading goalscorer that season with 18, and scored plenty of winners, I can barely remember any details about the games. With Rochdale, I could tell you every goal I scored, every chance I missed, every kick I received. With Forest, most games from 2006-07 and 2007-08 roll into one, which probably tells you everything about about my relationship with the coaching team.

Of course, it was an honour to play for such a big club, and to have been their leading scorer for a season is something I look back on with a lot of pride. I just wasn't enjoying my football as much as I should have been.

✳✳✳

You look through the Forest squad from that season and the quality was ridiculous. It was a really great bunch of guys, and it was good fun to play alongside them. That was vital, because if you're not getting on with the gaffer, then it's really important you're enjoying your time in the dressing room.

There were a lot of leaders in that group, too. Big personalities. Neil Harris was already leadership material, Jack Lester and Ian Breckin were leaders, and there was no doubt that Wes Morgan and Luke Chambers would become captains at some point in their careers. When there are so many leaders in a group, it tends to mean the dressing room is really strong. It also meant that things could spark up quickly because egos would clash and people weren't afraid to say it straight, but problems got defused quickly in those situations.

Wes Morgan was quiet to start with. He was pretty young then, but he was funny too. His nickname was the Bear and he used to call me the Polar Bear, which we probably shouldn't think about too much! But what a player. The skills he had for a centre-half even at a young age were unbelievable. When he came out of his shell he was like a big kid, laughing and joking all of the time. I knew he'd end up at the highest level because he had everything: quick, strong, aggressive and full of skills. I'm absolutely delighted to see what he's gone on to achieve, winning a Premier League winners' medal at Leicester City.

Kris Commons was such a good player. Technically he was outstanding. Jack Lester was another who was brilliant technically; he could unlock anything. He had the best hips in the world! Like with Wes Hoolahan at Norwich, if Jack was on your team in training the likelihood was you'd win the session because he was that good.

He was probably the angriest man I've met on a football pitch as well! Constantly chuntering and moaning and swearing and raging. But those hips didn't lie, and he could put passes on a plate for you.

Luke Chambers was a great guy, which probably disappoints any Norwich fans reading this! We signed him in January of the 2006-07 season and he was one of those blokes you'd go to war with, you'd have a pint with and you'd leave your kids with.

Another guy I got on really well with was Gary Holt. Three-lungs Holt. He was coming towards the end of his career but he was still running around relentlessly. Always on the charge. We're pretty similar in ways. He's a very funny guy, but doesn't suffer fools. He's quite stern, and if he doesn't like something he'll tell you. I like it when people are open and straight to the point. No pissing around.

It's your relationships in a dressing room that really keep you going, and they can last a lifetime. So although I wasn't enjoying my football as much as I'd have liked, everything off the pitch was going great. And it was about to get even better.

∗ ∗ ∗

On Friday December 15, I'd got back from training and Fay was upstairs wrapping Christmas presents. She'd had a few pains in the morning, but said she was feeling fine now. So I went back downstairs and played a bit of *Call of Duty*, as you do.

At about 3pm my phone went, and it was Fay from upstairs. Bit lazy, I thought. She told me she thought she'd weed herself. The mood suddenly changed. This could be it! Fay rang her twin sister Adele, who'd already had a little girl, and she told Fay that, yep, you're definitely in labour.

We jumped in the car, but it was rush hour and it was a nightmare trying to get across Nottingham. Then, halfway across, Fay declared she was absolutely starving.

"What?!"

"I haven't had anything to eat! Pull over and grab me a sandwich."

"You're pregnant and about to pop, and you want a sandwich?"

"I've not had anything all day!"

"But we have to get to the hospital!"

"JUST PULL OVER AND GET ME SOMETHING!"

So I screeched into a petrol station, ran in, grabbed a sandwich and chocolates and then realised we could be there for a while so grabbed something for me too. I rushed back out and pulled away, with Fay moaning that I've got the wrong sarnie.

We eventually made it to the hospital car park, and I was panicking and jumped straight out of the car. But Fay wasn't moving.

"What are you doing?"

"I've got to eat!"

"In the car? Why do you need to eat in the car? You can eat when we get inside!"

"As if they'll take me seriously if I go in there stuffing my face with chocolates!"

So I had to get back into the car and wait for Fay to finish her gourmet hospital car park meal.

We finally got into a room at 5pm and Fay was already in a lot of pain. I thought she must be quite far gone, but the nurses didn't seem to be in any sort of rush. A doctor came in and asked if anyone had assessed how far along Fay was... because she was five centimetres dilated. I went outside and rang her mum to tell her to start driving and to step on it!

By 9ish, just five hours after we'd left our house, Evie was in my arms. We hadn't known the sex of the baby, and when she came out, I didn't even think to ask. They just handed me this little baby and it was the cutest little thing I'd ever seen in my life. Obviously Fay had been given her first, and she also hadn't thought to ask whether it was a boy or girl. We were just so relieved, and blown away by this beautiful baby we had in our arms. It was actually a nurse who had to tell us it was a girl!

This amazing bundle of joy was in my hands, and I was stood there thinking, 'My life has just changed completely.'

There were no tears from me. Not through any ideas of manliness or any crap like that; I just don't understand how anyone can cry when they have a baby. For me, it was sheer relief that Fay was no longer in pain and that her and the baby were both OK.

Fay wanted to get home because everyone was coming down, so we left the hospital at about half 11. I hadn't even had time to eat my sandwich.

When we arrived home around midnight, James Perch was over to say congratulations even though we had a game the next day. Nathan Tyson was around with his missus too. Fay's mum and sister turned up gone 1am and it was just a lovely place to be. Lots of love in the house.

Looking back, it's a surprise to me that I actually played the next day. We lost 3-1 at home to Leyton Orient, but all I remember was everyone asking questions about Evie.

Straight away after that game things were different, because the football became irrelevant almost as soon as it was over. My mentality changed that day. I used to get really pissed off after games if we'd lost or the ref had nagged me, and I would bring that home with me. As soon as Evie came along it didn't matter anymore, because when you walked through the door you had a small human to look after.

To give you an idea of how becoming a dad changes you as a player, people always ask me what it was like scoring a hattrick for Norwich in the East Anglian derby against Ipswich. How did you celebrate? I bet you had a great night out? Well, I'd done the media, walked into the players' lounge with the matchball, kissed Fay, and then Evie came over and asked if I could get her a drink. So I was straight back into dad mode. Then she was like, "I want to go now, I'm bored! Can we go, can we go, can we go?"

So I grabbed the kids, grabbed some food, got home, had a bottle of wine and the game didn't get mentioned again! Fay wasn't bothered I'd scored a hattrick either, so while all of my teammates were getting on it and celebrating I was putting the kids to bed and sitting in front of the telly. One of the best days of my football career, and I toasted it like I'd just come home from a 9 to 5 job. However, in all honesty, that's absolutely the best way to celebrate.

Evie and our younger daughters changed my whole mindset and shifted my focus, and I started putting even more effort in to be the best I could be. To do even better for them.

* * *

Evie immediately put my problems at Forest into perspective. While I still wasn't happy with feeling undervalued by the coaching team, I got into a place where I could put that to the back of my mind and just go out and enjoy my football.

We were right in the playoff mix, and I felt I was playing well and contributing to the team. We finished fourth, which meant we'd play Yeovil in the playoff semis. Frustratingly, I'd done my groin and missed the first leg at their place, but we won 2-0 and appeared to be cruising into the final. The vibe around Nottingham was amazing. Everywhere you went people were wishing us good luck and talking about Wembley.

It didn't quite turn out like that, though.

My groin wasn't much better for the second leg so I had a place on the bench. The City Ground was rocking, I got on in the 76th minute, with the game at 1-1 and the tie 3-1 to us on aggregate. Still cruising, and there was a party atmosphere in the stands.

Football always kicks you in the gut when you least expect it, though.

In the 82nd minute, Yeovil got a lucky break when a curling shot hit the post and rebounded in off poor Alan Wright. Still 3-2 up, though, and we had plenty of experience in our squad to see it through. There were no alarms, but you could sense the nerves in the crowd. Just four minutes later the wily old striker Marcus Stewart got on the end of a cross and headed in for Yeovil.

3-3. We couldn't believe it. The crowd was silenced. I'd been on the pitch for only 10 minutes and we'd gone from sauntering to Wembley to back level. It was OK though. We still had the experience and the better players, and felt we could shift the momentum. But just before full-time, David

Prutton picked up a needless second yellow card with a tackle in the middle of the pitch, and suddenly we were down to 10 men. What the hell were we doing?

That was when the crowd turned, and quite rightly. We'd chucked it away. Yeovil were full of energy, and it was no surprise when they took the lead in extra-time. Somehow we equalised a minute later, but my groin was hanging off and I could barely move. We were right up against it, desperately clinging on for penalties, but inevitably Yeovil scored a fifth. In truth, it felt like we'd been put out of our misery.

The scenes at full-time were horrible. The crowd were chanting Stuart Pearce's name because they wanted him to take over as manager, Wes Morgan had a scuffle with fans and I just felt humiliated. Sitting in the dressing room after that was one of the lowest moments I had in my career. How do you explain something like that happening? Arrogance? Naivety?

With my groin in bits it would have been a miracle if I'd made the final had we got through, but it's still one of the biggest disappointments in my career. I'd have loved nothing more than to have been promoted with that group of players. But we'd blown it in spectacular fashion.

***

At 26, maybe my chance to play in the Championship again had gone. If we'd been promoted I could have had a real go at the second tier. I was sat in that dressing room after the semi-final thinking, 'I've got another year in this division. I'm going to have to start again.'

I was low, but I knew I'd had a good season. It had been difficult because of my problems with the gaffer, but I knew I was appreciated in the dressing room and in the stands.

I'd been voted Player of the Season, which was an unbelievable achievement. A massive honour. To get my name on the trophy felt phenomenal, especially when you look at some of the names who'd won it before: Peter

Shilton, Gary Birtles, Des Walker, Stuart Pearce, Nigel Clough. It was also nice to get that sort of respect from the fans in a season in which the club had tried to sell me; to end up being the leading scorer and winning Player of the Season in those circumstances meant a lot to me.

To lift a trophy voted for by the fans is absolutely amazing. That's your legacy. You're on that trophy forever.

***

At the end of the season, Fay's sisters Adele and Rachel were talking about emigrating to Australia. That would have a massive impact, as Fay was really close to them. Because they were heading out to take a look around Perth, me and Fay went with them to stay with Jane Grice, my host parent when I was at Halifax, and her family who were now living out there.

We also took Fay's mum, as well as Evie. She was just six months old, which was fun on such a long flight!

At this stage, me and Fay hadn't been trying for another baby, but we had the attitude that if it happened, it happened. After 10 days over there, Fay felt really sick. She thought she might need a pregnancy test, but I was convinced it was something she'd eaten.

Unknown to me, Fay had bought a pregnancy test when we'd gone into town, and when we got back she shouted to me to come upstairs. I got up there, and she showed me the pregnancy test. "Oh my god! You actually are pregnant!" "I told you I was right!"

I was thrilled, and so was she. It was brilliant news.

Fay was 23, we'd already had Evie, had got married, and she had her own home. But she turned to me and said, "You'll have to tell my mum." She was still scared to tell her own mum that she was pregnant! Her mum was obviously delighted when I told her, and we had a lovely meal out in Perth that night to celebrate.

What brilliant news to end the football year.

MY TOP 5...
WORST FANS

1. IPSWICH TOWN

Obviously.

2. SWANSEA CITY

It was fun and their abuse pumped me up, and for most of them it was just cartoony abuse. Some of them were properly viscous though!

3. GILLINGHAM

I have no idea why they hated me, but they did. They didn't like me at all but I couldn't tell you why. I bet they could tell you though!

4. BURY

They used to give me so much stick when I played for Rochdale. They'd always shout crap at me, but I liked it.

5. SOUTHAMPTON

There was a bit of rivalry between them and Norwich, and I got a very 'soft' penalty against them at home. Although they should love me, really, because I went and missed it.

CHAPTER 13

NOT A LEFT-WINGER, NO PUNCH-UPS AND HOSPITAL VISITS

2007-08

"Did you punch Colin Calderwood?"

It's a question I was asked hundreds of times when Colin came to Norwich as Chris Hughton's assistant in 2012. Everyone seemed to accept it as fact: Grant Holt and Colin Calderwood had a punch-up during their time at Nottingham Forest.

Sorry to disappoint anyone who likes a bit of football gossip, but it didn't happen. We might have come close to it once – more of that shortly – but we never came to blows.

I'd had an operation on my groin in pre-season, but luckily my recovery took only two weeks. I'd also handed in a transfer request during the summer as I felt I wasn't being offered a good enough deal despite being the club's leading scorer, but we got there in the end. So I went into the season hopeful of starting off from where I'd left off the previous season: scoring plenty of goals.

However, right from the start of the campaign I was being picked in tough away days, and then put on the bench for a lot of the easier games at home. It was a common theme of the year. To make matters worse, I wasn't playing up top where I wanted to. Instead, Calderwood pushed me out to the left of a front three. The gaffer knew I'd work hard out there and run all game.

There was a problem, though: I wasn't a left-winger. I was a striker.

Not only was I a striker, but I was a striker who'd been the leading goalscorer the previous season. Wherever I played I would always give my all and put a real shift in, but it started to piss me off.

The team were doing pretty well, although in truth we should have been running away with the league. Instead, we were hovering around the playoff positions and the fans were grumbling. The pressure was building on the manager, and the players were feeling the strain.

It started to come to a head for me at the end of January. I'd done a tough away game at Millwall, then a tough home game against table-toppers Swansea, then a tough away game at Bournemouth, who were battling against relegation and were really horrible to play against. Then we had Millwall at home next up, which was the sort of game you'd really fancy your chances in, especially in front of your own fans, but I was dropped to the bench.

I had 30 minutes away at Leeds after that and did really well, so with Swindon up next at home I was hoping to get a start. Now, I think, is when the "Did you punch Colin Calderwood?" question came from.

On the Friday before the game I was walking to training, and as I got through the gate, Colin pulled me over. "Holty, can I have a chat?" I knew exactly what was coming.

"No, I'm sick of this," I told him in the middle of the training ground. "I've had enough. I'm doing all of the tough away games, I'm working my arse off on the left of a three and you keep dropping me because I'm not scoring goals, but I'm playing as a left-winger. I want to play up front. I'm sick of this."

"Well, you're not scoring."

"Well, you're not playing me down the middle. How am I supposed to score when you're sticking me out wide?"

Colin was under pressure at the time as we weren't setting the world on fire, so I knew he had his own troubles. But I wasn't having it. I told him I was fed up. He gave me a bit back, which he was entitled to do. By this time, more people were arriving to training so we put an end to it. Calderwood told me I wasn't allowed to join in with training, and he'd see me after.

So I thought, 'Fuck it, fine' and walked to the changing room. I sat down and the kit man Tel asked what was going on because he'd just been instructed to take me off the squad list for tomorrow's game. I couldn't believe it. Dropped for a small argument. Fuck him.

Fay was very heavily pregnant with Erica at this time, so I was already a bit stressed and irritable, and I was chuntering away to myself, getting into a lather when I should have been calming myself down.

The boys came back in from training, and I was sat there telling them the gaffer's an idiot for dropping me. Colin heard about this, and he marched into the dressing room and called me a disgrace.

I lost it.

I got up in his face and went at him again. "I'm working my nuts off every single week here to do a job in a position I don't want to play in. I do it for the team, I do it for the lads, I do it for the fans. I don't do it for you."

It was heated, but we never got anywhere near blows. Just a bit of screaming and shouting. I think he was mostly pissed off about me telling the lads he'd booted me out of the squad. It was basically me being arrogant. He was under a lot of pressure in a difficult job, and I was 26 then. As you get older you appreciate how difficult a job management is, but I still think he could have handled it better. We both could have.

We've laughed and joked about it since. We get on really, really well now, and have done since he came to Norwich. But back then we just never saw eye to eye.

He left it by telling me to fuck off home and think about what I wanted for my future, and I happily obliged. What I hadn't expected was to go from one stressful situation right into another.

$$* * *$$

Evie hadn't been very well that morning, and just after my fall-out with Colin I'd got a phone call from Fay asking if I could come home because Evie hadn't got any better. Funny you should ask, Fay, but actually I seem to have found myself in a position where I can come home early!

Erica was due about seven days later, so Fay was already under a lot of stress and I got home as quickly as I possibly could. Evie just wasn't right. She was really limp, had been sick, wasn't keeping anything down and couldn't stand on her legs. We took her to A&E, and all thoughts about my bust-up with Colin were completely forgotten now.

A&E sent us back home. They said it was a viral infection, but Evie just kept deteriorating and we went straight back to the hospital. That time we were admitted to the ward, and were told she had gastroenteritis. She was really, really ill.

We ended up staying the night at hospital. Evie wouldn't eat and didn't want the catheter in her arm. We had a real concern for her. Finally she got to sleep around 3am, but the doctors had to take a syringe of her swollen knee. I picked her up and she was so limp. I had to put her left knee under my leg, her right knee over my leg and I locked her tight. The needle was absolutely massive. Huge. They drained 5mil of fluid off her knee, and the scream from her lungs was something I never want to hear again. She was wriggling and crying and I felt like the world's worst dad.

Colin called me in the morning to ask if everything was all right with Evie, and he told me to forget about training on Sunday and to come in on Monday. He asked after Fay, and made sure everyone was OK. I said good luck in the game that day, and that was that. No mention of the bust-up.

We finally got Evie out on the Saturday night, which put us at ease. It had given us a real scare, and I'd felt so helpless. It put everything that had gone on with Colin just 24 hours earlier into perspective.

On the Monday morning I went into Colin's office. He asked how Evie and Fay were, and then we had a proper conversation. We both said sorry for the way we'd approached it on Friday, and we set our stalls out and cleared the air, which is what we should have done in the first place. He was honest and said he didn't see me playing as the No.9 because Junior Agogo was doing well, and that I did a good job for the team on the left.

Even though we'd cleared the air, nothing had changed really. I wanted to be the striker, and Colin wanted me on the left. Gridlock.

I didn't have much time to think about it, however, because a week after going into hospital for Evie, we were back in to bring little Erica into this world. Fay had to be induced, and she was in so much pain because of an injection she'd been given in her leg. She drifted in and out quite a lot because of the drugs, and every time she woke up she said her leg was killing her. I'd never seen Fay in so much pain, and it was horrible to see.

So again it was pure relief when Erica came out. This time we already knew she was a girl, and it was a beautiful moment to have another little cutie in my arms and for both her and Fay to be fine.

It had been quite a week, but we couldn't have been any happier.

CHAPTER 14

COLD SHOWERS, MEETING HOOLAHAN AND LEAVING FOREST

2007-08

Clearing the air with Colin was one thing; that was the easy part. Getting back into the team and playing up top was another thing entirely. It just wasn't going to happen. I knew it, the gaffer knew it, my teammates knew it.

Although I started the couple of games after our fall-out, I was pushed out on the left again and got hooked at half-time away at Southend. Me and Colin knew where we both stood now, and although we had a new respect for each other, it was pretty clear I wasn't part of his plans. Not as a centre-forward, anyway.

It was no surprise when a few clubs started showing interest in taking me on loan for the rest of the season. Word had obviously got out I wasn't all that happy, and news spreads very quickly in football. When you needed a new club, it wouldn't take long for the phone to start ringing.

Bristol Rovers were keen on me, and I quite fancied the thought of going there. My old pal Rickie Lambert was playing for them and doing really well, the city was cool and I was told I'd be starting up top, which is what I most wanted.

While the football side sounded good, it was hard to justify it on a family level. We'd just had Erica so the thought of moving almost 300 miles away from Carlisle, where Fay would be living, was unappealing. It wouldn't have been fair on Fay, and she had been massively supportive through every step of my career.

The move was knocked on the head and my phone went quiet for a couple of weeks. Don't get me wrong, though; it's not like I was desperate to get out of Forest if nothing materialised. After all, we were challenging for promotion and it's good to be involved in a dressing room when you have a massive incentive like that to aim for. Having to stay wouldn't have caused me to sulk; as ever I'd have got on with giving my all for the team.

However, out of the blue there was interest from Blackpool to take me on loan. It was a bit of a shock because they were in the league above, competing in the Championship for the first time in 29 years. I was immediately interested. It was closer to Carlisle, and I'd be playing in the second tier for the first time since my first season at Sheffield Wednesday.

The manager Simon Grayson sold me the dream about playing in the Championship. It felt good that he believed I could do a job at a higher level, especially as I'd barely scored a goal all season. He was judging me on my goal record as a striker, rather than as a winger.

Blackpool were battling to stay in the division and the idea of helping them stay up was really appealing. That sort of pressure got me going, like it had at Rochdale when I first joined them. I also had no doubts about scoring goals at that level. There would be good players around me, and when that happened I always backed myself to score.

It was a no-brainer, and the loan deal was done in March.

***

You could tell Blackpool were on the cusp of doing something special. There was a really good vibe about the place, the players were fighting for each other and the fans were loving it.

Bloody hell, though, the place was old-school. And when I say old-school, I mean the oldest of old-schools. It was like stepping back in time.

The training ground was basically two wooden huts put together and it was situated right next to an airfield. It was also alongside a beach, which meant you were usually training in gale-force winds whipping off the Fylde coast. Cosy.

There were three or four showers between everyone, and two of them worked if you were lucky. Sometimes the water was even warm, just as a treat. You washed your own kit, which was unheard of in the Championship, and to be honest the set-up was worse than what I'd had at Workington and Barrow! It was amazing that they were competing in the Championship with those sort of facilities, but it showed what an incredible rise they'd had, and what a great job Grayson was doing.

Although it was a shock to see a club just one level below the Premier League with that sort of training ground, it didn't bother me at all. I was well used to those sort of facilities from my time in non-league just five years previously, and I had no problem mucking in and knuckling down. After all, who doesn't love a cold shower after three hours of training in the pouring rain on a freezing day by the Irish Sea?

The lads at Blackpool embraced all of that, and they had to. There was a really good unity, and that mentality probably came from not having all of the usual luxuries. You had to love it or you'd be out.

The only thing I found difficult was washing my own kit: it's not so easy when you're living out of a suitcase in a hotel. I made sure I went out of my way to be nice to the hotel laundry staff, because those poor guys had to handle my sweaty training gear on a daily basis!

✱✱✱

Blackpool had a good team, including the little fella Wes Hoolahan. He would go on to play such a massive part in my career at Norwich City, and he was unique. A magician; a joy to play with. A huge talent who should have played in the Premier League for most of his career, and who should have won over 100 caps for Republic of Ireland.

I'd played against him before and you could see what a good player he was (even though he had dived to win a penalty!), and I was looking forward to seeing him in training. It was clear early on that he was a big fish at Blackpool, but he had absolutely no ego. Everyone loved him.

One of my earliest training sessions there, a couple of days before a game, summed up how Wes was at the time: a loveable, talented rogue who lived for playing football.

The session had started, but there was no sign of Wes. The manager asked if anyone knew where he was, and someone piped up that he was on a flight back from Dublin. The next minute, Grayson's phone went off and it was Wes: "I'm almost here, gaffer! Sorry I'm late! You'll see me land in a second!"

A plane flew over, and landed on the strip right next to the training ground. Wes hopped out, and he was wearing Blackpool shorts, one long sock, one short sock, someone else's boots, and some rascal old t-shirt that he must have found in a cupboard somewhere.

Some of the boys were laughing – including me – but a few were raging about him being late because we had an important game coming up. The manager told Wes to do his warm-up, and that amounted to literally jogging two laps and declaring, "That's me ready, gaffer."

Wes joined the session, and Ian Evatt, who was one of the real leaders of the group, was moaning at him about being late. Fair enough. But Wes had a unique way of silencing the moaners: he got the ball and put it through Evatt's legs, dribbled to the goalkeeper Paul Rachubka, chopped him and put him on the floor. That had me chuckling, but Wes was only just getting started.

Next, the cheeky sod pretended to score but instead kept the ball. Paul dived at his feet again, and Wes popped it around him, leaving Paul on the floor for a second time. Evatt scrambled around to tackle him but Wes, cool as you like and with a massive grin on his little face, nutmegged him again! He finally stopped toying with them, flicked the ball into the net, took his top off and ran away celebrating, whirling it around his head. Evatt gave chase looking like he was going to kill him, and all of the boys were in stitches.

When you saw Wes doing stuff like that nearly every day in training you quickly realised how brilliant he was. He was completely different to anyone I'd ever played with. The only man who I saw beat players more often was Paddy McCourt, when I was at Rochdale. The difference was that Wes could consistently dominate a game: if you gave him the ball, he would relentlessly make something happen. He always carried a threat whenever he had the ball at his feet. Well, whenever he had the ball at his left foot, anyway. He didn't seem to need his right!

You can measure how good a player is by looking at how many teams he could immediately improve by playing for them. Well, Wes could have left Blackpool and walked into any other team in the Championship and have made them better.

The one thing holding Wes back was that he didn't mind a drink and a night out at that age, and I think he was indulged because everyone loved him. It wasn't until his first or second season at Norwich that he really started to look after his body properly – and he will happily admit that. He became a brilliant athlete, supremely fit, and was in better shape at 36 when he left Norwich than at 25 at Blackpool. If a good coach or manager had got hold of him at a really young age, you'd be talking about him as one of the finest Ireland players of all time.

* * *

Unfortunately, my loan to Blackpool was a complete waste of time. If I had done well there it could have led to the chance of establishing myself in the Championship, but it just didn't work out like I'd been told it would.

Things can change quickly in football, so assurances can be difficult to stick to, but there were promises made which weren't kept. I'd expected to go there and hit the ground running, but found myself on the bench and coming on in the last five minutes. I trained hard and trained well, but the opportunities didn't come along. Four matches and only 20 minutes of action tells its own story.

Simon Grayson did an unbelievable job at Blackpool, and keeping them up that season was an unreal achievement. However, I ended up calling him The Jetsons, because whenever I wanted to see him he suddenly zoomed off and disappeared like in the cartoon. He didn't seem to like a confrontation, or maybe he just didn't like speaking to me!

* * *

It looked like Forest would end up in the playoffs, and Calderwood wanted me back in the building after my loan ran out at Blackpool. It was great to hear he wanted me to be part of the group, and of course I wanted to play.

I watched Forest's last game of the season, on May 3 at home to Yeovil. We were third, a point behind Doncaster Rovers. We needed to win and for Doncaster to lose at Cheltenham, who in turn needed a win themselves to secure their survival. Typical last-day drama.

There was a TV in the box with the Doncaster game on, and goals were flying in in both matches. We won 3-2, Doncaster lost 2-1 and we leapfrogged them into second to win automatic promotion on the final day of the season. It was a strange feeling. I was absolutely delighted for the lads, and proud of the hard work I'd put in on the pitch throughout the year despite the difficult circumstances. I'd been with Forest for two-and-a-half seasons, and for that to culminate in my first-ever promotion still felt special, even though I was 90% sure my future lay elsewhere.

I had to travel back up to Blackpool afterwards because I was on the bench for their final game the next day. We got a 1-1 draw against Watford – I played the last three minutes – and that point ensured Blackpool stayed up. Not a bad couple of days!

The following day was Forest's end-of-season dinner, and then all of the players and staff headed off to Marbella. Although it was a fun trip, it quickly became clear while out there that my Nottingham Forest career was over. In situations like that you can just tell by the way staff are around you; like they've already accepted you'd be moving on. It was time for me to find a new club and a new adventure.

* * *

My time at Forest taught me a lot. The biggest thing that happened while I was there was having the kids. As I mentioned before, my mindset changed. When I left the building and walked through the door at home, the football was done. My life became better because I could switch off and concentrate on the family, whereas before I'd spend the whole weekend thinking about the game.

Naturally that helped me as a player, because it caused me less anxiety and stress. I was a happier footballer. I'd gone to League One with a big club and showed I could score goals at that level. I'd won Player of the Season for the first time and had won promotion for the first time. All of that was massive experience for me, and made me a more all-round player.

Being played out of position also taught me you can't always have it all your own way. The argument with Colin made me realise there will always be more pressure on a manager than there is on me as a player. All I had to worry about was going out and playing football; Colin had to worry about every little detail. It gave me more empathy towards managers and coaches.

Even though I didn't agree with the club's decision to let me go, I could understand why they were doing it. They just didn't see me fitting into the way they wanted to play in the Championship, and they were honest about that. They were wrong, but they were honest.

Being at Forest also taught me how important the dressing room is. I already knew that a happy dressing room usually meant a happy team, but Forest really showed how vital it is to have a group of lads who all had each other's backs. This was really important with Neil Lennon, who has spoken bravely and eloquently about his issues with depression.

Lenny had come in at Forest with big expectations. He'd arrived in the summer of 2007 and, although he was 36, was still a great player. Moved the ball, dictated play, got stuck in. He had everything. I've never seen anyone keep a ball as well as he did. He always kept it moving, and always wanted it. He was fantastic around the dressing room; just a nice guy. Everyone got on with him really well. He seemed settled enough, and had a good pre-season.

Only he will really know what was going on, but he was struggling off the pitch. It's not right for me to talk about it in detail, I don't think, but you could see he had bad days, and days when he couldn't come in.

When you're with a group of people for a length of time, you become really in tune with what's going on with everyone. Dressing rooms aren't as testosterone-filled as a lot of people might think. You quickly know if someone's not happy, and naturally take care of people in that sort of environment.

What fans don't always realise is that football isn't the be-all and end-all for players. It's secondary to any issues in the dressing room, such as depression, or illness. That will always come first, ahead of the footy. When you walk onto the pitch, obviously you're 100% focused on the game – especially as it can help take your mind off any issues – but if anyone is struggling in the group, that becomes the main focus.

If someone doesn't seem happy, a teammate will speak to the manager or a member of senior staff and tell them something's not right. A player is always more likely to be 100% open and honest with a manager than with a player, even if you're really close. There's always a game at the weekend, and you don't want any of your teammates to be worrying about you when there's a match to focus on.

When a player has an illness, whether it's physical or mental, no one thinks they're being selfish for not being in training, or for not being able to give 100%. You want them to get better and to be healthy as a person, and that's far more important than having them on the pitch. If someone needs to be away, they need to be away. There's no animosity about it at all.

I've been in dressing rooms where lads have been off for a while through injury or illness, so everyone splits their win bonuses and gives it to them. You do really take care of each other in there. Obviously it's competitive, and it can get a bit macho and you can fall out and there'll be sharp words, but when there's an issue the dressing room always rallies around. It's always people before football.

A football club is not just about the footballers, though. Far from it. We're only a small part of the set-up. Right from the manager all the way through to the cleaners, they all have a really important role at a club. So you make sure you treat them all as part of your family.

When I was in the Premier League with Norwich, a drinks company did a thing called sightings, where every time you were snapped on camera with their product, you would get paid for the sighting. Every penny we got from the sightings went to the staff. Cleaners, receptionists, security, physios, kit men: everyone involved in helping the players throughout the season got that money.

You have to look after everyone, because they're still doing the same hours you are. They're going on the road, they're missing Christmas Day, Boxing Day and New Year's Day. You look after your own because they're going to make you better, and because it's the right thing to do.

When a club is facing relegation you 100% know that might mean people will be let go at the end of the season. Someone who works in a kiosk might lose their job, or someone who works in accounts won't be kept on permanently, and they might have a family at home. So you really care about that: it drives you, because you've always got that in the back of your mind. Like any walk of life, there are selfish footballers who probably don't care about that side of thing, but the vast, vast majority do care.

Having such a good, close group at Forest who looked after each other meant I left there quite happy. I'd done my job, and I could hold my head up high knowing I'd given everything for my teammates.

I had another year left on my contract which meant there was no pressure on me, so I wasn't panicking about having to make a really quick decision. I knew there'd be offers coming in, and it would be a case of finding the best club for the next stage of my career.

I had really enjoyed the feeling of winning promotion with Forest, and I wanted more of that. The next move had to be to a club I thought had a real chance of doing something good, or somewhere with an ambitious manager or a chairman who knew where they wanted the club to go.

CHAPTER 15

HOROSCOPES, DROPPING DIVISIONS AND SHREWSBURY-BOUND

2008-09

I opened the door to the chairman's office at Shrewsbury. The first thing I noticed was a massive luxurious red carpet. Huge, grand oak desk. Behind it sat Roland Wycherley: pristine white hair, luxurious suit, pocket square to match his tie. A real dapper gentleman. You just knew he had a Bentley parked outside.

"Hello, Mr Chairman."

"Don't worry about those formalities," he said. "Call me Roland."

"Nice to meet you, Roland."

Then he threw in a bit of a curveball: "So you're an Aries then."

I nodded.

"That means you're fiery. I like that in a player."

I'd never had star signs brought up in a meeting with a chairman before. It was mad, but I immediately liked him for it. He had something of the old-school chairman about him, and he was really easy to warm to. He'd made me wait, though. I'd travelled down to Shrewsbury and had met their manager Paul Simpson, who I already knew a bit, in the morning.

The gaffer told me the chairman would arrive later, because he liked a lie-in in the morning and eggs for breakfast. Fair enough.

Simmo showed me the New Meadow, where Shrewsbury had moved to the season before. He took me around the training area, and talked me through who he was signing, and it sounded like a good squad he was putting together. He was going to go with two up top, with wingers who'd put the ball into the box for me. It sounded ideal. Exactly what I needed after Forest.

It all seemed great, but I'd wanted certain reassurances from the chairman.

An hour later, I was sat in Roland's office confirming my star sign. He then leaned in and sold his vision to me, and why he wanted me to sign for his club. The management team had been talking to him about players they wanted to bring in, and going through a list of names.

"I'm a bit old now so I drift off occasionally," he said. "But we were going through the list of centre-forwards, and Paul would tell me his thoughts on them. It went quiet and Paul said, 'There's one name I want to chuck in there, but I'm not sure we can afford him. However, if we can get him, I think he might win us the league. But I don't think we'll get him so I've not put him on the list'."

Of course Paul had done that on purpose; he knew it would get a reaction from his chairman. Roland's ears had pricked up immediately and he demanded to know who it was. Out of Paul's mouth came, "Grant Holt."

Roland said his mind immediately went back to when I had played against them for Rochdale, on the opening day of the 2005-06 season. "The ball came into the box," Roland told me. "You absolutely bullied our centre-half, put him on his arse, and fired the ball into the corner past Joe Hart. I've never forgotten you since that day.

"So I asked Paul to find out how much you were, and told him I'd pay it if we could afford you. Paul found out what Forest wanted, and I told him to do it straight away. And now we're sat here."

This is where the negotiation started. Roland was fine with my wage demands, but knew I wanted further reassurances: a three-year deal for security. A wage increase if we got promoted. A wage increase if I scored a certain number of goals. A clause in my contract so if someone came in and bid a certain amount for me, I'd be free to walk out of the door.

Roland thought about it for a long time and said, "I'll give you a three-year deal, and I'll give you your increases if you score a certain number of goals and we get promoted."

He also agreed to a valuation that, if met by another club, meant I would be free to go. He wouldn't write it into my contract, however, because if clubs knew my valuation there would be no chance of them going above it. But he gave me his word, and I was happy with that.

We shook hands and he said, "Right, let's get the paperwork done!"

Woah. Slow down! I had to put the brakes on and tell him I'd only come down for an initial chat. He wasn't having it though; he wanted a deal done there and then. I needed to speak to Fay and think about it. Nottingham Forest owed me my last payment, so I couldn't sign that day anyway. But Roland asked what I was owed, told me to go get some lunch with the gaffer and to come back up in an hour.

He looked me in the eye and said, "You're not leaving the building until we get this contract agreed."

Some players might have found that a bit weird, but I enjoyed the fact he'd sold me his vision, had told me what he expected, hadn't caved in to my demands straight away and was making me work for my money in terms of goal bonuses. He was ambitious, and wanted to take Shrewsbury up, but he wanted to do it in the right way without spending loads of money and putting the club into debt. He seemed like a very solid bloke.

I had lunch with Simmo and called Fay, before I headed back into the chairman's office. While I'd been downstairs he'd phoned Forest, and had sorted it out: he would pay me what they owed me that day, straight into my bank account. Forest would then pay him back.

The chairman was giving me his own money to get the deal done, and when someone does that, you know they're backing you to the hilt. I agreed the deal on the spot.

I'd travelled down there to have a look around and to have a chat, and I left having signed for Shrewsbury Town.

***

It wasn't just Roland who'd convinced me to join Shrewsbury. Simmo had a big part to play in it; he's from Carlisle and one of the best players to ever come from the town.

Paul Murray also had a big influence on the decision. Although I didn't know him, he was another Carlisle lad and he'd just moved from Gretna to Shrewsbury. He was a really fantastic footballer who'd been unlucky with injuries.

Before I'd gone down to take a look around Shrewsbury, Muzza had called me. He'd bought a house near the training ground and said the second bedroom had my name on it if I wanted it. He'd be driving up to Preston a couple of times a week because that's where his family were, so we could share the driving load, too.

Fay was going to stay in Carlisle with the kids, so I wanted to be somewhere not too far away from home, and to live with someone who I could get on with. Although I didn't know Muzza, I knew from a couple of phone calls that we'd get on brilliantly. It made my decision to say yes to Roland much easier.

Before I headed to Shrewsbury for the first time, I called Colin Calderwood. He told me it was up to me whether I wanted to go. He said the usual stuff along the lines of, "If you want to leave that's fine. If you don't want to leave then that's also fine. You can come back and have a shot of getting into the side." Basically, they were the lines you heard when the manager wants you to leave the building but doesn't want to explicitly say it in case you decide to stay!

My only doubt about joining Shrewsbury was having to drop down to League Two. But I just wanted to go somewhere, play football and enjoy myself. I knew I was going to play regularly at Shrewsbury, the manager wanted me, the chairman was really backing me, they were signing good players, and it felt like a really good challenge.

I was 27 and had started to accept my chances of having a real go at the Championship had gone. I thought the only way it would happen was if I did really well with Shrewsbury and helped them get promoted to the third tier and then we'd use that momentum to get promoted to the Championship. But even then, I'd be 29 or 30 and they might be looking for someone younger to play up front. So it was looking unlikely.

There were absolutely no thoughts of playing in the Premier League. If I'm honest, I'd never really seen that as an achievable goal. That didn't bother me, though. Not long ago I'd been working in a warehouse and playing non-league football, so everything I'd achieved since then felt like a bonus.

However, joining Shrewsbury was the first time I'd gone to a club where I was the big fish. Despite stepping down a division, it felt like a step up in terms of responsibility. I was the club's marquee, record signing. Everything was on my shoulders, and everyone knew who I was.

When I'd gone from Rochdale to Nottingham no one really knew my name, but at Shrewsbury everyone was aware of what I'd done. There had been a bit of pressure at Rochdale because I'd been brought in to help keep them up, but I was an unknown then. It had almost been a free hit. This time, I was going to a club with a bit of a reputation behind me and was expected to score the goals that would fire them to promotion.

***

I was a far better player when I joined Shrewsbury compared to when I'd signed for Forest. I'd played with better players, learned what to do against better defenders, and now I had all of that knowledge and experience to use in League Two, so I felt very comfortable there. My runs were better, my positioning was better, I could get away from defenders better.

The standard in training was not as high as it had been at Forest, and that can be quite difficult to get used to. At times certain stuff was sloppy. However, because I'd been around a bit, I knew how to put that to the back of my mind and quickly adapted to it. I certainly never thought of myself as being too good for that level; there were guys in that squad who had played to a higher standard than I had.

Even though I scored on my debut – a penalty in a 4-0 home win – it took me a while to get back into the swing of things at Shrewsbury, and to adapt back to playing in the fourth tier. I had to learn to strip my game back again. There was less linking play and moving the ball around, and more going back to basics: get in the box and get on the end of a cross.

I think that period of adapting led to me picking up five yellow cards in my first 10 games. A lot of it was frustration; maybe not getting the passes I was used to. Then, from October onwards, I started banging the goals in.

MY TOP 5...
BEST OPPOSITION PLAYERS

1. GARETH BALE

He could do everything. Untouchable. Pace, power, clever, great shot, great vision.

2. LUKA MODRIC

He was a joke. He made the toughest things look effortless. He never looked like he was breaking stride, but he was on a different level.

3. DAVID SILVA

We called him the ghost because he didn't look like he touched the floor. He floated around, and every time you thought you had him he'd get away and find space that hadn't been there a second earlier. He was no Wes Hoolahan, mind you.

4. ROBIN VAN PERSIE

His movement was ridiculous. He was phenomenal to watch when you were on the pitch. His runs were so clever, and he could score all sorts of goals.

5. ASHLEY COLE

He was the modern-day left-back ahead of his time. Brilliant defensively, a terrific cross and beat people for fun.

CHAPTER 16

FLAG VANDALISM, FIVE GOALS IN A GAME AND GHOST PENALTIES

2008-09

The Shrewsbury fans took to me from day one. I think they appreciated the job I was doing, they saw I was happy to work really hard and, of course, I was scoring goals. Banging a few in tends to help your relationship with fans, funnily enough.

They had a song for me, 'Holty Is Superman', and it did feel brilliant to have the fans sing my name. They also had a massive flag of me hanging in one of the stands. That was great, of course, but the thing I remember most about the flag was the infamous case of Moustachegate.

One day, me and Paul Murray got pulled into Paul Simpson's office. "Right, who was it?" he asked, which was a bit cryptic as I had no idea what he was talking about.

The Head of Operations was in there too, and he told us people were really unhappy with what we'd done.

"I honestly don't know what you're on about!"

"No? Well, someone's sneaked into the ground, climbed to the back of the stand and drawn a moustache on your face!"

I burst out laughing. "You what?!"

"The fans aren't happy because someone's put a moustache on your flag. They're not cheap, those flags."

"So why am I here? As if I'd draw a moustache on my own flag!"

"But it's your flag."

"Exactly! I'm not going to graffiti my own flag!"

Muzza, who'd been quiet up to this point, crossed his legs and calmly said, "Sorry, don't know anything about it."

"So you never touched the flag?"

"Why would I touch the flag? I don't know anything about it. I've got better things to do with my time."

They told me to find out who did it so, like any good detective, I headed to the crime scene. To be fair, the culprit had done a good job. The 'tache was bushy, but subtle enough so it didn't look ridiculous. Some nice work.

All along, I knew who was responsible. It was of course Muzza, but he denied it. I bloody knew it was him though; I had no doubt in my mind it was something he'd think was really funny. I played along, even though he wasn't admitting it.

Next stop was the dressing room, where I found all of the lads. "The gaffer's just pulled me in about my flag," I told them. "So, come on, who's drawn a moustache on my face?"

As expected, everyone found it hilarious. Then Muzza popped up with, "We need to find out who's done this. It's a disgrace." I couldn't believe his cheek!

The Head of Ops called us back in again after training. He asked if I'd found out who'd done it, and I said no. He asked Muzza if he knew who'd done it, and he said no.

"Is that right?" He said, before calmly opening his laptop, turning it around to face us, uploading a video and pressing play. It was the CCTV of the stadium, with a shadowy figure by the flag.

"Right lads, I don't suppose you recognise the fella drawing the moustache on there do you? Look familiar by any chance?"

As soon as he said that, Muzza's shoulders starting bouncing up and down from laughing.

You could clearly see him on the CCTV, walking up the stairs, stopping every few steps and looking around to make sure no one was watching him, like the Pink Panther in those cartoons. He got his pen out, had another look around, drew the moustache and then ran back down the stairs like a naughty schoolkid.

I was in hysterics, and to be fair everyone was laughing. Muzza was always like that, forever thinking of ways to keep himself entertained. He was a brilliant guy, and living with him really helped me settle in. We quickly became really good pals.

The two of us lived in a chalet in the grounds of a massive house that one of the club directors owned. Our rooms didn't have windows in, but they had a skylight in the ceiling. They were perfect for afternoon naps – and footballers love an afternoon nap – because you'd stick a towel over your skylight and it'd be pitch black.

The trouble is, if you didn't set your alarm you wouldn't know how long you'd been sleeping for when you woke up because it was pitch dark whatever time it was. I'd go for an hour's sleep and then wake up four hours later with 20 missed calls from people wondering if everything was OK!

Me and Muzza would commute back to Carlisle and Preston together, so it worked out well. I don't think I'd have joined Shrewsbury if he hadn't been there, because I knew I needed someone to travel back home with. There were groups of lads from Liverpool and from Birmingham at the club, who would spend a lot of time back in their cities, so if I was going to go there then someone to hang out with was vital. Either that, or I'd tear my hair out.

We had tennis courts at the back of the chalet, and we'd use those to help keep us fit. We also had a local butcher's which was run by a guy called Bert; Bert the butcher. We became friends and he had a rule where if I scored at the weekend we'd have T-bone steaks on the Monday for free. What an incentive! He probably hadn't banked on me scoring 28 goals that season, though, so he must have got sick of the sight of me scoring.

Not only that, but Burt had to give us two sets because the deal was Muzza would also have a steak when I scored. Now, I don't want to say Muzza was piggybacking off my goals, but he was definitely piggybacking off my goals!

We'd help Bert with tickets for the game, and he'd dish them out to his farmer buddies around the villages. We also went shooting with him. I'd wear a big wax jacket, flat cap, all of the gear. We used to collect our own shots, and Bert would pluck the birds for us. It would give us something to do – and something else to be competitive about – because there's a lot of downtime when you don't have your family living with you.

We stayed in a lot, which was different to when I was at Rochdale. We didn't spend hours in the pub or have takeaways on a Friday night. We watched box-sets, and played a lot of Scrabble and dominoes together – competitively of course.

Shrewsbury was quiet. Peaceful. There's not much to do there, but it's a lovely place and was really relaxing. There wasn't a massive football culture in the town, not like in Nottingham where you always had people coming up to you to talk about the game. In Shrewsbury you could happily sit in a coffee shop for hours and not have anyone bother you. That suited where I was in life.

I was looking after myself much better than when I was at Rochdale, although those cravings for curry fried rice and battered sausages never went away! I'd just have it after the game instead of before...

FLAG VANDALISM, FIVE GOALS IN A GAME AND GHOST PENALTIES

✱✱✱

We had a good side that season, and we were outstanding at New Meadow. The fans were brilliant and really backed us, but we had one major problem: winning away from home. We won our first away game of the season at Exeter, but then didn't win away again in the league until the penultimate away game at Rotherham, and then we got our third in the next game at Dagenham & Redbridge, which took us into the playoffs.

If we'd won just a few more on the road we'd have got automatic promotion. We could never quite work out why we couldn't do it away, though. We played the same way and felt we put in good performances, but we drew so many on our travels.

It was strange, then, that in October we'd gone to Wycombe Wanderers in the Football League Trophy and smashed them 7-0. That was the night I scored my first-ever professional hattrick, at the age of 27. Then a minute later I'd scored my first-ever quadruple... and then five minutes later I'd scored my first-ever quintuple!

I hadn't been expected to play in the match, but I'd picked up a one-game suspension in the league so the gaffer wanted me to start to keep me in a good rhythm. Wycombe, who were in the league above, had a decent team out, and we were pretty strong too.

I'd scored four in my first 10 games of the season. It was decent, but most strikers will tell you they want to average a goal every other game, and this seemed like a decent opportunity to get on the scoresheet. I wasn't wrong: I'd already scored a couple by the break and we led 3-0.

We played really well after half-time, but I actually started to find it annoying. We were moving the ball around, controlling possession and passing it about nicely, when in actual fact I just wanted them to play me in because I was desperate for that hattrick.

With 26 minutes to go Shane Cansdell-Sherriff hit an absolute worldie into the top bins, and that sucked the life out of Wycombe. Here was my chance. Finally, with 10 minutes left, I managed to grab my third with another header, and I thought, 'Right, that's done. My first hattrick. Nice work, Holty.'

It turned out I wasn't done, though.

A minute later, a long ball was flicked on and it fell nicely to me. I smashed a left-foot volley from 25 yards which went in off the stanchion, and suddenly I had four. I was just thinking, 'Oh my god, I've scored four!' I felt like a child down the park; I couldn't really process it. Scoring four goals in a game just sounds ridiculous!

Andy Cole had scored five for Manchester United when they beat Ipswich 9-0 when I was a teenager. I always liked Cole, so now I wanted to equal that. The more I scored, the hungrier I got. Five minutes later I struck one sweetly into the bottom corner, and oh my god I'd got five! Five in one match! I was that kid in the park again, celebrating like I'm Andy Cole!

You'd think I'd be pretty happy with five, especially for someone who'd never scored a hattrick before. But I realised I'd got two headers and gone left foot, right foot, left foot, so now I had a chance to get a perfect double hattrick. Andy Cole had never scored a double hattrick, let alone a perfect double hattrick!

On 90 minutes I hit an unbelievable volley and thought, 'This is it! The perfect double hattrick!' But their 'keeper made a stunning save, tipping it on to the post. What a bastard! After all, they were 7-0 down so he could have just let it in! It wouldn't have made any difference.

It was weird to be disappointed after scoring five, but I was gutted to not get my sixth. I've got the ball still, and of course it's also a big honour to be in the Johnstone's Paint Hall of Fame...

✱

I was absolutely flying after the win over Wycombe. I scored seven goals in November and rarely went more than a couple of matches without a goal. We were right in the hunt for the playoffs when it came to March, and we headed to Gillingham in the middle of the month.

We knew it would be a real test for us. We'd spanked them 7-0 at home in September, so they'd be looking for revenge. They were also ahead of us in the table, and we were desperate to keep pace with the top six.

Things did not start well. We were 2-0 down just after half-time and I was getting absolute pelters from the Gillingham fans. I'm not even sure why – I'd only scored once in the 7-0 win – but the abuse was relentless. That just fired me up though, and made me more determined. I wanted to shut them up, and I always played better when I had some fans to shut up.

In the 79th minute Moses Ashikodi won a penalty for us. Someone booted the ball miles away, and there were arguments about the decision. It took ages for me to get the ball and to put it down on the spot.

I calmed myself, and ran up to take the penalty. Then something strange happened. You know how sometimes you get the sense of someone being right next to you in your peripheral vision? You don't actually see anyone, you just sense them. I suddenly got that feeling in my final stride, but I still managed to hammer the penalty into the bottom corner. I wheeled off to my left to celebrate, but their 'keeper Simon Royce had shanked the ball in anger and it absolutely smashed me in the back of my head.

The force of it hitting me made me bite down on my tongue, which hurt like crazy. Roycey came up to me straight away to apologise: "Sorry, sorry, I was just kicking it away!" I told him not to worry, and that was when I realised I was bleeding from my mouth. I'd bitten a chunk out of my tongue and I couldn't speak properly!

Not only that, but it also dawned on me the ref had blown up, and instructed the penalty to be taken again. I couldn't believe it! On what grounds?!

Well, it turned out that the feeling of someone being right next to me was literally someone being right next to me. Ashikodi had encroached so far into the area that he'd almost been level with me when I'd struck the ball. I'd never known anything like it.

I looked at Ashikodi like, 'What the fuck were you thinking?' and he shrugged and said sorry. He'd just had a moment of madness. All of their fans were laughing, I was bleeding from my tongue, and I had to take another penalty in a massive game against a promotion rival. No pressure.

Roycey was saying to me, "I know which way you'll go this time!" and I turned around to make sure no one encroached this time. Ashikodi was stood about 10 yards back! I told Roycey I was going the same way, but I sounded ridiculous because I was lisping so badly due to the massive hole in my tongue. I was pissed off, so I decided to run up and smash it as hard as I could into the opposite corner. The ball flew in, and I wheeled away again and shouted through a mouthful of blood, "Don't kick the ball at me again, Roycey!"

I cupped my ear at the Gillingham fans and they went even more ballistic. They crumbled under the pressure in the last 10 minutes, and I ended up scoring the equaliser, heading home a Chris Humphrey cross in injury time. I ran the whole length of the half to the dugout; everyone was going mad and jumping on each other. Moments like that are what you play football for.

Sadly, though, it would be Gillingham who would end up having the last laugh.

CHAPTER 17

THE SOUND OF SILENCE, BURY BURIED AND WEMBLEY WOE
2008-09

A dressing room can be the quietest place in the world. There might be 20 blokes in there, and barely any room to breathe because you're huddled in so close, but the absence of sound can be deafening. No shouting, no banter, no taking the piss; nothing. It is the silence of defeat, of despair, of plans ruined and of dreams broken. It is the hush of wondering if those bruised bones had been worth it, of time away from family, of failure.

One of the lowest points of my career was standing on the Wembley turf after we'd lost 1-0 to Gillingham in the Playoff Final. I was the last Shrewsbury player to leave the pitch, holding back to watch every single Gillingham player climb those steps and lift the trophy to huge cheers from their fans. It was agony. At the time, I told myself I'd stayed out there because the horrific feeling of losing a Wembley final was something I never wanted to experience again. So I put myself through their celebrations in order to bank that feeling and use it to make me work even harder.

In truth, I think the real reason it took me so long to get off the pitch was because I knew what it would be like in the dressing room. I dreaded having to go in there, to leave the pitch, with everything getting slowly quieter as you walked down the tunnel and entered the dressing room to silence. The only muffled sound would be the Gillingham celebrations in the dressing room across the way, just to slam home what you'd missed out on. It would be a realisation that the season was over, and you'd achieved nothing.

So I lingered on that famous pitch, where I'd celebrated as an 11-year-old in the Smiths Cup. Watched the Gillingham players hugging and high-fiving as they came back down the famous Wembley steps, trophy in hand. I took it all in, and then turned to head down the Wembley tunnel and into the quietest place on earth.

***

As crushed as you feel after losing a Playoff Final, in time you learn to enjoy the journey that took you there. That last month of the season was a proper whirlwind, and the drama of our win away at Dagenham on the last day of the season will always live with me.

To put it simply, Dagenham needed a point to get the final playoff spot and we needed three. We'd beaten them twice already that season: 2-1 in the league and 5-0 in the Football League Trophy. I'd scored in both matches, and felt really good going into the game at Victoria Road.

It was must-win, do or die, winner takes all. The usual clichés. We were really confident, though, and started on the front foot. Bang, I headed in Chris Humphrey's cross in the 19th minute, and then Chris doubled our lead not long after. 2-0 up and playing confidently. Dagenham pulled one back just after half-time, and the game became really cagey. They only needed a point so were desperate for another goal; we needed a win so were desperate to protect our lead.

It was proper backs-to-the-wall stuff, with their crowd right behind them, and the relief at the final whistle was huge. There was certainly nothing quiet about that dressing room.

We'd sneaked into 7th, so faced the side in 4th in the semi-final. That suited us just fine, as it was a club we were desperate for revenge over: Bury. They'd beaten us 2-1 at their place in April, and it had been a really tasty game. Tackles flying in, words on the pitch and stronger words in the tunnel, and their fans were really giving it to us. You get used to fans abusing you, but that day it was really nasty.

We said after the game that we'd love to get Bury in the playoffs, and that's exactly what happened. We couldn't wait to play them.

We absolutely smashed them at our place in the first leg. Battered them. But we couldn't find a way through and they scored late on thanks to a lucky own goal. They acted like they'd already won the tie; celebrated like they were already at Wembley. They got in our faces in the tunnel post-match, and a few of our players gave it back. I had no interest in getting involved while the tie was only halfway through, and headed straight to the dressing room.

A few of the lads were moaning when they came in, so I just went on a rant. "I tell you what, fucking shut up. Everyone just calm down. When we play Bury at their place, just remember what they're doing right now. Celebrating like they're already promoted. We were good today and played them off the park, and we can do that again.

"We won away at Dagenham, so that away curse is gone, and we'll fucking beat that lot. Just remember when we're tired in the game, remember the way they were already celebrating. Use it."

Three days later we went to their place. Luke Daniels saved a penalty for us on the hour-mark, as well as the follow-up. Brilliant double save. That galvanised us and we bombarded Bury for the last 20 minutes. With two minutes remaining, a long ball was sent into their box and Kevin McIntyre smashed it in.

The away end absolutely erupted. It was an amazing moment, not least because Kevin had only just come back from a broken leg. We'd got back into it but were on the back foot again when Steven Leslie got sent off at the start of extra time. To this day I still don't think it was a red card, and it halted our momentum.

Not long after, I got elbowed in the sternum. Caught an absolute treat. I could barely breathe, but the physio told me to carry on. A minute later, I tried to set off for a ball in the corner, but I just couldn't catch my breath. I was gasping. There were only 15 minutes left, but we were already down to 10 men and I just knew with me on the pitch it would be like playing with nine men. I was desperate to stay on, but running was beyond me. I was hindering the team. The gaffer substituted me, and I got dog's abuse when walking off. The match was now out of my hands.

The game went to penalties. As the main penalty taker it was really difficult not to be out there to influence it. It was a feeling of powerlessness. I needn't have worried, though. Luke – who'd made a string of unbelievable saves when we were down to 10 men – saved two penalties and we scored all of ours. We were going to Wembley!

It was great to beat them after the shit they'd given us, and I couldn't resist saying something to their boys when we were in the tunnel. It was like I'd lobbed in a hand grenade. It all went off: shouting, pushing, shoving, squaring up. I ducked out of it though because I was still too winded to get involved. Pulled the pin, did a runner!

A camera crew came into the dressing room and everyone was singing and dancing. Yet I just sat there, watching everyone celebrate. I wasn't that excited because I knew we hadn't won anything, yet. All we'd done is get to Wembley. That meant nothing. Of course I was delighted to have won the semi-final, but we'd achieved nothing. To do that, we needed to win at Wembley.

* * *

The week leading up to the final was intense. Lots of press, plenty of attention and really hard training sessions. We were right up for it.

We knew we were taking a good crowd and that the atmosphere would be brilliant. We'd beaten Gillingham 7-0 at our place and drawn 2-2 at theirs, so we were confident. Despite those results, I actually thought Gillingham were the best team in the division. They moved the ball really well, and their manager Mark Stimson had them well-drilled. Wembley has a massive pitch, and their game would suit that.

That's exactly how it turned out: in the first half they gave us an absolute shoeing, moving us about the pitch at will, but they didn't score. We came into it in the second half and moved the ball better. Although we were having more possession, we barely created a thing and my only chance was a blocked shot. I ran my arse off, and it was a pleasure to do so on the Wembley pitch. But nothing would fall for me.

It looked to be heading to extra-time, but disaster struck. They won a corner in the 90th minute; we were man-marking, but whoever was supposed to be on Simeon Jackson lost him. He darted to the near stick and headed it in. One lapse of concentration, and it looked like we were done.

We kicked off and the ball went into the corner. Maybe one last chance? We got a throw-in, and the ball was crossed to the back post. I was unmarked, the ball was looping towards me and I set myself to get into position to leap. I screamed my name – "Hoooolty's!" – and jumped. The ball never reached me, though. Graham Coughlin heard my shout too late, got up and headed it wide. I just know I would have scored. My chance – our chance – had gone. Gutted.

The whistle went, and we'd lost at Wembley. For 30 seconds I stood still, taking it all in. Not knowing how to react. It was almost a trance, but I snapped out of it and pulled a few of our lads up from the ground, telling them we'd had a good season. Anything to shake the feeling of emptiness. All of that time invested into the season, wasted.

Our aim had been to win the league, and we hadn't. Then our aim was to win the playoffs, and we hadn't. All gone in 90 minutes. You can't explain the feeling until it's happened to you. You're just hollow.

As I've said, I didn't want to leave the pitch. I also didn't want to go upstairs to see family and friends because they'd be so disappointed for me. Their sadness for me would be too difficult to take; like I'd somehow let them down. It was an overwhelming feeling of bitter disappointment.

Disappointment for the manager because he'd worked so hard. Disappointment for the chairman because he'd put his money in to try and get us up. Disappointment for the fans for backing us all year, and going to Wembley and seeing us lose. Disappointment not to have got Shrewsbury back up to the third tier. Disappointment my 28 goals counted for nothing.

The journey back was an absolute killer. Awful. Not much talking. A lot of tired blokes, all realising that the season was done.

CHAPTER 18

THE BIG QUESTION, ANKLE PROBLEMS AND SIGNING FOR NORWICH

2009

There is one question I ask myself more than any other about my career: if Shrewsbury had won at Wembley, how would my journey have panned out?

Simeon Jackson's 90th-minute winner meant we remained a League Two side, and me a League Two player. But if Simeon had missed, and Shrewsbury had gone on to win and get promoted, would I have left to join Norwich City? Almost certainly not.

Promotion would have meant I'd have achieved my goal of getting back to League One, so in that scenario I would almost certainly have stayed no matter who came in for me. Would we have been good enough to get another promotion to the Championship? We'd have given it a right good go, but I don't think we would have had quite enough quality.

I would have been 29 at the end of that season, and still in League One. At that age, it's very unlikely a Championship club would have come in for me, even if I'd done well. I'd have probably spent the next few years playing in League One or League Two, and been quite happy with it. It would still have been a good career, and one I would have been really proud of. But it would have been a very different journey for me.

So, although losing at Wembley was the darkest day of my career, it was also the day that set off a series of events which would lead me to, improbably, playing in the Premier League.

THE BIG QUESTION, ANKLE PROBLEMS AND SIGNING FOR NORWICH

✱✱✱

I'd had an ankle operation at the end of the season to remove a piece of floating bone and a spur, but the pain was still there when I returned for pre-season. To make matters worse, I'd also broken my toe during a training week in Spain (I did it in training, obviously. I definitely didn't do it stubbing my toe against a wall while wearing flip-flops. Definitely not).

Despite having two dodgy feet, I'd had interest from Colchester United in League One. Marc Tierney had joined them from Shrewsbury, and he called me to tell me their manager Paul Lambert was really keen on me. But Colchester weren't meeting Shrewsbury's £400,000 valuation of me, so it seemed like a non-starter.

After returning from Spain, my agent told me Bryan Gunn had called him. He was the manager at Norwich, and was very interested in signing me. So interested, in fact, that they were going to put in a bid.

I wasn't expecting that. They'd been in the Premier League pretty recently, and my brother used to wear the famous speckled top (some would call it the famous birdshit top) from when they'd been in Europe in the early 1990s.

I knew about them beating Bayern Munich in 1993, and that they'd had some really good strikers like Chris Sutton, Dean Ashton and of course my old Wednesday teammate Mark Robins. It was a big club. Wes Hoolahan was there, and I knew Matt Gilks and Sammy Clingan who had both played for them and enjoyed it. Also, Bryan Gunn was a bit of a legend for any kid growing up in the 1980s and 1990s.

Their interest changed the goalposts. I really fancied playing for a team like Norwich, as they would be expected to challenge very strongly for the title. It was like when Forest came in for me while I was at Rochdale; I hadn't been expecting a side of Norwich's stature to show any interest in me. They had been relegated to League One for the first time in 50 years, but had a really good side. Colchester also had a decent chance of going up, but Norwich were far more attractive.

They were going to meet my valuation, so the move could happen sharpish. Although it was really far from Carlisle – Norwich is really far from everywhere, let's be honest – Fay was pleased because she'd heard it was a good place to bring up kids.

After training, the Shrewsbury chairman and the gaffer pulled me in. Norwich had met my valuation, but Roland wasn't happy with the structure of the deal. I trusted his instinct, but asked him to try and get the deal done as it was a fantastic opportunity for me.

It was in Roland's hands now, and me and Muzza ended up going to the pictures that evening to pass the time. The next morning, Roland told me the deal had been agreed. I popped back to Carlisle to see Fay and to pick up some bits, and then it was time for a 300-mile road trip to Norwich.

***

My god it's a long way! Luckily, my brother was off work so he joined me for the journey. After what seemed like an endless amount of road, we eventually pulled up at the Holiday Inn at Carrow Road.

It was absolutely roasting in Norwich. It had been cold in Carlisle so we were in jeans and jumpers, but it was about 30 degrees. There's a retail park near the ground called Riverside, so we headed to Morrisons for a toilet break, and across to Next to get some summer clothes. With social media now, you probably couldn't casually pop across to a large shopping area for a wee and a spot of shopping when you're about to sign for a club, but back then no one really knew who I was anyway, so there were no strange looks as we queued up in Next to buy shorts and t-shirts.

We checked in at the hotel, showered, and then I headed across to the ground with my agent to meet Bryan Gunn for the first time. He was really warm and friendly, but businesslike.

He showed me around the ground, and it was the first time I'd been to Carrow Road. Obviously I'd played at Hillsborough, so it's not like I was blown away, but I was impressed. It immediately felt like being back at a bigger club. The training ground, Colney, was excellent, and a level above anywhere else I'd been at.

Bryan went out to take training and I was left to chat with the physios. One of the first questions was about my ankle. "Oh it's fine, of course!" No way did I want to tell them it still felt buggered.

They sent me up to the hospital for scans of my heart, knees, hips and ankles, which was a much more intense medical than I'd had before. I went up there with Paul McVeigh, who had played in the Premier League for Norwich and was re-signing after a couple of years with Luton Town.

My phone was dying and I didn't have my charger, so I turned it off. It took ages to get my MRI, and my brother had been ringing me and leaving messages while it was switched off asking where the hell I was. He was just moaning because he was hungry.

My agent had also been trying to get hold of me, and he had good news: the deal had been agreed with Norwich's chief executive David McNally. The money was more than I'd been expecting, so I was really pleased. Couldn't have been happier.

Well, when I say it was agreed, that all depended on the results of the medical. I was sure that would all be OK, so me and Steven headed to a local pub called the Woolpack. He had a pint and I had a soft drink because I was trying to be good, but that didn't last. We were a few pints in when I got a call saying I had to go back to the hospital the following day to get another scan on my ankle. Uh-oh. I had a little panic, but no more than a bit of anxiety. My ankle had been causing problems, but I wasn't worried that anything was seriously wrong.

Following the second scan, Bryan told me to come to the training ground the following morning. This was starting to drag a bit, and I was getting pissed off. Bryan asked me to keep a low profile and stay at the hotel in case anyone spotted me, but I wasn't having that. I told him, "To be honest, I'm not going to sit in my room. It's not my fault the signing is dragging, so I'm going to go out for some dinner with my brother and if I'm seen I'm seen." I think after that he knew what he was getting with me.

The next morning – now my third day down in Norwich – I met the physio at Colney. They'd got the scan back, and the results showed that the spur on my ankle was still there. Not only that, but the floating bone was back. Unbelievable. I knew something hadn't been right after the surgery.

Although it was good to know for certain what was wrong with my ankle, I was worried. Was this going to mess up the deal? The physio said I might need another operation. Could I play all year on it? Probably. Might it flare up again? Maybe.

I felt in limbo, and really angry about my operation. Gunny was honest with me, and said my ankle was causing a lot of problems for him. The club were skint, and I was the only signing they were going to make involving a fee. Not only that, but the money had been raised through donations. Understandably, he was worried about risking that cash on someone who might need another ankle operation.

However, by this point I just wanted an answer. I said to him, "Ring who you need to ring – Delia Smith or David McNally – and tell them it either gets signed this afternoon or I'm leaving and I won't be back. It's up to you guys. I'm not mucking around anymore. I'd love to sign here, but I have other clubs who will come in for me."

The next few hours were excruciating. It was a bold move to lay it on the line like that, and I was beginning to doubt whether it had been the right thing to do. Finally, my phone buzzed and Bryan's name flashed up.

"I've spoken to Delia and the board, and everyone's agreed. We want to sign you. Welcome to the club."

Huge relief. I was a Norwich City player.

THE BIG QUESTION, ANKLE PROBLEMS AND SIGNING FOR NORWICH

✱✱✱

Gunny told me I'd been at the top of his list of targets. He'd seen me play and thought I'd fit in really well, but hadn't been sure whether he'd be able to get me in because most of the transfer kitty had gone. But one of the club's directors, Michael Foulger, had donated his own money in order to help sign me. Without that Norwich wouldn't have been able to afford me, and hearing that was pretty special. It was clear they really wanted me at the club.

The physios did an amazing job with my ankle, and I could play on it happily within a week. That's no slight on Shrewsbury, by the way, but Norwich had a much bigger medical department. It meant I could join in properly with all of the training and hit the ground running.

I was put up in the Holiday Inn while I looked for a place to live with Fay and the kids. Being in the hotel suited me really well, because loads of the new lads were staying there: Matt Gill, Owain Tudur Jones, Michael Nelson, Stephen Hughes. You could see the Carrow Road pitch from my hotel room, and I couldn't wait to get out there and play.

It was the first time I'd signed for a club where I was familiar with so many faces. Gilly had won promotion with Exeter, Michael Nelson with Hartlepool, I knew what Wes could do, I knew what Gary Doherty could do, Jon Otsemobor had been at Liverpool, Jamie Cureton had scored goals everywhere, Paul McVeigh had been at Spurs and been brilliant for Norwich, I'd played against Chris Martin and Michael Spillane when they were at Luton, and I knew Adam Drury had been in the Premier League. It was a really good squad.

Then I heard Norwich had sold around 20,000 season tickets, and it stopped me in my tracks. It was their first season in League One for 50 years but they were still selling out the stadium. Incredible. You just knew we could blow the league away if things went well.

I was a better player than I'd ever been. Not only that, but I suddenly found myself having a very real chance of playing in the Championship again. We just had to make sure we started the season well.

MY TOP 5...
CHOCOLATE BARS

1. SECRET

Gutted this isn't made anymore. I loved it as a kid.
Chocolate casing with a creamy mousse. Perfect.
They were the best bars.

2. TOPIC

Another one you don't see very often now.
Hazelnut, nougat and caramel; great diversity.

3. TWIX

Solid. Very solid.

4. BOOST

Lovely bit of caramel, with a small dollop of biscuit.
Phenomenal.

5. NOUGAT BAR

You either love it or hate, and I love it.

CHAPTER 19

1-7 (SEVEN), GOALKEEPER CALAMITY AND GUNNY'S DEPARTURE

2009-10

I knew I'd made the right choice coming to Norwich. Clubs that have just been relegated can often have a vibe of decline. Morale is low, fans are bitter, players are tired. The whole place smells of failure. But I didn't find that at Norwich. There was an expectation on the club, and a buzz you could feel when you were walking around the city. A chance to start over again.

Everyone in the city supports Norwich. It's probably one of the only places I've been where it's very rare you'll see a Manchester United top or an Arsenal or Chelsea shirt. I really liked that. You got the sense very early on that they belonged at a higher level and needed to get back to the Championship quickly.

I was their big signing, and was seen as the guy who would bag the goals to get out of the division. That meant people knew who I was, which was different to when I first joined Forest. I had more of a reputation now, and a track record of scoring goals. That brought with it more pressure, which was exactly what I'd wanted.

The fans took to me early in the pre-season games, probably because I was doing more running in those matches than I needed to in order to get up to speed with my fitness. I was making unnecessary runs and pressing when I shouldn't, but it was helping me to get fit. The fans saw that as me putting a real effort in, and it gave me a reputation as a really hard worker right from the start.

The standard in training had gone up from Shrewsbury. You had to be better and work harder. However, I wasn't sure we'd definitely clicked in pre-season. Although there was a good vibe around the place, I wasn't 100% convinced we were gelling properly. There was something missing; maybe an extra bit of energy. It was hard to pin down.

Despite these little concerns, we felt pretty good going into the opening game of the season against Colchester United at Carrow Road.

A few of us felt Colchester were going to be a tough side that year. They had good players, with a really solid spine. It would be a stern test, but I'm not convinced everyone in the dressing room thought that. There was something about the atmosphere which made me think that maybe some players weren't quite prepared for what League One would be like.

Despite that, I was confident. I genuinely thought we had a brilliant chance of winning the title, and believed we'd beat Colchester. I wanted to lift trophies, and I wanted the first game to be a statement.

Just not the statement it turned out to be.

* * *

It was a lovely, sunny day. We walked out of the tunnel to a packed stadium and a huge roar. The fans had stuck with the team, and there was a buzz of expectancy about the place. After a few years of underachievement in the Championship, a lot of fans were probably thinking that relegation had brought with it the opportunity to win matches and enjoy football again.

The atmosphere was great, and it felt good to finally be out there and playing in front of a big crowd. We were brilliant for the first 10 minutes: moved the ball around, played good football, got stuck in. I felt at home immediately. Then suddenly Colchester scored a horrendous goal from our perspective: a bad back pass, and our goalkeeper Michael Theoklitos came off his line, flapped at the ball and let in Kevin Lisbie. How had that happened? We barely had time to recover before Theo had pushed a tame shot right into the path of Clive Platt, who made it 2-0 after just 13 minutes. Shell-shocked.

In less than 15 minutes, all of that pre-season expectation and positivity had disappeared. Carrow Road was silent. Can we start the season again?

1-7 (SEVEN), GOALKEEPER CALAMITY AND GUNNY'S DEPARTURE

Theo has unfortunately gone down in Norwich folklore for that performance, the one and only time he played for the Canaries. He was a great guy; he'd come over from Australia and everyone liked him. However, I must admit I'd had my doubts about him in training. He didn't seem like he was a good shot-stopper, and didn't fill me with that much confidence. But I'd been wrong about teammates before, and as Gunny was a former 'keeper I put my trust in his judgement.

It got worse for Theo, though. He had to pick the ball out of his net for the third time in 19 minutes. Already 3-0 down. Fucking embarrassing. I'd never known anything like it. Everyone was looking at each other wondering what the hell was going on. They were shit goals to concede, but I was thinking, 'This can't get any worse. Let's chill out a bit, tighten up, get settled.'

Well, that never happened.

Just three minutes later Colchester won a free-kick from a shite pass from one of our boys. David Fox, who would join us the following season, was standing over it. I thought, 'I've seen him score free-kicks before. He couldn't could he?' He could.

I was stood in the wall, and I remember it sailing over us and thinking, 'Phew, it's straight down the middle of the goal. Easy save'. But I heard a roar from the away fans, turned around and saw Theo picking it up from the back of the net. How the fuck had that gone in? It was right down the middle! It turned out that Theo had misjudged the flight and dived over it. Poor guy. I looked up at the scoreboard. 0-4. Just 22 minutes in. Please swallow me up.

Next thing I knew, a couple of Norwich fans had run onto the pitch towards the dugout and thrown their season tickets towards Gunny. At the time, I didn't think much of it. I was still in shock from the scoreline, and it was only after the game when I realised I'd never seen anything like that before. It was a disgrace, really, and no way to treat a club legend. I bet they regretted their decision very quickly.

Colchester got their fifth before half-time, which was another awful goal. I just wanted it all to end and start over again. Colchester had been first to every tackle, had wanted it more, had been far more up for it than we were. We were crushed, and we still had a whole half to go. The crowd was going ballistic. I'd never heard boos that loud before, and too right as well.

Not a word was said when we got into the dressing room. On my debut, I didn't think it was my place to say anything. Then Wes, who didn't often say much in these situations, just shouted out, "What the fuck was that? The goals are fucking shite, we're defending like c*nts." No one said anything to Theo. He was sitting there, on his debut, absolutely gutted.

As a manager, you can do one of two things when you're 5-0 down at half-time. You can either launch into the players or you can go jovial and put it down to one of those things. Bryan tried angry, but it didn't quite go as he'd planned. He screamed and shouted a bit, and chucked a bottle of sun cream in a rage. I imagine he thought it would be an angry statement, but instead the sun cream squirted out of the bottle and flew absolutely everywhere, splattering all over people's suits.

As soon as it happened, he apologised for it. Now, saying sorry probably isn't the best way to strike fear into your players, but Gunny is a respectful man. A real gentleman. He's a brilliant guy, one of football's nicest blokes, and being angry just didn't suit him.

But what can you do in that situation? You're 5-0 down in the first game of the season and two people have run onto the pitch and chucked their season tickets at you. Gunny told us to do our best in the second half, to do everything properly, to be professional.

That didn't happen, though. Colchester nearly scored twice within five minutes of the restart, and the crowd just lost it. We were shot. Somehow Cody McDonald scored for us, and we had a bit of a rally for at least a whole three minutes. That was quickly ended when Colchester scored a sixth, and then they banged in another in injury time to make it 7-1.

Seven. Seven! Embarrassing.

Lovely August day, opening match of the season, title-challengers, my debut, and we lost 7-1 to the club I could have joined. Oh, and it was Norwich's biggest-ever home defeat in their 107-year history. Perfect.

We walked off. Huge boos. A few of us went over and clapped the fans – the few who were still in the ground, anyway – because it was only right to do so. More boos.

***

Everyone was quiet in the dressing room. It was depressing; eerily silent. Bryan said a few words, as did coaches Ian Crook and Ian Butterworth. I said my piece, telling everyone I was here to win the league, that I'd been promoted from League One before and that we needed to work harder, run further, and be fitter than everyone.

After the game I went to the players' lounge to see my old Forest teammate Gary Holt, a former Norwich player who had been on the bench for Colchester, and his wife. It wasn't quite the catch-up I'd been expecting two hours earlier. As I was leaving I bumped into Paul Lambert, the first time I'd seen him since all of the Colchester links. I thanked him for his interest, and said good luck for the rest of the season.

I ended up walking out of the ground with Theo. We just chatted away, and I tried to tell him that these things could happen in football. He was low, though, lower than a snake's belly. As he was heading out to the car park, his phone rang. It was in his bag, and as he tried to get it out – and you won't believe this – he dropped it! It slipped right out of his hand. I didn't know whether to laugh, cry or give him a hug! There were fans watching, and I just thought, 'Poor sod!' He picked his phone up and said, "To be fair Holty, I nearly caught that one!"

The first thing I saw when I got back up to my hotel room was the bloody pitch through my windows. I drew the curtains immediately. There were 200 messages on my phone. Ignored them all. I phoned Fay, instead.

"Are you all right?" she asked, cheerfully.

"I'm all right. Take it you haven't seen the score?"

"No, did you win?"

"No, we didn't. We got beat 7-1."

"Oh no, that's not a great start! Did you see Gary?"

And in that moment, Fay asking if I'd seen Gary Holt, I calmed down. There were more important things than football. We talked about the kids, and about her day. I had a bath, chilled out, went through the game and analysed my performance in my own head. I went downstairs to get some food with the boys, talked about how shit the game was, how crap Theo had been, and we put it behind us. There was a sense we'd put it right in training ahead of playing Yeovil in the Carling Cup on Tuesday.

* * *

We travelled down to Yeovil on the Tuesday morning, and it would be an extended break in the South-West because we had Exeter City on Saturday.

We thought there would be changes to the XI for the Yeovil game, but there weren't actually that many. Ben Alnwick, who was on loan from Tottenham Hotspur, started in goal, but the gaffer had told the press Theo was always going to sit it out because it was a cup game. Probably true, but also very convenient.

We had a point to prove as a team, and I really wanted to beat Yeovil because of the playoff semi-finals with Forest. I desperately wanted to shove a performance down their throat. However, we were crap in the first half. We couldn't get to grips with them. We knew we had to up our game, and we did in the second half. I grabbed a late hattrick, which was a fantastic feeling, and we won 4-0.

That helped put the 7-1 behind us, and personally it was nice to get off the mark with a hattrick in only my second game. Although I didn't think our performance was all that great, I was happy we'd got the season going.

1-7 (SEVEN), GOALKEEPER CALAMITY AND GUNNY'S DEPARTURE

We travelled from Yeovil to our hotel near Exeter. We all went out for a big dinner on the Wednesday evening and we were allowed to have a drink, which I don't think some people at board level were too happy about. It probably didn't create a great impression four days after the Colchester game.

Following training on Thursday, I was waiting in the hotel for Adam Drury to go for a coffee. David McNally wandered across and asked for a quick chat. I assumed it would just be about my hattrick the other night, or to ask how I was settling in.

It wasn't either of those things. Instead, he told me the club had let Bryan go.

I was shocked. Despite the Colchester game, we'd just won 4-0. Who gets sacked after a 4-0 win? After the surprise subsided, I just felt disappointment. Bryan had brought me in and shown a lot of faith in me as his marquee signing. He was also a really good guy, and it felt harsh. As players, we'd let him down big time.

At a team meeting later that day Bryan came in and told everyone the news. It was very difficult for him because he hadn't seen it coming. For a Norwich City legend, that meeting must have been so difficult for him. It was horrible to see, actually. Hard to watch. I'd never had any problem with him at all; he was the gaffer to me.

As with any time a manager goes, some players were happy, others weren't. And that was that. Gunny was gone. McNally came in and told us Butterworth and Crook would take charge until we appointed a new manager.

We got a draw at Exeter, but it was a bit of a nothing game. We didn't play particularly well, and there was a real feeling with everyone that we were in limbo. I was worrying, as there was no way of knowing who was going to come in as manager. I'd just signed for three years, Fay hadn't even moved down, and I'd only played three matches. Who knows, Colin Calderwood could walk through the door!

CHAPTER 20

INTRODUCING PAUL LAMBERT, HURTY TOOTH AND CAPTAIN HOLT

2009-10

It was on the bus to our midweek match at Brentford that the identity of our next manager was revealed.

There'd been a lot of speculation about who might be coming in, but we'd done our best to put that to the back of our minds while preparing for the game. It's tough when you're in that sort of limbo because, as good as the training might be, and as well as you might practice, you've always got it hanging over you. Will the new boss rate me? Will he totally change how we play? Will he bring his own staff in? Will I fit into his style? You basically ready yourself for an overhaul.

It was Wes who broke the news to us. He stood up on the coach and announced, "I know who the new gaffer is!"

Everyone immediately sat up. Some played it cool, pretending not to care, others shouted at Wes to hurry up and reveal all.

The two words which came out of Wes's mouth were a total shock to me: "Paul Lambert."

No one had expected it. There'd been no rumours, no links, no whispers. Nothing. It wasn't a name that had been mentioned at all. We couldn't believe it, especially because his team had battered us 10 days earlier. How had we managed to get him?

I think Wes had heard from David Fox at Colchester, and then a few minutes later I got a text from Marc Tierney saying the same thing.

Lambert had told the Colchester boys he was joining Norwich, so the news spread quickly.

After the shock, I realised I'd never been so happy to hear Paul Lambert's name. A bloke who'd been trying to sign me all summer and knew what I was about. A manager who really rated me. I'd never been so relieved!

We heard he was going to be at the game against Brentford, but we were surprised when he came into the dressing room ahead of the match. He said, "I won't tell you anything to do with tactics tonight, but I do expect you to run around as hard as you can." That was it. He went off, we went out, and we were absolutely shite.

We weren't at it at all and lost 2-1. I thought we were unfit, but I can't really comment on why that was, because I wasn't there for all of pre-season. But, after four games, I didn't think we were in good enough shape.

Lambert came in the next morning with his new coaching team: Ian Culverhouse, who was a Norwich legend and had played in the side which finished third in the Premier League in the early '90s, and Gary Karsa. They'd both been with Lambert at Wycombe Wanderers and Colchester.

After going through the video from the Brentford match, Lambert told us he didn't think we were fit enough or disciplined enough. It was no surprise to me. He told the boys that anyone who wanted to leave, or didn't want to be there, could walk out of the door. He only wanted men who were desperate to be at Norwich City.

The following day would be a training session in which players would be mixed and split into three teams. Whoever played best would start against Wycombe at the weekend. As simple as that. He didn't give a shit if you'd played in the Premier League, or had played 250 games in League One, or had scored goals wherever you'd been. He would judge you on how you did in training.

I loved that. It was a great first impression of him, and I really liked the idea of everyone having to prove themselves. It got my competitive juices flowing.

***

On the Friday night before the Wycombe game, I woke up in bed to my mouth thudding. What the hell was that? It took me a while to realise it was coming from my tooth, and the pain was absolutely killing me. It was like it had its own heartbeat.

The tooth had been a little painful throughout the day, but a couple of painkillers had sorted it out. Now, in bed, that pain had tripled, and I was out of painkillers. It was around 2am, and I was wide awake the night before a massive game.

I called reception to ask if they had any paracetamol, but apparently hotels aren't allowed to issue medication. I tried to force myself to sleep, but the pain was just too much. I texted the physio, asking him to call me as soon as he woke up.

All I could think of was my tooth, throbbing away like someone punching me repeatedly in the jaw. I tried putting boiling hot water on a flannel and pressed it to my face, but it made no difference. So there was only one thing for it: putting some gear on and heading out at 2am on a Friday night in search of drugs.

The hotel is only a couple of minutes from Prince of Wales Road, which is full of late-night bars, cheap takeaways and thousands of people on the piss. It's definitely not a place where you want to find yourself stone-cold sober early in the morning on a weekend.

Norwich was still unfamiliar to me, so I headed up a back road off Prince of Wales. I couldn't think straight because it felt like someone was hitting me in the face with a brick, but I stumbled across an all-night garage. I grabbed the strongest painkillers they had, as well as some heat patches that were supposed to be for stiff backs.

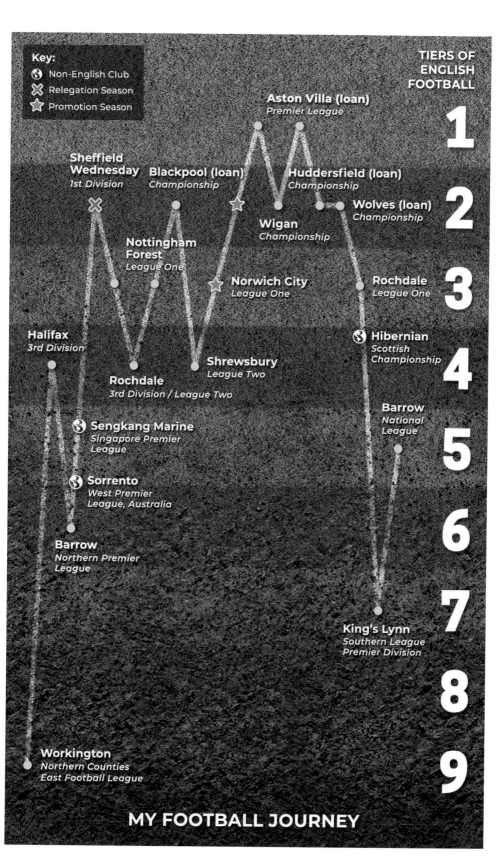

Key:
🌐 Non-English Club
✖ Relegation Season
★ Promotion Season

TIERS OF ENGLISH FOOTBALL

1
2
3
4
5
6
7
8
9

Aston Villa (loan)
Premier League

Sheffield Wednesday
1st Division

Blackpool (loan)
Championship

Huddersfield (loan)
Championship

Wolves (loan)
Championship

Wigan
Championship

Nottingham Forest
League One

Norwich City
League One

Rochdale
League One

Halifax
3rd Division

Hibernian
Scottish Championship

Shrewsbury
League Two

Rochdale
3rd Division / League Two

Barrow
National League

🌐 Sengkang Marine
Singapore Premier League

🌐 Sorrento
West Premier League, Australia

Barrow
Northern Premier League

King's Lynn
Southern League Premier Division

Workington
Northern Counties East Football League

MY FOOTBALL JOURNEY

Family!
Me in the
middle, posing,
with Steven,
Rachael and
Mum on holiday,
with Mum and
Dad below.

Great
hat, Holty!
My dad,
below,
probably
could've
done with
my sombrero...

Kids! The day after Erica's birth, just a week after my bust-up with Colin Calderwood.

Hattrick! Hattie makes it three beautiful daughters!

Childhood sweethearts!
Fay, the love of my life.

Wembley! Walking out onto the famous pitch, and lifting the Smiths Crisps trophy.

Trophy winner! With St. Edmund's.

Non-league glory! Celebrating with Stuart Williamson
as Workington beat Mossley to win the title in 1999.

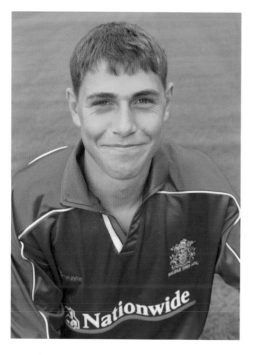

Young and handsome!
Halifax headshot.

Off the mark! My first
Football League goal, for
Sheffield Wednesday
at Brighton.

Champagne celebration! Getting soaked after sealing
promotion to the Premier League with Norwich.

Derby win! Celebrating my hattrick against Ipswich.

We are Premier League! On the Carrow Road pitch with Evie and Erica and, below, on the bus parade through Norwich.

Tensing! Showing the Swansea fans I'm not such a fat lad after all.

Final season! Scoring for Hibs against Aberdeen in the Scottish Cup semi-final.

Eyes on the ball!
Scoring against Liverpool
at Anfield.

I walked outside, and with the distant throb of dance music and drunken shouting, I got the paracetamol out and rubbed it into my gum. As I stuck my finger in there, something popped. Sssssss. It had been an abscess, and my god the pain when it exploded. The excruciating pain. But also the relief. The blessed relief! But then my mouth was filled with a disgusting taste, and – sorry, readers – I had to spit the mucus out into a drain.

What a sight I must have been. Half two in the morning, rubbing stuff into my gum, moaning to myself, spitting into a drain.

A few people had clocked me when I headed back to the hotel. "Haven't you got a game tomorrow?" "Shouldn't you be in bed?" "Are you pissed the night before a match?" I don't think anyone believed me when I told them I'd been on the hunt for painkillers for an abscess. To be fair, I wouldn't have believed me either!

Despite popping the abscess, it was still killing me, so I whacked the heat patch on, got into bed and finally drifted off. I was shocked back awake by my phone ringing at 7am. It was the physio, of course, who'd got my message. He organised painkillers to be sent to the local pharmacy for 9am, so I got a couple of hours kip before heading out to pick up the pills. My face had got massive at this point, like I had a huge boil on my jawline. At this stage I didn't really care, though, and I pocketed the pills and headed back.

The plan was to grab a little more sleep, and get up at 12 to head to the ground. But my phone rang at 11. Who the hell was it now? Paul Lambert. The gaffer. Just what I needed.

"All right, gaffer?"

"Fucking hell you sound well!"

"I'm dying!"

"Get a grip, you've just got toothache." The physio had obviously let him know.

"Gaffer, I'm in so much pain!"

"Don't be ridiculous, it's just a bit of toothache. I need to have a chat with you, come see me now."

What did he want? I clambered out of bed, absolutely knackered, gum still sore. Got changed, and headed to the gaffer's office at Carrow Road. Knocked, headed inside.

Lambert looked shocked at the sight of me, and his eyes fixed on the massive lump on my jaw.

"Jesus, you look like the elephant man!"

"That's right! Not just a bit of toothache, is it!"

I told him the full story, laying it on thick about the pain and the lack of sleep. He asked what I was thinking about the game that day.

"What do you mean?" I asked.

"Well, do you want to play?"

"Of course I want to play. I'll either have pain lying in my bed or pain playing out there, and I'd much rather be out there."

"Good answer. And just to let you know, you're starting and I'm taking the armband off Gary Doherty and giving it to you. I want you to be captain of this football club. I want you to lead by example, and I think you'll thrive."

Wow. I couldn't believe it. I was stood in the gaffer's office, a face like a smashed-up pumpkin, nine hours after spitting my own pus into a drain, and I was captain of Norwich City.

To be given that honour after only a couple of weeks was massive. I hadn't expected it at all. I'd been captain a couple of times at Rochdale, but that was it. To do it for a club like Norwich City was genuinely humbling.

INTRODUCING PAUL LAMBERT, HURTY TOOTH AND CAPTAIN HOLT

How did I celebrate being given the armband? By having my abscess lanced off in the dressing room.

Lambert had a novel way of letting you know the team for the day. He would read out the starting XI and subs really quickly, like rapid fire, and then say something like, "Make sure you fucking win" and walk straight out again. You barely had time to process it, or to ask if you'd heard your name or not. Cully would then take over, tell us the formation and remind us of our tactics. That first match, Wes wasn't in it, Doherty wasn't in it. That made us all realise this manager meant business.

We went out there and put Colchester right behind us. We played really well and beat Wycombe 5-2, and it could have been more. I got my first two goals at Carrow Road, which really settled me. However, the gaffer made me play the whole 90 minutes despite knowing I'd had very little sleep, which probably tells you everything you need to know about him!

It felt like we'd started the season again, and the whole dynamic changed. The fans were loving it, we had finally clicked on the pitch, and there was a real positivity about the place. It was great to sit in the dressing room afterwards and take it all in. Out of nowhere, it suddenly felt like someone had come over and given me a whack. I just slumped. I felt absolutely knackered. The day had caught up with me.

I did my media stuff, and went straight back to the hotel to sleep. I was too tired to go for dinner or to celebrate with the lads. I ordered all of the crap I could on room service, got it all down me, and fell asleep around 8pm. What a whirlwind.

CHAPTER 21

KILLER SESSIONS, LAMBERT'S HAIRDRYER AND WES'S REVELATION

2009-10

We didn't know what had hit us. The lads were slumped on their benches in the dressing room after a training session, stunned. No one said a word. We were dead on our feet, looking around at each other with a vacant expression on our faces. Wow.

If anyone had thought beating Wycombe meant the coaching team would take it easy on us, they were wrong. Very wrong. The training sessions became really tough. Or, to put it another way, ridiculously fucking hard.

The gaffer hadn't been joking when he said we were unfit. The intensity in training had gone up massively under the new regime, and the incentive we were given was that it would slow down after the New Year. The plan was to be at peak fitness by Christmas.

We were basically having our pre-season three weeks into the start of the campaign. Not ideal when you're playing every week, and sometimes twice a week, but I was 100% behind it and so were the rest of the boys. We knew we had to be fitter, and the only way to do that was to train like lunatics.

To start with, all I wanted to do after sessions was have a big bath, not talk to anyone and head back to the hotel to sleep. But it didn't take long to start producing results. Instead of wanting to slump straight into bed, you soon started feeling fine after a session. Don't get me wrong; you knew you'd been put through your paces, but day by day you got more used to it. I started feeling fitter than ever.

We were also working on structure relentlessly, and training in a diamond. I'd not really played in that formation before, but I enjoyed it. It gave me a strike partner, the full-backs provided plenty of width and loads of balls into the box, while having a No.10 gave the strikers more space to operate in. It suited our squad perfectly.

Culverhouse led most of the sessions, but the gaffer was always watching. Sometimes all of a sudden Lambert would blow his whistle if he didn't like what he was seeing. He'd tell us what he wanted to see, and then stand back again. If he was really pissed off and thought we weren't focused enough, he'd stop the sessions and make us all do sprints.

Cully was very demanding. If you weren't living up to his expectations in a session he'd tell you straight away. There was no arguing with him, either. He was always insisting that standards needed to be high, and he wouldn't let you slack. His sessions were phenomenal: always interesting, really clear, and he got the best out of everyone. He was a fantastic coach; probably the best I played under.

It was obvious very early on that Cully and Lambert bounced off each other. Gary Karsa was Head of Football Operations and was very much the guy in the background. It's fair to say he did the stuff the gaffer didn't want to do. Sorted the press out, collect the fines, set up the sessions. Importantly, he was often the go-between for players and the manager. It worked, because the gaffer and Cully didn't have time to do it all, so Karsa took a lot of pressure off them. It was a good dynamic.

I was surprised it didn't seem to work out for them at Aston Villa after they left Norwich, and I have no idea why it didn't. You don't know what goes on in the background, but it was a shock to see them part ways. All I know is that when they were at Norwich the three of them worked together brilliantly.

There was an impression from outside the club that Karsa and Cully were closer to the players, and that Lambert would keep himself separate. That's not true. You knew where your boundaries were with the gaffer, but he'd happily be part of the team, and you could chat away with him like he was a pal.

However, always in the back of your mind were the absolute roastings he could give people; bollockings that would make anyone witnessing them properly flinch. When he was in full flow, his roastings were like a hurricane. You would never answer back to him when he was using the hairdryer treatment, but I always made sure I kept eye contact. As hard as it was, I wouldn't look away.

There were two instances with him that always make me chuckle. One time, we were in the dressing room at half-time during a midweek home game, and for some reason it was boiling in there.

Lambert was going mad because we'd been having a beast of a game. The tactics board was already on the floor, the boys were looking everywhere apart from at him, and Lambert was in full scary Glaswegian mode. Our kitman, Riggers, was stood behind the gaffer's right shoulder while he was ranting away. Because of the heat, Lambert was trying to get his jacket off but the zip got stuck. He was flapping about with it, and everyone was dying to laugh but no one dared.

He finally ripped the jacket off and, without looking, chucked it behind him to Riggers. What he didn't notice was that the zip had whipped Riggers right in the eye. Oof.

We'd all seen what had happened but the gaffer was oblivious. Riggers was hunched over, holding his eye and desperately trying to not scream out in pain; everyone else was trying to not laugh. Eighteen lads, all attempting to think of something to stop them from sniggering. No one could concentrate on what the gaffer was saying. Eventually, Lambert left us with a, "Fucking get yourself sorted for the second half." As soon as the door closed behind him, all of the boys erupted with laughter. Poor Riggers, his eye red as anything, could finally let out a scream in pain.

KILLER SESSIONS, LAMBERT'S HAIRDRYER AND WES'S REVELATION

Another time, after a draw, Lambert came in and was going ballistic because someone had cost us the game. In the middle of his hurricane he slammed a fist down on a table in the centre of the dressing room. Unfortunately, someone had piled all of the post-match food on this table. So, when the gaffer banged it, a plate of chicken wings flipped, and in what seemed like slow motion, looped up and smashed on the floor.

Lambert didn't miss a beat, though, and continued with his rant. A broken plate wasn't going to stop him. I looked at Cully, because I knew he loved those chicken wings. He'd always eat them. His face just fell, like a child who'd had a treat taken away from them. After Lambert left the room, with all of the boys reeling from the bollocking, the first person to speak was Cully: "Who fucking puts the food on the table there, everyone knows Paul goes mad after games!"

The gaffer had that fear factor, but most of the time he was one of the lads. His family hadn't moved down to Norwich with him, so he used to hang around after training a lot. He'd sit in the dressing room with the boys, and you'd end up having a good chat about the team we were playing that week. It wasn't formal, at all. Just a conversation. But you'd walk away from it with really good information in your head about what to expect from the game. Was Paul doing it because he was dropping the seed in about how we should play at the weekend, or was he just having a chat because he was a bit bored? Who knows, but all of the boys enjoyed it when he joined us.

It was a similar scenario when we travelled back from away games. The gaffer would often give it a couple of hours – and all journeys back to Norwich were usually at least four hours – and then he'd come and sit with the lads for an informal debrief (if no one moved for him to sit down he'd quickly shove someone off their seat!). That was really good, because when you stepped off the bus you felt like the game was done and behind you. It was clever management.

***

It wasn't just Paul who would hang around after training. Every player lived within 20 or 30 minutes of the training ground, so all of the lads would end up staying for longer at the end of the day. No one had to rush off because they lived in a different city.

When I was at Rochdale there were probably only four or five lads who lived in town, while everyone else drove in from different cities. That meant most players would be off straight after training. It was the same at Shrewsbury. But at Norwich, people would just chill out after a session. Some would go to the club gym, some would have a rub with the physios, some would sit in the canteen.

That really helped everyone to bond, and it also meant wives and families would get to know each other. As a team we'd go for dinner or on a night out and everyone would always come. It was rare that people ducked out of them, as we all enjoyed each other's company.

It was important to socialise as a team, and we used to head out into Norwich regularly. Don't get me wrong, Norwich isn't as lively as London or Manchester or any of the big cities, but it had a good nightlife. You were never short of options if you wanted a drink.

Wes was lively on a night out, while Matty Gill would take props with him. That often meant putting on a fake sleeve tattoo or wearing a fake 'tache or glasses. It doesn't sound funny, and to be fair it probably wasn't! But after a few drinks, you laughed at anything.

I wasn't a bad drinker, and Nels – Michael Nelson – could hold his booze. My tipple was always beer, and then Disaronno. Two drinks, nice and easy. Everyone was pretty much beer, lager, get on with it. There were no wine connoisseurs, put it that way. Chrissy Martin was the biggest drinker. He used to be able to drink straight vodka! But he could handle it. On the flipside, Adam Drury could hardly speak when he'd had a few. Russell Martin, when he arrived in December, quickly became the dad of the group because he didn't really drink.

KILLER SESSIONS, LAMBERT'S HAIRDRYER AND WES'S REVELATION

The younger lads in the squad would have their little group, too. They were more interested in chatting to girls because they didn't have any wives or girlfriends, and they'd leave us old fellas at the bar.

In those days I could grind out hangovers. I was sick a lot the morning after a night out, though. Rather than a fry up to help my hangover I'd usually find another pint in the morning worked best!

***

While all of the lads bonded quickly, there were clouds hanging over a few players at the start of Lambert's time at the club.

It was a surprise when Wes was made to train with the Under-18s after the Wycombe game. Lambert had already managed Wes at Livingston so knew what he had to offer, and I don't think there was any malice to the decision. It was as simple as Wes wanting to play in the Championship, and Lambert only wanting players committed to Norwich. It was fair enough on both sides.

It's not like Wes was banished from speaking to the boys in the first team or eating with us, it was just that he wasn't involved in training. He didn't kick up a fuss; that wasn't his style.

Everyone knew what a talent Wes was, though, and that he would be far too good for League One. It got to the point where Wes said he wanted to stay. Lambert told the club that he really wanted to keep Wes because he could be a massive threat in League One, and that was that. Wes went straight back into the team for our home game against the early leaders Charlton Athletic in mid-September. It was great to have the little fella back.

The match felt like a real marker for where we were as a team. It had been a mixed bag since we'd beaten Wycombe, with a win, a draw and a loss from the three games. We went 2-0 down to Charlton quite early on, but I thought we'd played well and fancied us to get back into it. I put Wes in with a throw-in and he scored just before half-time, and in the 92nd minute I got on the end of a Chris Martin cross to grab an equaliser.

It was thoroughly deserved because we'd battered them in the second half.

It was a decent result, but the most memorable aspect of that game was that it was the very first time Wes had played as a No.10 in his career. He'd always been a left-winger who would drift inside, because that was the only way most sides could fit him into a 4-4-2 formation, which was what most English teams were still playing.

He was an absolute natural as a No.10; an unbelievable player in that role, and yet it had taken until the age of 27 for a manager to play him there. Mad. The position was perfect for him; it gave him license to dictate the game in the final third, to play those clever passes, to pick up space between the opposition's midfield and defence. You could tell very quickly he was going to cause people utter mayhem in that position, and defenders wouldn't know how to deal with it.

We were starting to look fitter than other teams, and a flurry of crucial late goals started to create a mentality that we were never beaten. We knew we had what it takes to keep going right to the whistle, and our ability to score last-gasp goals became a key feature of the team.

After our hammering by Colchester, the season was starting to take shape. Fay and the kids had moved down to Norwich and we'd bought a house, I had settled into the city, the goals were flowing and the promotion push was just about to begin.

MY TOP 5...
HOUSEMATES

1. JAMIE CLARKE

We had a great laugh while at Rochdale. He had his daft
moments, but we bounced off each other really well.
He took his dog for a walk while sleep-walking once.
I had to chase him down the street to bring him back in.

2. PAUL MURRAY

Despite him defacing my flag at Shrewsbury, he's a great pal.

3. MICHAEL NELSON

Really chilled. I lived with Stephen Hughes at the same time
at Norwich but, erm, sorry Hughesy!

4. RICHARD EVANS

We were dead young when we lived together at Wednesday.
He was so down to earth, and really relaxed. Good Welsh lad too.

5. ADY PENNOCK

You've got to get on when you're in your mid-30s, and me
and him could talk football 24/7 while back at Barrow.

CHAPTER 22

GIANT SHIN PADS, LAST-MINUTE HOWLERS AND SWEET REVENGE

2009-10

In October, we headed to my hometown of Carlisle on the back of two big wins. It felt like we were starting to motor. The gaffer gave his team talk in the dressing room, geeing us up, and with a spring in my step I went to grab my boots from my bag.

The boots were present, but there seemed to be something quite important missing. I turned to our kitman, Matt, who had just been brought in.

"Matt, where are my shin pads?"

"What do you mean?"

"My shin pads. Where are they?"

"They're in your bag."

"Where?"

Matt came over and, after a poke around, agreed they definitely weren't in there. He looked around, a bit lost. Some of the boys started asking where their shin pads were too.

It quickly became obvious that Matt had forgotten everyone's shin pads. Every single one. Not just one; all of them. This was a problem.

The gaffer found out, and he was raging. He couldn't believe it. How do you forget to pack everyone's shin pads? Poor Matt was shitting himself, bless him, with 18 lads looking at him like he was the world's biggest idiot.

Obviously I knew the area, so I ended up giving Matt directions to a local Sports Direct.

"How am I going to pay for them though?" he asked.

Before I could answer, the gaffer interjected: "I'll tell you how you're going to get them, you're going to use your card and pay for all of the shin pads, son."

Matt returned half an hour later, with a bag full of shin pads. Drama over. Or not. There was another problem: all of the shin pads were size large. Little Wes tried them on: "Fuck me, I'm not playing fucking cricket! I can't wear them. They look like cricket pads!"

The gaffer went nuts again, and sent us all out onto the pitch. I was having a right giggle at Wes because they looked absolutely massive on him. "Where's your cricket bat, pal?"

It didn't seem to deter him too much though. Wes ended up scoring the only goal in a 1-0 win, and he celebrated by taking a shin pad off and giving the crowd a wave with it! The only surprise was that he didn't need to use both of his hands to lift it up.

Three wins on the bounce, five unbeaten. Next up: a trip to Elland Road to face the league leaders, Leeds United. We were going into the game confident. We were eight points behind them in 6th, and we knew it was a brilliant chance to claw back some ground.

***

It was a proper game. Two good sides going at it, both looking to win. The atmosphere felt like something in the Premier League, and I thought we rose to the big occasion. Until the 90th minute, anyway.

Bradley Johnson, who Norwich would buy when we got to the Premier League, scored early on for Leeds, but I equalised by bullying him at the back post (to this day he still says it was a foul. He is wrong, though. I was just too strong for him!).

The clock ticked around to 90 and, although we'd battered them second half, we were happy with taking a point from the game.

Fraser Forster had a goal kick. Maybe time to get the ball up the pitch for one last attack. Or not. Kick, shank, straight to Jermaine Beckford, goal. Head in hands. Fraser on the floor. Their crowd going berserk. What the fuck had just happened?

We'd dominated them, so to concede an injury time winner from a howler was a nightmare. We knew what was coming in the dressing room. The gaffer walked in, it all went quiet, and he started stroking his lip thoughtfully. He looked at Fraser.

"Tell me about that kick then, eh?" he said. "We were comfortable, we'd got a good point, and you go and do that. What were you thinking? I don't believe it. You've killed us!"

Lambert went quiet for a few seconds, before deciding to launch into Fraser again. Then quiet again, then angry again. It was like someone turning the radio on and off. Then he moved on to a couple of others who'd been facing the wrong way when the goal kick had been taken. On and on he went.

I think Lambert went big on us because he didn't want standards to drop. He didn't want anything sloppy coming into our play. We couldn't afford to make mistakes like that if we wanted promotion. However, even though we'd lost, the boys came out of that game feeling positive. Leeds were supposed to walk the league and we'd gone to their place and absolutely battered them. Play like that, and we'd be moving up the table in no time.

Personally, it was nice to score because of my dad. It would have been the perfect scenario for him: his son scoring at Elland Road, but Leeds still getting the win. I wish he'd been there so we could have talked about it after the game, but it was great to be able to pay homage to him with a goal. He'd have liked that.

GIANT SHIN PADS, LAST-MINUTE HOWLERS AND SWEET REVENGE

***

We bounced back with a win against Scunthorpe and then we rolled into Stockport. We had to laugh when we got there, because the pitch was a total shambles. They'd mown one side of it lengthways and it was practically barren. The rest of the pitch wasn't great because there'd been rugby played on it the night before. We were basically playing football on a ploughed field.

Going from Elland Road, which felt like a Premier League ground, to a pitch like that summed up League One for me. You always had to adapt your game, because you never knew what the next challenge would be.

Our game plan had to change to basically attacking down the left side in the first half and then the right side in the second half! I scored a couple, but I didn't know much about my first one: their goalkeeper came for the ball, caught it and literally dropped it on my head and it went in! I ran off like it was the best goal in the world.

We won 3-1, and it showed we could really battle and fight on a shit pitch. It also put us five points off the automatics. We really started picking up in December. We beat Huddersfield 3-0 just before Christmas, the coldest day I've ever played football on. Freezing. We just wanted to get the game done because we were having our Christmas do in London that night. It was 0-0 at half-time and the gaffer told us if we didn't win then the party would be cancelled! We worked our arses off in the second half, and then jumped on the train afterwards.

We were in fancy dress – I remember Josh Dawkin came as a can of spam – and it was a great night out. We had plenty to be happy about. We were in the top six and chasing the automatics, and we knew we could still get even better. After the nightmare opening game, we'd come a long way in four months, and we were beginning to get plenty of plaudits. People were talking about us as title-challengers again.

Most of the compliments seemed to be directed at me, Chrissy and Wes. It still happens to this day; fans saying we were always going to get promoted with the three of us in the team. But it wasn't about us. We had really good players behind us, and we'd have been nothing without them.

So many times Korey Smith would break play up from nowhere, or Simon Lappin would cover a huge amount of ground because Adam Drury had gone up the pitch to get a cross in, or Fraser Forster pulled off a world-class save, and it would go unnoticed. All of that allowed the three of us to go and do what we could do: create and score goals. We wouldn't have done that without everyone else dominating the midfield and at the back.

The three of us complemented each other brilliantly. I was the old-fashioned No.9. I'd stay high, work people and run the channels. Chrissy could float and score from anywhere, which made him really difficult to mark. Wes roamed and looked for the ball everywhere, pulling those strings.

I get asked if I took Chris under my wing at all because he was only 21, but you definitely didn't need to do that with him. He could certainly look after himself. If there was one boy who wasn't short of confidence it was Chrissy. People used to hate playing against him, and I think he got a bit of a bad reputation because he just hated losing. He'd do anything to win, but he was a great guy off the pitch and really fun to be around.

Wes had got more serious since I'd had that short spell with him at Blackpool. The League One season with Norwich was a big one for Wes, and being under Lambert was probably the making of him. He was in much better condition, and took training more seriously. You could see the results on the pitch, and he looked far too good for League One. It was a pleasure to play with Wes and Chrissy, but even more of a pleasure to be a part of that squad. When we got on a roll, it felt like nothing could stop us.

* * *

We kept on churning out results, and we sauntered into Colchester on January 16. Revenge mission. It was more than simply wanting to get our own back, though: they were 4th in the league and we were 2nd, so there was far more than revenge at stake.

On the morning of the game, Lambert told me to control the players and make sure they didn't react to any of the stick they were going to get from Colchester fans. The gaffer knew he was going to get a load of crap himself because of the way in which he'd left to join us. He said not to worry about him, though: he wouldn't react.

We had a job to do, and it was important to keep our cool. He asked me to lead by example and keep my emotions in check. Easier said than done, but sure thing, gaffer.

I was with Paul when we came out of the tunnel for the first time. He got about five steps onto the pitch when a group of Colchester fans in the boxes started shouting, "Lambert you're a traitor, your team's shit, you're a twat." Stay cool, don't react.

Paul turned around and screamed, "Fuck off! What the fuck do you know about football you fucking idiots!"

I couldn't believe it!

"You just told me to keep my emotions in check and to not respond!"

"Ah fuck them, do what you like today!"

Of more concern to me was the pitch. It was a joke. Squelching everywhere. The ball kept stopping in practice and there was no way the game should have been on.

Me and Cully went in to the see the referee, Mike Dean, with Colchester's captain Magnus Okuonghae and their manager Aidy Boothroyd. Cully was saying the pitch was disgraceful and that we shouldn't be playing, but Colchester wanted it on. One of Boothroyd or Okuonghae said we were scared to play on that sort of pitch, and I replied, "Are you kidding me?

We'll beat you whatever we play on, but the pitch is an absolute disgrace." It was just big talk, but they were already pissing me off.

Colchester had a record crowd in. It was only 10,000 but they were properly noisy, as were our fans who'd come in big numbers. Colchester's chairman Robbie Cowling had been talking to the press in the week leading up to the game, saying how much he wanted to beat us. That just gave us more reason to want to go there and absolutely smash them, though. He did his team no favours by blabbing to the media.

We got shit from the crowd from the moment we walked out, but most of it was reserved for Lambert. He loved it though, and made a point of giving the travelling fans a couple of waves while he was being booed.

We quickly shut their fans up in the 16th minute. Chris Martin scored a lovely left-foot strike from outside the area, and that was just the start. Colchester played well, actually, and caused us problems, but we were really clinical. I put Chrissy through on half-time and he somehow kept control of the ball in the mud and slotted home. Bang. The gaffer punched the air, which the home fans hated, and tensions were already high after a scrap between Wes and Marc Tierney which got Mike Dean pulling out four yellow cards. A proper battle, and I was loving it.

Unsurprisingly, at 2-0 down some of the Colchester lads were getting in the ref's ear about the state of the pitch. At half-time there was a huge argument between the two teams about the pitch, and then Chrissy waded in with, "I'm on a fucking hattrick, there's no way this game's getting called off you c*nts!" The gaffer was involved too, and it was all getting a bit stupid.

Doc smashed home a third a few minutes after the break and we utterly dominated after that. They were still trying to get the game called off, and the ref pulled me and Okuonghae over. He said the game was going to go the full 90, and if one more of their players told him to call it off, he'd book them. Perfect. That was us sorted.

We kept going and ended up 5-0 winners, and even had room for Wes to miss a penalty. I scored the fifth, getting on the end of a huge kick downfield from Fraser, and to celebrate I did a big dive into a huge puddle. Mud went everywhere, and I carried on skidding for ages! It was like I was a kid again.

It was a proper statement win and it showed again that we could roll our sleeves up and get dirty. We were fighters. Our fans were bouncing. They'd been singing 'Up the football league we go' all game, and it did feel like we were becoming unstoppable.

I loved that win. It was brilliant to get our revenge after their fans had been giving it to us at our place. They'd also been trying to make the game into an East Anglian derby, but that existed only on one side. The Norwich fans did not give a shit about them.

We were scoring lots of goals, we were winning from behind, we were dominating. We had Leeds in our sights, and we wanted the title.

CHAPTER 23

TOO MUCH RED WINE, PIZZA HUT AND WINNING THE TITLE

2009-10

The day we finally topped the table for the first time that season, I got sent off and ended the night blind drunk and being taken home by Paul McVeigh and Darren Huckerby.

We had Brentford at Carrow Road after our win at Colchester, and I got given a red just before half-time for foul play. I don't think it should have been a sending off, but there was nothing I could do about it. It had been goalless at the time, but Chris Martin scored to give us a 1-0 win with 10 men. A phenomenal effort.

We were top only on goal difference, and Leeds had two games in hand, but it felt really good to have somehow clawed back that 11-point gap. However, it made my sending off even more frustrating, as that meant a three-game ban for me.

Rather than going into town to celebrate the win, me and Stephen Hughes decided to grab some food at a nearby pub called the Rushcutters. We had a glass of nice red with the food and then we thought, well, we might as well get a bottle. We enjoyed that so much we fancied another bottle, and quickly we'd had two down us. We got a phone call from one of the lads saying there were a few of them out in town, so, with the booze starting to take a hold of us, we headed into Norwich.

Everyone was on the beers but me and Hughesy thought we'd be sensible and not mix. Instead, we ordered a third bottle of red wine. Funnily enough, we had got a bit rocky by now. We moved on to a new bar, but still thought it was sensible to not change to beers and got another bottle of red. That meant we'd both had two bottles each, and it was really starting to kick in. So much for a quiet night at the Rushcutters.

We headed to a club, Mercy, and everyone bought shots. Red wine and shots; famously a great mix. Someone gave me a drink called a Crucifix, which was Red Bull with three shots. Classy stuff. I knocked that back and headed to the VIP area, but my head was killing me.

You know when you've gone past the point of no return? Well, a feeling of nausea hit me suddenly. I couldn't make it to the toilet; in fact I couldn't even make it five yards. Out it all came: I threw up all over the VIP area. I couldn't even get my hands up in time to cover my mouth. It was like the girl in *The Exorcist*, and this huge tube of red liquid projectiled out of me. Red everywhere. Carnage. There were a couple of victims who got struck, the poor bastards, and I thought that, yep, it was probably time for me to go.

McVeigh and Hucks got hold of me and dragged me outside. You know you're in a bad way when those two are the sensible ones in that situation! I was totally out of it, and they got me in a taxi and hopped in with me. We pulled up outside of my driveway and Macca and Hucks tried to help me to my door.

"Let me have some dignity, let me walk to my own house," I told them. I stumbled four steps, and collapsed like a tree being felled, right on to my face.

I woke up in the morning, lights on, bucket next to me. Somehow, though, I felt as fresh as a daisy. I couldn't remember how I'd got home, so I phoned Macca. He told me the full story, and asked, "How's your mate?"

"Who?"

"Hughesy"

"I don't know, why?"

"He was even worse than you! When we left, Hughesy had been resting his head on an electricity box outside the club for 45 minutes to get some kip!"

✳ ✳ ✳

Despite feeling fine on the Sunday, I felt rough as a dog when I got in for training the next day. The gaffer had heard what had happened on the Saturday night, but was fine with it. He knew that everyone needed a blow-out occasionally. Because I was suspended following the sending off, he told me to go home for a week. Fay and the kids had moved back to Carlisle because she'd been missing home, and going back up there to be with them would be exactly what I needed.

It was a relief to have that week off. I hadn't realised how tired I was. Playing week in, week out, with the tension of a promotion push rising, while playing all season on a dodgy ankle, had exhausted me. The red card probably showed that my mind wasn't quite in the right place, and that my decision-making wasn't great. I think the gaffer probably realised that, and it was really good of him to give me that week away.

It came at the perfect time. I recharged the batteries and returned ready and refreshed for Brighton in mid-February. Elliott Bennett, who would join us in the Premier League, scored early for them but I grabbed an equaliser late on and Doc popped up with the winner. Another come-from-behind late winner, and it was great to be back on the pitch and ready to push on in the final 15 matches of the season.

✳ ✳ ✳

One hundred and fifty-nine days after we'd lost at Leeds United to go 11 points behind them, they came to our place. We were top and eight points ahead of them in 2nd, with the chance to go 11 points clear. Funny old game.

All the talk ahead of the match, on March 27, was how both teams' fortunes had changed. They'd been on a poor run, and we were heading into the match full of confidence on the back of six wins in our last eight games.

TOO MUCH RED WINE, PIZZA HUT AND WINNING THE TITLE

For a whole week we'd had people coming up to tell us to get revenge for the loss at Elland Road. We were more than happy to oblige.

We knew a win would keep us 11 points ahead of third, with eight games remaining. There was no mindset of playing it safe for a draw; Lambert told us we had to go and show everyone we were the best team in the division.

It was a red-hot day and the atmosphere was amazing. Once again we had over 25,000 in the ground, which was incredible support for League One. However, we struggled to break them down. They were really solid, and we couldn't seem to find a way through but the crowd stuck right behind us.

With a minute to go we were settling for a point, but you just knew you could never say never with our team. Hughesy bent in a cross, and there was Chrissy Martin at the near post, brilliantly getting in front of his marker, to glance in a great header. The whole place erupted. Everyone was going nuts. Ballistic.

It was relief more than anything because we felt it had cemented automatic promotion and we were buzzing after the game. That was the first time I'd really experienced a proper promotion run in, because I'd been on loan at Blackpool when Forest went up. I was loving it; it was special to play in a team that was the best side in the league and showing it every week.

✳ ✳ ✳

We bumped back down to earth in the next game in quite some style. 2-0 down after 12 minutes to relegation-threatened Tranmere. Two penalties conceded; Fraser Forster sent off. Brilliant. Not long after, they went 3-0 up from a clear handball.

It got even better: Lambert got sent to the stands, and Karsa followed him soon after. I pulled one back, but the game washed out after that. Everyone was a bit stunned in the dressing room. Most of us blamed the referee, because sometimes you convince yourself it's the ref's fault in order to cover up the fact the team hadn't actually played that well.

We had Stockport at home three days later, and they were rock bottom. Miles from safety. This was the first time a few nerves crept in. Promotion was so close, and we were desperate to get it done. You do worry about blowing a big lead; when it's yours to lose the pressure changes, and that day we were nowhere near our best. We had to hold on to a 2-1 lead for 65 minutes, and it got really nervy in the second half. The full-time whistle felt as good as any goal we scored that season.

I'd scored what turned out to be the winner in that game, and it was my 30th goal of the season. I was the first Norwich player to get 30 goals in a season since Ron Davies in 1963-64, and only the fifth to ever do it at the club. It was a huge honour. I felt great and was in the form of my life, but it took a massive backseat to my desperation to be promoted.

I picked up a yellow in the next game, a draw in a really fiery match against MK Dons. It meant I'd be suspended for the next two matches, and I was absolutely gutted. The booking was a disgrace. There was nothing in it, just a little shove. MK Dons ended up with nine yellow cards, which told its own story, and we were indebted to Chris Martin, who scored a great free kick in injury time to get us the equaliser.

Because we were so close to getting promotion, it was a nightmare to not be involved. We lost our next game at Leyton Orient, and we were awful. I was in the stands, and it was horrible to watch. It killed me not being able to influence the game. So with our next trip, to Charlton, the gaffer told me to head home to Carlisle and rest up while I was still suspended.

***

A win over Charlton coupled with Swindon failing to beat Walsall would mean we were promoted. The fans were desperate for us to do it at The Valley, because that was the scene of Norwich's relegation the previous season. But Charlton were a good side and in the playoffs; everything pointed to a really tough game.

My viewing platform of choice was *Soccer Saturday* on Sky Sports. I was sat at home, with my kids running around, watching Jeff Stelling and crapping myself each time they headed to The Valley for a report.

It seemed every time they went there, it was to say that Fraser had pulled off an amazing save. It sounded like Norwich were getting battered. Maybe I should have just gone to the game, because watching on TV for updates was even worse. After the half-hour mark they went back to The Valley and I thought, 'Oh god, here we go again.' I clenched everything in fear, but the score flashed up as 1-0 to Norwich. "Michael Nelson has put City in front! He's buried a Simon Lappin corner!"

I shouted in celebration and jumped up in my living room. "Get in!". I called out to Fay, "Nels has scored!" Even Fay was excited! My mum called me to tell me Norwich had scored, bless her. "I know, Mum!"

The second half was torture, with Fraser pulling off more saves. It got to about 70 minutes and I just couldn't handle it anymore. How did I cope with the nerves? I went out to get pizzas for tea.

I got in the car, Radio 5 Live on. Goals going in everywhere, but not at The Valley. I got to Pizza Hut, and headed in. Now I couldn't even listen to what was going on. Instead I looked at the scores on my phone; kept refreshing them. Nothing happened as I waited for the pizzas. I picked them up, got back into the car and put the radio back on. Swindon had drawn. If we held on, we'd be promoted.

"And over to The Valley... Norwich have done it! They've secured promotion back to the Championship!"

"Fucking get in!" I sat there screaming in celebration, the car bouncing as I jumped around in my seat like a lunatic. It must have been a right sight for people walking past! My phone kept going off, and my mum called to say Norwich had won. "I know, Mum!"

I got home, and texted Nels. "Well done on the goal you big bastard!". He called me straight away and put his phone on loudspeaker, with all of the boys screaming down the phone celebrating.

"We didn't need you did we!" Nels joked.

"I'm just having a beer and a pizza so go fuck yourselves and I'll see you Monday!"

I was sat at home, I'd just turned 29, and it was sinking in that I was now a Championship footballer. I'd been captain, and my goals had been pivotal. My wife and kids were around me, and, honestly, I couldn't have been happier.

I was a bit gutted I wasn't there for the celebrations that night. But my mind was now focused on winning the league. I was really buzzing for the chance to play in our next game against Gillingham, because beating them would seal the title.

* * *

On the Thursday before the game, Lambert told me that if we won the league on Saturday against Gillingham, it would be my last game of the season. I was a bit gutted, because I'd wanted to try and break the all-time goals record for Norwich in a season, but understandably the club wanted my ankle operation done a week earlier. It made sense, and it also meant it sounded like they definitely wanted me in the Championship next season. Brilliant news.

The atmosphere was sensational. A real party vibe at Carrow Road, and we played with all of the confidence of a side that had just won promotion. As usual, though, it still took us until quite late to score, and we won 2-0.

Paul took me off with five minutes remaining, and I soaked in the standing ovation. It felt great to walk off, title sealed, fans standing to applaud. What a difference it was to coming off the pitch after our 7-1 spanking by Colchester on the opening day of the season.

You won't be surprised to hear we all went out that night. The players, the coaching team, the club staff, everyone from behind the scenes who had been a part of it all season. So many people had worked their arses off, so we felt it was important we were all out together. The fans were all celebrating too, so it was just a really lovely party atmosphere across the city. It felt like the whole of Norwich was a carnival of celebration. I certainly wasn't on the red wine that night though; just kept it to beer!

I had my ankle operation that week, and the lads beat Bristol Rovers 3-0. We then rolled into our last game of the season, which just happened to be Carlisle at home. Talk about fate. To be at Carrow Road to lift the trophy against my hometown club was brilliant. I couldn't have planned it any better.

Before the game I'd picked up the Player of the Year award, and when my name was called out as the winner the place absolutely erupted. Even the Carlisle fans were clapping, which was really nice.

Me and Nels were sitting in the South Stand for the game, because we'd both had operations. To get there we had to walk around the pitch and we got a standing ovation all of the way round. The fans were singing 'We fucking love Grant Holt', which is something I'll never forget. We got to the Carlisle fans and I didn't know what to expect, but we got a standing ovation off them too, which was lovely. It made me quite emotional, actually, because they could quite easily have booed me. I had friends in the away end, people I'd grown up with, so it made the day even more special.

As for the game, it was a dead duck for us. We'd been pissed all week so it was no surprise we lost. No one seemed to care, and the fans were there to see us lift the trophy at the end of the game. To hold that above my head, out on the Carrow Road pitch, with champagne flying everywhere, was a phenomenal feeling. A real 'wow' moment in my career. At the age of 29, it was the first trophy I'd lifted and it was very much worth the wait.

There was a lot of press to do, and I did an interview with BBC Cumbria's James Phillips. I would go on to work with him, and he's told me since that he couldn't believe I'd made the time to go and speak to BBC Cumbria that day. But my upbringing has always been important to me, and Cumbria is a big part of who I am. He asked me about my journey from non-league, and not having had the chance to play for Carlisle, and it really sunk in then that I'd come full circle. Lifting a trophy, medal around my neck, talking about Carlisle. A special feeling.

Back in the dressing room, beer and bubbly was everywhere, and we were chucking everyone into the communal bath. We even threw the gaffer in. He clambered out, grabbed everyone's trackie bottoms and chucked them into the bath. What he hadn't realised was that loads of them had mobile phones in! No one really cared at that stage though; everyone was too busy having a brilliant time.

It was the most satisfied I'd been in a dressing room up to that point. I was sat there, with the League One trophy next to me, completely content; thinking about having my chance in the Championship, of how far I'd come since I'd given up on professional football eight years earlier. These are special moments in your career, and I was old enough by then to really try and savour it.

What a contrast it had been from sitting silently in the dressing room at Wembley with Shrewsbury Town at the end of the previous season. From May to May, total despair to sheer joy. The title had been no fluke, either. We'd won it by nine points, which was a phenomenal effort in a season when League One had a lot of quality sides fighting for promotion.

It had been a privilege to share that dressing room with all of the lads; there was no one in there who didn't deserve it. Everyone in that squad had played their part in winning the title, no matter how much game time they had. A true team effort.

CHAPTER 24

COURT CASE, TRAIN DRAMA AND AN UNFORTUNATE RED CARD

2010-11

It had been over seven years since my first Championship match, when I'd come on as a 71st-minute substitute for Sheffield Wednesday against Watford. So who did the fixture list computer throw up for our first game of the 2010-11 Championship season? Watford, of course.

Since my seven matches in the second tier for Wednesday, I'd played 314 games and scored 127 goals. I'd got married, had two beautiful daughters, and played for five different clubs. There might have been one or two yellow cards along the way, too. Those 20 minutes for Blackpool aside, my return to the Championship had been a long time coming.

I'd felt comfortable in that league as a 21-year-old, and since then I'd developed into a much better player. There was no reason at all why I couldn't score goals in the division.

While I was buzzing for the chance to show what I could do on a bigger stage, absolutely none of us at Norwich were thinking that promotion was a possibility. Of course you enter every season with the goal of winning the title, but realistically you also know it's massively unlikely. We'd just come up from League One, and it was very rare to see back-to-back promotions. There were no thoughts of the Premier League.

However, we knew we could compete. We had a good group of players and we'd also made some really good signings. Simeon Jackson, who'd scored that Wembley winner against Shrewsbury for Gillingham, was a fantastic purchase. If I could have picked a striker from League One to play alongside it would have been Simeon, so I was delighted he was coming in. He was a livewire and worked his arse off, and everyone said he was a really good lad.

The gaffer brought in a lot of midfielders. David Fox, Andrew Surman and Andrew Crofts joined us, and they offered real quality. I knew Foxy would be perfect for what we wanted to do in terms of keeping the ball moving, and his set-pieces were top-class. Surs could link play really well, and Crofty had brilliant drive and never stopped running.

Fraser Forster went back to Newcastle, and that was a real blow because he'd been massive for us. He'd been far too good for League One, and he would have dominated the Championship. Our number two Declan Rudd was a really fantastic 'keeper but at the age of 19 he was still a little bit too young to establish himself, so when the club brought in John Ruddy from Everton it gave everyone a massive lift. We also had Elliott Ward and Leon Barnett arrive, which gave us proper depth at centre-back.

I thought the club did a brilliant job in recruitment that summer. We already had a great group of players, but they found that balance between adding quality without completely changing the team. We couldn't wait to get started.

* * *

I'd had a great summer back in Carlisle with Fay and the kids, and everyone still seemed on a high when the lads returned for pre-season training. I'd moved in with Nels and Hughesy, my ankle was fine after the operation and there was a real buzz in training. It was a lot of hard work, but we'd be really fit going into the season so everyone embraced it. Well, I say embraced it. There's only so much embracing you can do of running around like a lunatic and almost killing yourself every day.

We knew it would get even tougher during a training camp in Germany, so we decided to have a barbecue for the lads at our place the day before heading out there. It would be a good way for the new boys to get to know everyone.

On the day of the barbecue we had a pre-season friendly against local side Dereham Town in the afternoon. During the warm-up I pinged a ball and hurt my thigh. Hmm. That didn't feel good. But I put it down to fatigue from all of the work in pre-season and started the game. Bad idea, of course. I came in at half-time and the thigh was killing me.

The physio was concerned. "When did you feel it go?"

"Just before the game."

"Before the game! Why did you play on, you idiot?"

"I thought it was just fatigue!"

"Fatigue? I think you've pulled your thigh!"

That didn't go down well with the gaffer, and I was pissed off with myself after feeling good in pre-season. What an idiot. But I wouldn't have a scan until we were in Germany, so I put it to the back of my mind. There was no point shitting myself about something that could be fine.

The lads all piled around our house after the game. The plan was to have a couple of beers, enjoy the barbecue and then everyone would leave at 10. After all, we had to be at Norwich airport in the morning. A few brought their cars, so weren't drinking. Total professionals.

The first sign of the night not quite following our intended plan was when the boys who'd brought their cars had a beer. After all, everyone else was drinking, so it was only fair. But a couple of hours into the night, all of the drivers decided they'd get a taxi instead, and the drinking properly started. There was no stopping us now.

Inevitably, most of us ended up going into town. Because so many of the lads had come in shorts they had to borrow jeans from me, Nels and Hughes to go into the city. It was lucky Hughesy was a small fella, or Wes could have been in trouble!

At no point did anyone turn around and say this was a bad idea. It's funny how an early start never seems so bad after you've had a few beers. All of the new boys were getting on really well, so it felt like a smart plan to keep on drinking. You wouldn't want to end a bit of team bonding, would you? All of these beers would be for the good of the squad in the long run!

I ended up getting home at about 2am, seven hours before we were supposed to be at the airport. I wasn't too wasted, though. My thigh had been hurting so I'd been quite sensible about my drinking. Others were much worse than me, and Hughesy and Nels hadn't even come back yet.

The house was an absolute state, with beer bottles and cans everywhere. Total tip. If it got left like that, it would absolutely stink when we got back from Germany, so at 3 in the morning I decided to start cleaning everything up.

Half an hour later Nels and Hughesy stumbled in wondering what the hell I was doing. Did they help? Did they fuck. Instead they went straight to bed, which was probably fair enough because they were utterly steaming. I ended up cleaning the whole house. It was a bit of OCD, and I also think I had a bit of wired anxiety about my thigh which kept me going.

With every single bottle and can bagged, I got to bed and had a couple of hours' kip. In the morning, I had to drag Nels and Hughesy out of bed. It was like looking after kids. They didn't have time to shower, because we knew the gaffer would have gone mad if we'd reported to the airport late. Clothes on, pile into my car, pull into the airport. Every minute another car would turn up, and a player would step out looking as rough as anything. Surs looked an absolute mess; he'd obviously enjoyed getting to know everyone!

The gaffer arrived and was assessing everyone, looking at us all like a dad watching his hungover teenage kid coming down for breakfast. I could see him thinking, 'Were you fuckers drinking last night?'

He came over to me. "Were you out last night?"

"What do you mean?"

"Were you drinking?"

I'd already planned my script, so I knew what I was going to say: "Course not, gaffer. I wouldn't be drinking with my thigh would I! All of the lads came round to mine for a barbecue, so people had a beer or two but that was it. I had one can, and then I was on the water."

He didn't seem to believe me, though. Funny that. "Look at the fucking state of some of them!"

"It was just a bit of team bonding, gaffer. Getting to know the new boys. That's how our group does it. You know what it's like!"

"Yeh, you'll know exactly what it's like when we get to Germany."

And with that I just thought, 'Oh shit, that's them done for in training.'

I went over to Nels. "The gaffer's just said to me, 'You'll know what it's like when we get to Germany'."

Nels looked at me like I'd just told him our hotel was haunted. His face was a picture of pure fear. I thought it was hilarious, because I wouldn't be training due to my thigh. I'd never been so happy to be injured!

So many of the boys were struggling on the flight and desperate for the toilet. There seemed to be a constant queue for the whole two hours! We got a bus to the hotel and it was the quietest journey ever. Everyone was falling asleep.

At the hotel, all of the boys were craving to get into their rooms and crawl into bed. The gaffer knew this, of course, so told us to check in, come straight down for dinner, and then we'd be training at 4. Everyone slumped; they knew it was going to be an absolute killer of a session. Bedtime seemed a long way off now.

I would put a lot of money on that session only being added in after

Lambert had seen the state of everyone at the airport. I was crying with laughter because I knew they were all going to get beasted in training, and, yep, the gaffer and Cully absolutely ran the life out of them. Everyone was dying afterwards, but still had to come down for tea.

I was rooming with Nels and he kept saying, "I just want to get into that bed, all I want is to get into that bed." Everyone scoffed their food down, and got away as quickly as possible; right up to their rooms and straight to sleep. I didn't see another one of them until the morning. Not one person flinched for the whole night. Normally we'd be in each other's rooms, playing cards or just chatting, but there wasn't a peep. No one stirred until morning.

We had a good week out there, and the new lads settled in really quickly. On the last night the gaffer put on a barbecue at the hotel, and it's fair to say all of the boys were a lot more sensible with their drinking!

The week didn't go so great for me, though. My scan showed a grade 2 thigh strain. That was a beast because I'd really wanted a good pre-season. There were a lot of people wondering whether I could carry on my goalscoring form into the Championship, so I'd wanted to get a good summer under my belt. I'd worked so hard, and had looked after my diet, so it was a really frustrating time.

It was probably more frustrating for our physio Neal Reynolds, though. I am the world's worst for being injured. I hate it. Poor Neal had to put up with me moaning and pissing about, and because no one else was injured, it was basically just me and him in a room together. He had the patience of a saint, but I was so annoying that it probably gave him even more of an incentive to get me fit.

* * *

Neal worked miracles, and got me back in time for the bench in our opening game of the season, against Watford at Carrow Road. However, the thigh injury had become the least of my worries.

The match had been moved to a Friday night for TV, which was great. Everyone loves playing on TV under the lights. But it also caused a problem: I was due in court that day. I'd got 12 points on my driving licence, and I was arguing one of the points. However, the court house was up in Shropshire. That made playing in Norwich, 200 miles away, a little tricky.

Apparently there were cameras outside the court waiting for me to turn up. They'd have been hanging around for a long time, though, because I didn't show. Nothing was going to stop me playing against Watford. In my absence I got banned from driving for six months. That meant it became planes, trains and automobiles for half a year, but luckily for me Nels would often drive up to Carlisle, so I'd get a lift with him a lot of the time.

That day, though, I was focused on Watford. The fact it was on TV immediately made it feel like you'd stepped up a level. There was a different atmosphere around the place, like you were in the big time a bit. It wasn't the Premier League, but it still felt like a world above League One.

We lost 3-2, but put in a decent performance. We'd competed well, and we knew we'd be OK if we played like that. It was good to get off the bench and have a run around, and it was great to see all of the debutants gelling. Surs, Crofty and Foxy played well and we created plenty of chances, which made me itch to be out there to get on the end of them.

I started the next game in the Carling Cup and scored a couple against my old friends Gillingham. We won 4-1, and it felt good to get some more minutes into my legs and to get up and running in the goals column. Most importantly, I also felt really fit, which was a relief after the injury. All of that sweating in pre-season had paid off.

Next up were Scunthorpe, in the league. We passed them to death but just couldn't seem to find the net. But in the 90th minute Simon Lappin put a great ball into the area, and I got ahead of my man and threw myself into a diving header, and guided it into the bottom corner. Bang! Three points, a last-minute winner and I'd got my first Championship goal since April 2003.

After a few games, it felt perfectly natural to be playing in the Championship. The quality was obviously higher than League One, and you were competing against better, fitter players. But we never felt overawed or out of our depth. It didn't take long to realise we belonged at that level, and we could do more than just compete. Teams expected us to be a pushover, but quickly found out we could do the dirty stuff really well, and that we had a lot of quality throughout our side.

We found ourselves in the top six throughout September. We hadn't expected to start so well, but it was funny because we weren't really setting the world on fire with our performances. Despite surpassing expectations, it felt like we could play much better. A lot of promoted teams might have been more than happy with a better-than-expected start, but we wanted to improve even further. There was no resting on our laurels.

A 4-3 win over Leicester City at our place at the end of September was a massive confidence boost. Our fourth was a 30-yard worldie from Wes; he couldn't usually kick it that far so he must have had his spinach that morning! Leicester were a really good side, and we'd dominated them for long periods. We'd gone back to the mentality from the previous season of, 'You score two goals, we'll score three'.

As we started to click, we went from being tough to beat to being a bit more attacking, and the Leicester result made a lot of teams in that division stand up and take notice of us. They probably started to realise that our start had been no fluke.

***

You don't realise how useful driving is until you have to get a train – or several trains – from Norwich to Carlisle. After a 1-0 win over Middlesbrough in October, Nels wasn't driving back up so I couldn't nick another lift off him. Instead, I had the pleasure of the great British rail network to look forward to.

I had to get the 6 o'clock train or I wouldn't have been able to make it back, which meant I didn't have time to change into normal clothes after leaving Carrow Road. So it was a case of Norwich City trackie on, hoodie up, and coat zipped up to cover all of the branding. I just wanted a nice quiet journey without being noticed. However, the station was mobbed and full of Boro fans. Great. I got on the train and it was heaving, with no seats anywhere. All of the reservations had disappeared.

I grabbed a seat by the toilet. Real classy. My hood was still up, but this Boro fan went to the loo and looked at me like he'd recognised me. I really couldn't be arsed to engage with anyone, and he came back out of the toilet and looked at me again. He went to sit down with a bunch of mates who were all Middlesbrough fans, and then one of his pals also went to the toilet and looked at me.

Then a third mate came over and said, "Are you Grant Holt?" "Yeh I am, yeh". "No way! What did you think of the game, you lot were good weren't you!"

This could go one of two ways: I'm rude and they kick off, or I'm polite and I spend the next hour until Peterborough station talking to them. So I went for the friendly option; said we'd played well, but that Boro had been good and it was a really close game. That was the prompt for his mates to all come over to stand near me, and we were suddenly into a full tactical deconstruction of the game. It was a proper debrief all the way to Peterborough. They were good lads, though, and even offered me a can!

We got to Peterborough, and I was stood at the platform waiting for my connection when a train pulled in and a whole horde of Derby County fans got off. Oh god, here we go, I thought. As a former Forest player the last thing I wanted was to be spotted by their rival fans. A lot of them clocked me but didn't say anything, so I dodged a bullet there. Maybe I hadn't made as much of an impression at Forest as I'd thought!

Trouble over. Or so I'd thought.

Next minute, another train came in. Would you believe it, it was full of Ipswich fans. Not only was I in Norwich gear, but their team had also just been beaten by Forest. Double trouble. Honestly, I'd never shit myself more in my life. I put my hood up even more, and edged closer to a group of police officers. It felt like there were thousands of Ipswich fans, but there were probably only about 10! A lot of them looked at me like they recognised me, but I don't think they could quite believe a Norwich City player would be standing on the same platform as them. Luckily they didn't have much time to do a double-take, as they were rushing to make their connection.

After what seemed like forever, my train came in. I had a first class ticket but, and I really should have seen this coming, so did a bunch of Boro fans. They clocked me straight away, and the whole way up to Newcastle they were talking to me about football. I couldn't even put my headphones in because I didn't want to be rude.

It was a long old train journey, and they were getting drunker and drunker and louder and louder. But they were all jovial, and it probably helped when they found out I was from Carlisle. I was from the north, so I was one of them!

It was fine, really. I love a good chat about football. It was only because I was tired that I'd wanted a bit of peace and quiet, but the Boro fans were all good guys. It might have been a different story if it had been a train full of Ipswich fans, mind you.

***

It was one of the last train journeys I would have to make to see Fay in Carlisle, because she was going to move back to Norwich again very shortly.

The reason? She was pregnant. Number three was on the way!

I found out while I was on the golf course. I'd been playing a round with Wes and Adam Drury. I was on fire on the course, had just hit a great drive right down the middle of the fairway and was about to take my second shot when Fay called.

I answered but told her to wait so I could take my next shot. Phone on the floor, ball right onto the green. Nice. I started chatting away, and she was saying something about moving back down to Norwich. I told her to do whatever she thought was best and I'd support her. It didn't have to be straight away.

Fay was like, "What are you on about? Of course I'm going to have to move back down." I just repeated, "It's up to you, I don't mind if you do or you don't. Whatever's best for you." That's when she said, "Have you seen my text message?"

"No?"

"Well check it!"

So I looked at my texts, and flicked through to find the last one from Fay, which I hadn't seen. It was two words: 'I'm pregnant!'

I couldn't believe it! Wow! Amazing news. But my god she must have thought I was being rude and uncaring, telling her to hold on while I casually took a shot, and then saying I didn't mind whether she moved back to Norwich or not!

We'd been talking about having another baby, but we thought while she was up in Carlisle and I was down in Norwich it was best not to. But a weekend in London had changed our minds, thanks to an encounter with a gypsy. Yep, true story. We'd been in Covent Garden and gone to see one of those gypsy fortune tellers. She'd read our palms, and said to Fay, "Ooh, you've been talking about having another child haven't you. Well, you're going to have another one!"

Obviously it's nonsense (or is it? Make your own mind up!). But it made us think harder about having a third, and we'd decided to go for it. And to think that fortune tellers get such a bad reputation...

* * *

Norwich had a little stutter after that win over Boro, but we looked to be back on course when we were 3-1 up at Reading in the first half. We'd played some great stuff, and I'd got myself a goal too.

Just before half-time, I remember the ball coming inside. I stepped over Ian Harte to get my arse between him and the ball. I knew I'd be in if I could get a touch and turn him. As I stepped across, I rolled him and he went down like he'd been stamped on. I hadn't got anywhere near him, but he was having a right good roll around on the floor, and as I turned around the Reading players were all running over. Then the ref, Michael Oliver, came over and got the red card out.

I couldn't believe it. "What the hell, Michael?"

"Holty, you've just stamped on him!"

"I've not touched him! I stepped right over him!"

But he wasn't having it. I told him he'd be embarrassed when he watched it back. Ridiculous decision.

Lambert nailed Oliver in the tunnel at half-time, and I waited for him as well and had a second go at him. I was fuming. We laugh about it now, though. Whenever we see each other he always says, "Remember that red card at Reading!" Funnily enough, yes I do! He's a really good guy, though, and a brilliant ref.

Back then you knew he'd be a top referee because he communicated really well in the right manner. I hated it when referees ignored me when I was trying to have a bit of dialogue about a decision, but the respected ones, like Michael, always explained their thinking. A good referee gives their decision, talks you through it, and gets on with it. Even if you don't agree with their call, at least you know why they've made it.

Some refs in the Premier League have an ego and love to be among the top players; a bit showbiz. They like to be seen laughing and joking with the big names, but couldn't care less if you're not well known. I don't want to name any of those characters in particular *cough* Mike Dean *cough*, but the best ones treat everyone exactly the same. Michael was the best of the lot when I played.

I was raging at him that day, though, because Reading ended up drawing the game 3-3. Playing with 10 men had made a big difference, and the decision had robbed us of a couple of points.

Luckily, the red card was rescinded after the game, which was brilliant news. If it hadn't been, I would have missed my first-ever East Anglian derby.

MY TOP 5...
REASONS THE NORTH IS BETTER THAN THE SOUTH

1. HUMOUR

It's important to say here that the north starts at Stoke for me. Anything above there is north, so anywhere from Stoke and above has a better sense of humour than elsewhere.

2. THICK-SKINNED CHARACTER

People seem to take less offence and laugh at ourselves more easily. Apart from if it's someone from the south taking the piss, obviously.

3. THE PEOPLE ARE MORE CHILLED OUT

Life isn't 100mph.
We'll get where we want to in our own time, thanks.

4. CHIPPIES

The fish and chip shops are much better. In fact, any meal that you think of as being wintery is better in the north. Pies are better. Pastries are better. Hotpots are better, and I don't even like hotpots.

5. SCENERY

You're always 15 minutes away from unbelievable scenery. Mountains, hills, lakes, forests. Beautiful. Shame it's always raining though.

CHAPTER 25

ONE GOAL, TWO GOALS AND A THIRD GOAL AGAINST IPSWICH

2010-11

If there's one thing people ask me most about my career, other than 'how did a lump like you play in the Premier League?', it's my hattrick for Norwich against Ipswich in the East Anglian derby.

When I was starting out at Workington, I never thought one day I'd be cemented into the history of one of England's top clubs. Certainly not for the right reasons, anyway!

Barely a day goes by without someone mentioning the hattrick to me. I could be shopping, or in a cafe, or out for a pint of milk, and someone will wander over and tell me they were there that day at Carrow Road, or that it was their favourite moment as a Norwich fan. I've become so used to being asked about it, but you never forget what an honour it is to be remembered like that, and to have given thousands of fans such a great memory.

I hadn't played in a proper, big derby before. I didn't play against Sheffield United or Derby County while I was at Wednesday and Forest, so I was really looking forward to this one. I knew it was a big deal because it was a game I used to watch as a kid, and this one was on the BBC.

The build-up started about two weeks out. It was constant. In the press, on social media; people on the streets telling me we had to beat them. You had old Norwich boys like Darren Huckerby and Iwan Roberts talking about the game in the media, and how they hadn't realised what a massive deal it was until they'd played in their first East Anglian derby. That kind of stuff, from former players, made you realise you're going to be in for a dramatic day. It also made you realise you could write your name into history, too.

The game was at the end of November, and the return match at Portman Road wasn't until late April, so bragging rights would last for a long time if we won it. That made us even more determined; an extra bit of motivation. Another motivating factor was our respective positions in the table. Everyone thought Ipswich would be the bigger side that season because they'd had a bit of money behind them. Their fans fully expected promotion, and thought we might be relegated.

So it was pretty pleasing that, following a decent start, Ipswich had started to falter by the time we came to play them. It was still tight in the table, and we were only three points above them. But a win would put us back into the playoffs, and leave them only four points above the bottom three. Even more motivation.

Although we hadn't won in the five games since the Boro match, it didn't feel like a blip. We were still right amongst it and doing better than people had expected, and we were playing with confidence. What better way to get back on track than in your big local derby?

***

Lambert was playing the match down in the press, but privately he was telling us we were the better team; if we worked harder and ran further than them then our quality would show. It helped having a gaffer who had played in one of the biggest derbies in the world, for Celtic against Rangers. He knew what he was talking about, and that always goes a long way for a manager.

We had a boost earlier in the week when we'd signed Henri Lansbury on loan from Arsenal. He was an attacking midfielder and I knew he was a really good player, and people were raving about him and saying he'd go on to play for England. He added even more quality into our midfield, so much so that people often forget that Wes was on the bench for that game. That was huge strength in depth for a side that had been playing in League One six months earlier.

Lambert was actually banned from the dugout for the game, but a little thing like that wasn't going to throw us off. The last thing the gaffer said to us before we went out of the dressing room was to make sure we didn't do anything stupid early on. "Not a problem gaffer," I said. I was the captain, and knew I had to set the standard.

We walked out, and the roar was ridiculous. I'd never heard anything like it. I shook hands, did my usual jump in the middle of the pitch, and the noise just kept going. It was a freezing day, snow had been cleared off the pitch, but the atmosphere was absolutely red hot.

With Lambert's line about not doing anything stupid ringing in my ears, four minutes into the first half Jack Colback had the ball in the corner for them. I thought, 'I've got him here', and I banged into him; absolutely buried him. As I caught him, my elbow accidentally hit him on his way down. A huge roar from the crowd, and both sets of players came steaming in.

I thought, 'Fuck, this is a red card. I'm off'. I'd messed up. The gaffer was going to kill me. Luckily, I was saved by Grant Leadbitter, who decided to grab me by the neck. I reckon the ref thought if he sent me off he'd then have to send Leadbitter off too for manhandling me. I'm guessing the ref didn't want to show two red cards less than five minutes into the game. We both got yellows, and I couldn't believe I'd got away with it.

I looked up at the gaffer in the Directors' Box, thinking he was going to nail me. Instead, he just gave me a wink! From that tackle, and that melee, we were right on it and the crowd were fully behind us.

***

We'd started well and after 13 minutes the ball went down our left side. I thought there was a chance it might be cleared, so I moved across to that side in anticipation. Simon Lappin hooked it forward, and my instinct told me the bounce of the ball could be really awkward for their defender Darren O'Dea, so I got to work on putting him under pressure.

With the ball bouncing, I had a split-second decision to make: if I misjudged the flight of the ball and accidentally caught him while trying to nick the ball, I could be sent off. I was already on a yellow and lucky to be on the pitch, and I didn't want to give the ref another excuse to get the red card out. But the ball bounced kindly and I just had to have a go at it. I nicked it off him, and I was through on goal.

O'Dea was left for dead behind me, which gave me the time to open up my body and curl the ball into the corner. Huge roar, total relief, mayhem.

I could have been sent off 10 minutes earlier, and now I'd put us 1-0 up and written myself into derby history. I knew I'd always be in that film reel of Norwich scorers in the derby. What a feeling; this is what we played football for.

They equalised on 29 minutes but we were back ahead six minutes later with a goal from the training ground. We'd done a session on how square Ipswich's backline got, so we'd worked on moving the ball from side to side to shift the backline, and then Lansbury or Wes would slide the ball through the middle to me. We then practiced it in a small-sided game, but when Lansbury slipped it through to me I actually missed. Put it wide.

In the game, the ball was worked across the pitch just outside the area and Ipswich's right back stepped out. That was my cue to get from left to right, and Henri spotted my square run and put in a great pass through the middle. Cut their backline in half. As the ball came in I had a quick look at where their 'keeper was, and he was coming out of goal. That gave me a decision to make: try to round him or hit it early. I sensed I was being closed down, and I thought rounding the 'keeper would give the defender the chance to tackle me, so I took a touch and hit it low at the goalkeeper's feet. It went through his legs, and oh my god I'd scored twice in the derby!

I ran off, looking for a pitchside microphone. Why? Well, I'd said to Nels in the warm-up that if I scored I'd use the big mic as a pretend moustache to celebrate. We'd all been doing Movember for a friend of Nels' who'd been diagnosed with cancer, so we were all sporting moustaches of varying sizes. Mine was droopy and bushy, a proper gunslinger's 'tache – or so I thought, anyway. As soon as the ball had hit the back of the net, I ran over to where this huge mic was, picked it up and put it on my top lip.

I quickly realised that the microphone wire had actually got wrapped around my legs, which meant I nearly went over full tilt when the boys jumped on me. With the noise deafening, and the crowd cheering right in front of me, I was having visions of face-planting over the advertising boards. It wouldn't have been a great look live on BBC television, so I had to carefully turn full circle until I'd untangled the wires.

A couple of minutes later the odds swung decisively in our favour. I got slid through just inside their half and I turned Damien Delaney, but as I got away he grabbed my arm and held on. I had another split-second decision to make: I was quite far out still, so a goal wasn't a certainty. But Delaney was the last man, so going down would mean a straight red. Quick calculation, and down I went.

I was in the ref's ear straight away: "I was clean through and I'm on a hattrick here, you've got to send him off!" The red card came out, the crowd went ballistic, and that was effectively the game done. Now we could go and blitz them.

***

There was a melee in the tunnel at half-time, with the Ipswich boys saying I should have been sent off. I didn't care, though. I just laughed at them. In the dressing room, the gaffer told us to not do anything stupid because they'd be trying to even things up and get us down to 10 men. If someone kicked us, let them kick us, if there was a 40-60 ball we weren't sure we could get, leave it and sit off. His parting words were, "Now go and dominate them and bury them. Show everyone who's the best team in East Anglia."

We passed them to death at the start of the second half. But for all of our nice play, a bit of edginess crept in while we were only one goal to the good. Wes came on after the hour mark and immediately started picking holes in their defence. Suddenly we were rampant again. Wes took down a cross from the right and rolled in Chrissy Martin. I was free in the area, but I knew Chris was trying to shift it to get a shot off instead of passing to me. His angle was blocked, so now he didn't have much choice other than to pass it back to me. I was in the centre of the area, and the 'keeper's view was blocked by a defender, so I used the angle and side-footed it in the corner.

Bang! A hattrick in the derby, in front of the famous Barclay stand. What a feeling. I dived in front of the crowd, and all of the boys piled on top of me. You don't forget those sort of moments: 3-1 up, cruising, and I'd scored three against Ipswich.

The fans were properly enjoying themselves and singing "You're getting sacked in the morning" to Roy Keane, the Ipswich manager. It's rare you can spend the last 10 minutes of a massive derby enjoying it, and it felt great to knock the ball around against a beaten opponent, with the crowd in full voice.

Wes scored a great fourth goal, showing his class to put the 'keeper on the floor before chipping it over him. He then did his little forward roll to celebrate, which was hilarious. He probably took that celebration off Robbie Keane, but he couldn't manage the flip that Robbie did, so just stuck to a forward roll!

It capped a brilliant display, and it was a real marker to lay down. We came off that pitch bouncing. Not only were the bragging rights secured, but the result had taken us back into the playoffs, and given us our first win in a while.

I got the ball signed, and sat in the dressing room soaking it all in. I was told I was only the second Norwich player to score a hattrick in the derby, and it was a surreal feeling when it sank in that I was going to be forever written into Norwich City history.

CHAPTER 26

PREMIER LEAGUE DREAMS, BAD PENS AND SQUEAKY BUMS

2010-11

January 1, 2011 was the first time in my career I thought I might become a Premier League player.

I was 29, and had risen eight tiers since playing for Workington in the North West Counties League 12 years ago. Suddenly, one more tier – the final tier – was possible. How had that happened?

The Premier League had been unimaginable. At no stage when I was at Sheffield Wednesday or Nottingham Forest, or when I'd joined Norwich, did I think it could happen. And I'd been happy with that. I was more than pleased with being a professional footballer and scoring goals in League One and League Two for a living, with a hope that I'd get back to the Championship if things went really well. Premier League, though? Nah. No chance. Too far-fetched.

We were on a roll, though, after a good December which included a 2-1 win at Coventry. I scored both goals, with another late winner, but it was a crap game. However, the Norwich fans seem to remember it because of our celebrations in the snow when the winner went in.

I'd already said before the game that if I scored late I was going to jump in the snow surrounding the pitch. We got a corner late on, and I managed to hook the ball over my left shoulder and it flew in. I thought, 'Right here we go!' It was late on, we'd finally broken their resistance, and nothing was stopping me going into that snow. I wheeled off to the corner in front of our fans, belly-flopped into the snow and decided to do a snow angel.

I instantly regretted it. After all, who knew snow could be freezing cold?

Everyone bundled on top of me and then we did what you have to do when you're out in the snow: have a snowball fight. That was completely off the cuff, and I think it showed the spirit in the group. We were all enjoying the ride together. But my god, we were freezing our bollocks off for the last few minutes!

On New Year's Day, we got a huge 1-0 win against QPR at Carrow Road. They were leading the table, and an early Russell Martin goal was enough for us. That put us back up to third, just a point behind Swansea in second and five off QPR. And that's when the thought process changed.

Our mindset flicked from thinking we had an OK chance of making the playoffs, to believing that automatic promotion was on for us. And, of course, automatic promotion meant Premier League.

I was at an age where I was only ever going to get to the Premier League if we got promoted, and there were a lot of lads in that squad who were in a similar position. Premier League clubs were unlikely to come in and buy too many of us, so this would be the only way to get there. Our only chance.

That was a huge incentive for all of us. It's amazing what an unlikely shot at playing at the highest level can do to a team. There was no one who wasn't desperate to make the most of the opportunity, and when you've got 16 or 17 lads like that in the same squad, it becomes powerful. It's hard to stop that sort of momentum.

You think about being on *Match Of The Day* and everything that might come with being in the Premier League, but at the same time you try and play it down to yourself. We didn't really talk about it as a group; we just knew everyone was in the same boat. Instead of talking about the Prem together, we'd talk about promotion meaning we'd get to go to Las Vegas for our end-of-season celebrations. Focussing on Vegas became our way of talking about going up without putting too much pressure on ourselves; talk about the Premier League was very rare.

We didn't care about aiming for the Championship title, though. Who remembers who won the league? We just wanted one of those top two spots; it didn't matter which one.

Shortly after the QPR game, Burnley came out and said they had asked for permission to speak to Paul Lambert about becoming their manager. Norwich had responded by kindly telling Burnley to piss off.

It was unexpected, but it's normal for managers who are doing well to attract interest. The fact Burnley were below us in the table and still felt they were a more attractive club than Norwich showed just how far we'd come in a short space of time. Some clubs were treating us as small fry from League One, but you knew when you were at Norwich the potential there was massive.

The fans were panicking about Lambert and the press were all speculating about whether he'd go, but the players weren't that worried. It didn't really affect us. We just carried on training as normal. Rumours and comings and goings are part and parcel of football, so you just learn to get on with it. I've been sat laughing with friends in the dressing room one day, and the next day they're giving me a cuddle and walking out with a bag because they've got a move somewhere. You get used to that rotation of people.

None of us would have asked the gaffer about it, other than to joke with him a little bit. You'd get the boys saying to him something like, "Morning, surprised to see you still here!" You don't really talk about those sort of things with a manager. If he leaves, he'll come and tell everyone and that'll be that.

Lambert put it all to bed by telling the press he was happy at Norwich and there was no chance he was leaving, and that was the end to it. Time to crack on.

Not only did our mindset shift in the New Year, but so did that of the sides we were facing.

Teams had changed their ethos of how they would approach us. At the start of the season, I think a lot of sides just thought they'd turn up and win. We'd just come up from League One; we'd be pushovers. By the turn of the year everyone knew we were a good side. There was no surprise element to us anymore. All teams knew how we played, they knew our strengths and weaknesses. Instead of teams coming to attack, they would come to defend. Especially at Carrow Road, they would come to frustrate us.

That was a huge compliment, but it took a few games for us to adapt. You see a lot of promoted sides do well for the first half of the season but then tail off when they've been worked out and can't be flexible, but we were cleverer than that. Bizarrely, it was actually another last-minute winner that made us slightly change the way we approached games.

It was against Reading in mid-February. It was a really sweet stoppage-time winner, because I beat Ian Harte at the back stick to score, which was a nice bit of revenge for him getting me sent off at their place earlier in the season. The goal had come from David McNally catching a clearance in the Directors' Box, throwing it down to the gaffer on the touchline, who then chucked it to one of our lads for a throw-in. Ten seconds later, the ball was in the net. You can talk about a team effort, but that goal was taking the piss!

The win took us back to level on points with Cardiff, who were second. It was also our eighth injury time goal of the season. The crowd were loving it because of all of the drama, and that never-say-die attitude was amazing to be a part of. But Lambert told us we had to stop relying on last-minute goals, as great as they were. We talked a lot that week about getting our mentality right earlier in games, because we didn't want to keep giving ourselves a mountain to climb. In a long season it can end up wearing you out. The message was to tidy things up and stop the sloppy mistakes, or we can give up thinking about promotion.

* * *

Talking of sloppy mistakes, let's take time to remember Wes's penalty against Preston North End in March.

It was 1-1, and we got given a pen in the 72nd minute. Now, I knew Wes had scored a penalty against Preston while at Blackpool by chipping it straight down the middle. And as he stepped up, half of me thought, 'He might chip this again' and the other half of me thought, 'Surely he won't chip it again.'

Of course he chipped it again.

The 'keeper didn't move, and the ball plopped straight into his arms. Oh dear.

We knew Wes was going to absolutely get it in the dressing room from the gaffer if we didn't take the three points, and for the next 20 minutes I'd never seen a team work so hard to get a winner. We were trying to save Wes from a Lambert hairdryer, but the game ended 1-1.

The whistle went, and we headed back to the dressing room knowing what was coming. We were all raging with Wes a little bit, but we could never slag him off because that's just what he was like. We knew for a fact he could turn it on in an instant, and flip a match whenever he wanted to. He had moments in games when you'd think, 'How the hell has he just done that?'. He could win matches on his own, and that's why none of the boys, as much as we were pissed off with him, would criticise him for that penalty.

The gaffer, however, wasn't quite so forgiving.

"Go on then, tell me what the fuck you were thinking."

"I thought the 'keeper was going to dive."

"So that's your thinking? You thought the goalie is going to definitely dive. We're trying to get to the Premier League and you're dinking it; you're fucking chipping it? Are you winding me up? Just do it properly! Fucking about like we're all big time now! We're fighting for our lives here to get to the Premier League and you're chipping it. Honest to fuck!"

Everyone was looking down at their feet, half agreeing with the gaffer, half feeling sorry for Wes. It went quiet. Then, as Lambert started up again, Wes made the one fatal mistake I'd been hoping he would avoid.

"Well, it worked last time I did it," he said.

"Sorry, you what?"

"It worked last time I chipped it down the middle."

"And who was that against?"

"Against Preston a few years ago."

The last sentence was a mumble, because he knew there was no coming back from that. To chip a penalty was one thing; to chip it against the same team twice was another. Predictably, the gaffer went on the rampage again.

In all honesty, as horrible as it was to see one of my mates get properly destroyed, I was also buzzing a little bit because I knew I would be on penalties after that. I'd been wanting to get on pens ever since I joined Norwich, and me and Wes had both known another miss would mean I'd get my chance.

It was inevitable really, that we got a penalty in the next game. We were drawing 1-1 with Leicester City, and I did have a few nerves when I stepped up. But I buried it to give us the lead. We went on to win 3-2, and we should have scored more. It was a really good performance against a top side, and it put us back level on points with Swansea in third.

I got another penalty in our next game – both had actually been won by Wes – and we scored two late goals (sorry, gaffer) to beat Bristol City and move us into the top two with nine games remaining. Squeaky bum time.

PREMIER LEAGUE DREAMS, BAD PENS AND SQUEAKY BUMS

✳ ✳ ✳

The next two matches at the start of April showed how quickly things can change in football. First up, we smashed Scunthorpe 6-0 at our place.

I got a hattrick, then Simeon Jackson came off the bench and got a hattrick too in just 15 minutes. It was massive because Simeon hadn't scored since October, and needed that injection of confidence. That match also showed how much depth we had up top. We started the game with myself partnered with Dani Pacheco, a great lad who'd joined in March on loan from Liverpool. Then we both went off and were replaced by Simeon Jackson and Sam Vokes, who'd come in on loan recently from Wolves. We also had Chris Martin, who'd picked up a bad hamstring injury in February, and Aaron Wilbraham, who'd joined in January. With that sort of power, it was easy to forget we'd been in League One the season before.

However, none of that helped in our next game, against Swansea. We'd started the day four points ahead of them, but that gap was down to one point by the end of the match after they beat us 3-0. We'd taken the game to them but, fair play, they battered us.

The match had been played in a good spirit, so it was weird when they started celebrating like they'd won the league. It was like they'd sealed promotion, and I almost had a fight with the goalkeeper Dorus de Vries when he ran past and banged into me, which I thought was a bit distasteful. He was being a prick.

There was a bit of a scrap in the tunnel and I remember telling them that when we were drinking champagne and getting steaming in Las Vegas after we'd been promoted, we'd enjoy watching their shitty playoff game from our sunbeds.

It's funny where you can find a bit of extra motivation, and Swansea acting like dickheads gave us even more reason to go and get the job done. There was no way we were going to let this slip.

CHAPTER 27

CRUSHING IPSWICH, THE LOUDEST GAME AND JACKSON'S HATTRICK

2010-11

Some derbies are more important than others. Often, they have nothing riding on them other than local bragging rights. Occasionally, though, there is more at stake.

We faced Ipswich Town at Portman Road with only four matches of the season remaining. A win would take us back into the top two with three to go. A defeat would leave us a point behind Cardiff, who would have a game in hand. Quite a lot at stake, then. For us, at least. Meanwhile, Ipswich had won four out of their last five matches under their new manager Paul Jewell to get a bit of respectability in mid-table, and would have been desperate for revenge after we'd smashed them earlier in the season.

We thought we'd be in for a tough battle. Instead, we absolutely battered them.

It was quite surreal when we went to warm-up out on the pitch because there were hardly any Norwich fans in the ground. We were told there were huge queues to get in, so it was a weird atmosphere. Despite that, we started with a bang, Surs put us ahead after 13 minutes and I knew the game was already done, even then. Ipswich had tried to turn it into a kicking contest, but we were just too good for them.

After that there was a throw-in down the line, and Darren O'Dea properly elbowed me in the mouth. It was right in front of the linesman, but nothing was given. All of the Ipswich fans were giving me abuse because

I was right next to them and I was going mad at the referee, but he wasn't having any of it. My lip was bleeding and I was telling the ref, 'He's fucking elbowed me!' I couldn't believe nothing was given.

A few minutes later Foxy put in a corner, and I was so happy that Gareth McAuley bundled it into his own net. 2-0, and our fans, who had now all been let in, were absolutely bouncing.

I was still ranting about the elbow at half-time; still raging. I just wouldn't let it go. It nearly caused a melee on the pitch, and the gaffer came on and nailed the referee for letting it go. We just wanted to show that we weren't going to be bullied, and it fired us up even more.

Obviously Ipswich were trying to do everything to get me sent off in the second half because they could see I was still furious. We were given a free-kick early on, and me and David Norris ran away together, and he was grabbing me by the stomach; literally trying to drag me by pinching my stomach. He did that all of the way into the area; I'd never known anything like it. Pinching my stomach!

I got my own back at a corner when the ref wasn't looking. I went up behind Norris and scraped all of the way down the back of his calf and ankle. Nothing too painful, just a friendly reminder to not be a prick. We both laugh about it today, and he still can't explain why he thought of giving my tummy a pinch! Obviously I'm amazed with my famously lean physique that he managed to find anything to grab hold of.

In some ways, we were even more dominant than we had been in our 6-0 win over Scunthorpe. It was a proper battering. There was one period in the game where we must have put about 40 passes together without them getting near us. The only surprise was that we didn't score our third until the 73rd minute, when I set up Simeon.

Jimmy Bullard scored a worldie for them, but that just made us step up a gear. It was great that Russ Martin and Pacheco got on the scoresheet too, and we ran out 5-1 winners. By the time the game had finished, the ground was empty apart from a sea of yellow. We'd battered them so heavily that we'd taken over their ground.

***

People often ask me if I was gutted to not get on the scoresheet that night. Honestly, I didn't care. I'd played well, set up Simeon and was involved in Russ's goal, so I felt really pleased with my performance. The hattrick against them at Carrow Road was special, but there's always an amazing buzz after an away win like that. The only disappointment was that we didn't get a sixth, but you can't have everything.

What was really satisfying was that their fans had been saying we'd only beaten them earlier in the season because they'd been down to 10 men. Well, we'd just beaten them 5-1 with 11 men so what were they going to argue about now? The bragging rights were there for all to see; you can't really gloss over an aggregate score of 9-2.

We stuck the music on loud in the dressing room and it was a great place to be. Everyone was laughing and joking, just a bunch of pals having a brilliant time together. The journey back up the A140 was great. There was no drinking, just a real sense of satisfaction having smashed a team, and a belief we could go into the last three games of the season with real confidence. There was a contented buzz you only get after really special wins.

We didn't have long to think about bragging rights, though. Three days later we were into our next match, against Derby County at home. The reception we got when we walked out was phenomenal, as the fans were seeing us for the first time since the 5-1 win. I thought that was loud, but, by the end of the game, the noise levels would be off the scale.

***

Three games remained, but there were no nerves going into the Derby

218

County match. Our fate was in our hands, and this was a chance to cement our place in the top two. We started the match like a team who'd just beaten their rivals 5-1, and Simeon gave us the lead on the stroke of half-time.

They equalised not long after the break, but Simeon curled in a beauty of a second from outside the area, and I thought that was the match done. We were dominating, and I was convinced we'd see it out easily. But Derby got another equaliser in the 63rd minute, and suddenly we had to step up again. That's not always easy when you've been dominating, because it feels like a punch to the gut, but the crowd gave us a massive lift. As soon as Derby had scored, the crowd belted out 'On The Ball, City', as if they were telling us, 'Don't worry lads, you'll score another. No problem.'

For the final 10 minutes we were relentless. Russ was practically playing as a right-winger, putting in cross after cross, but it wasn't quite falling for us. We were like a wave; we just kept coming at Derby but they were putting their bodies on the line left, right and centre. I was trying to keep the boys calm, telling everyone to continue playing our football. The crowd stuck right behind us and kept us going, and we always believed the chances would keep coming.

Big John Ruddy pulled off a great save just before the end, which he'd been doing all season. But people often forget about his crucial save because of what happened next.

Henri swung in a corner in injury time, right through the crowded penalty area. I was near the goalline, and I watched Russ drive a shot goalwards. It's in! Yes! No! Blocked on the line! Shit! Off Simeon's chest! Is it in? It's in! It's actually in!

What a noise. Phenomenal. The only thing I can relate it to is the silence when a golfer is taking an important putt, and that anticipation as it goes towards the hole. Is it going in? Is it? Is it? Then it drops in, and everyone explodes.

Boom! Carrow Road erupted. Euphoria. The fans swarmed down the stands in front of us, people fell over the ad boards, all of us dived on each other, Ruddy ran the length of the pitch to join in. I'd never known a noise like it. The roar just kept going, all of the way to the final whistle. You must have been able to hear it across the whole of the city.

Even though we'd not won anything, it felt like it was now our destiny to be promoted. Nothing was going to get in our way. We got back into the dressing room, and heard that Cardiff had won. It made Simeon's goal even more important, because our fate was still in our hands. And I was buzzing for Simeon. He'd hit a real scoring streak since that hattrick at Scunthorpe and he'd become unplayable at times. Big players come good at just the right time, and he'd certainly done that.

I've probably watched that goal back more than any other and if I could go back to one game in my career and rerun it, then it would be that one. It had absolutely everything, and I'll never forget the wall of noise when the ball went in. Spine-tingling. Most importantly, it gave us three more points with just two games of the season left.

MY TOP 5...
GOALS

1. SHREWSBURY AGAINST ROCHDALE

Flicked it up and hit a left-foot volley into the top corner.

2. NORWICH AGAINST LIVERPOOL

The header at Anfield. The occasion, the setting, and it was
a bloody good header against world-class defenders.
That header showed everything about how I'd be that season.
I believed I wanted 50/50s more than anyone else.

3. SHREWSBURY AGAINST WYCOMBE

The fifth of my five in the League Trophy. To be able to say
I scored five goals in a match is pretty special.

4. SHREWSBURY AGAINST GILLINGHAM

I scored twice at their place, which felt great because it was
a big game and their fans had given me stick all match.

5. NORWICH AGAINST IPSWICH

The first goal of my hattrick was the best. It showed exactly
what I was: harrying and pressing, never giving up a lost cause,
wanting it more than a defender, and then having the
composure to finish really well.

CHAPTER 28

POMPEY PARTY, PARADES AND UNIBOND PREM TO THE REAL PREM

2010-11

"Right, no matter what happens I don't want anyone watching the game."

The words of Paul Lambert in a hotel outside Portsmouth on May 2, 2011. Our match was at 7.45pm at Fratton Park that night, but third-place Cardiff were playing at home at 5.15pm against Middlesbrough. It was the penultimate game of the season, proper squeaky bum time, and we were desperate for Boro to pull off a shock. A Cardiff defeat would guarantee us a place in the top two and promotion to the Premier League.

So, of course, there was absolutely no way we were going to follow the gaffer's instructions. He didn't want us distracted by their game, or to be mentally tired by putting ourselves through watching it. He was deadly serious about it. We were deadly serious about ignoring him.

We were supposed to be chilling out or having a nap before leaving for Fratton Park at 6pm. Because Nels had joined Scunthorpe in January to be closer to his family, I was now rooming with Russ Martin. We flicked the TV on, but because the coaching team were on the same floor as us, we had the volume down so no one could hear it.

Cardiff had been in top form, and everyone was expecting them to win and put the pressure back on us. So when Leroy Lita put Boro ahead after three minutes, me and Russ were both silently celebrating and fist-pumping. I quietly opened the door and looked down the corridor, and a load of the lads had done the same thing; poking their heads out to quietly celebrate. We didn't make any noise, not one sound.

Thirteenth minute, bang! Boro score again. Unbelievable. This time we're all out in the corridor, silently high-fiving and fist-pumping. Silent disco. Wes even did a roly-poly down the hallway and we were all crying with laughter, still trying to not make a noise.

We had to be down in the hotel lobby around 5.45pm, so we quickly packed and headed down. By the time we got there, Boro had scored another. We couldn't believe it. The Premier League felt like it was in our grasp.

Everyone was talking about it on the bus. For me, knowing the score and knowing what we had to do helped. It might have made others more nervous, but I always thrived under that sort of pressure. As a captain you've got to be in control; you can't let your emotions ride away, because everyone's looking at you. If I'd acted edgy or nervous, that would rub off on everyone. If I'd started shouting and fist-pumping every five minutes, it would have sent the wrong message. So I stayed calm and in control, like it was just another game.

I hadn't been back to Fratton Park since 2003, when I was with Sheffield Wednesday and Portsmouth were top of the Championship and we were bottom. They'd practically won the title to get to the Premier League so there was a party atmosphere at the ground, and now eight years later, I was there thinking, 'By the end of today I'm going to be a Premier League footballer'. I just wanted to enjoy it and get the job done.

Another reason I felt calm was because my mind had been distracted from the football all week. The hospital were concerned about the size of our third kid, Hattie, who was due later in May. We had a growth scan booked the next day and although everything was probably fine, I was a bit anxious about that. It put the game into some sort of perspective, which helped with my nerves.

✳✳✳

You could tell the gaffer was looking for a moment to explode. He'd been pissed off about someone laughing in the tunnel, and I'd seen in his eyes that he felt some of the lads thought the job was already done before we'd even kicked off. We knew we just had to win and we'd be up.

Back in the dressing room, Wes laughed about something. That was Lambert's cue: "What the fuck are you laughing at?" That stunned everyone into silence. He'd got everyone's attention. "We've got a game in 20 minutes and you're laughing your head off. Get your fucking mind on it. It's not done; you think it's done because Cardiff got beat. Well, it's not done. They're a good side, Portsmouth, and they're going to be right up for this to spoil our party. So stop fucking laughing and get your fucking heads sorted."

Lambert had deliberately waited for one of the big characters like Wes to step a tiny bit out of line. He knew Wes could take it and that it would send a message to the rest of the dressing room. It was a reality check, and it got everyone's heads back into the game.

We were waiting in the tunnel to come out, and some of the Portsmouth boys were shouting that we thought the game was already done and to show us what they were made of. I was stood at the front, and yelled out, "Right, come on then, let's get at it. Beat this team here, and we won't see them for a while." We walked out to a huge sea of yellow behind one goal; a huge roar from an unbelievable support.

We always did a pre-match huddle and I'd been wondering about what to say. I didn't want it to be the usual, "Let's do it right" or, "Get at these." As soon as we got into our circle, it came to me: "Look at this stadium, look where we are," I said, looking around at all of the boys. "Next year we could be at Anfield, we could be at Old Trafford, we could be on *Match Of The Day*. In 90 minutes we could all be Premier League footballers so let's roll these over, get at them quick and let's go and have a party."

No screaming, no shouting; just a nice easy conversation to remind everyone of what was at stake. It helped that Portsmouth had a good crowd in and, as always, they were making a lot of noise. That got us up for the battle even more, and we really tore into them.

***

Zak Whitbread missed a chance. I had a shot saved. We should have had a handball that the referee never gave. Elliott Ward missed. Simeon Jackson had a chance. We had one off the line. We were battering them, but we went in at half-time thinking, 'How the hell are we 0-0 here?'

There were no nerves, though. We'd dominated, and I knew we'd keep creating chances. It was just a case of taking one that came our way. The gaffer told us we'd been brilliant, and that whatever happened tonight we could be proud of what we'd done. That gave everyone a lift too.

We flew at them in the second half, and we were attacking the goal with our fans behind. Five minutes in, and the deadlock was finally broken. Foxy picked it up centrally about 40 yards out, and he shaped to cross and I got on the move on the right. He went left, though, and I turned around because I didn't know if Simeon had made his run to the back post. I watched the ball loop over Ritchie De Laet – what a ball it was, inch-perfect – and it fell to Simeon. Oh my god, he'd gone and scored! 1-0 up! One foot in the Premier League! Our fans went ballistic and we celebrated in front of them. That was the noisiest I'd ever heard an away following; the sound of joy and total relief.

There were still 40 minutes of the match left; 40 minutes to get to the Premier League. We used the goal celebration as an opportunity to regroup a bit as we were walking back for the kick-off; a quick get-together to refocus. We wanted to keep attacking, and that's what we did.

The longer we went without scoring another, though, the more the match became a battle. We kept the ball well, but Pompey were throwing men into the box and we were having to win big headers and clear our lines. We'd been doing that all season, and we certainly didn't mind having to turn the game into a physical battle.

Ninety minutes ticked over, and the board went up for injury time. Then, just like that, the whistle went for full-time. It was a blur; injury time had gone in a flash. I'd expected it to feel like hours, but instead the time flew by. And we were up! We were up to the Premier League!

The first feeling was sheer relief. That season had been a long-old journey; we'd never set out to achieve promotion and yet here we were, standing on the pitch with the Norwich fans streaming on, as Premier League players. Actual Premier League players. I was 30 years old, and I was no longer a Football League striker; I was no longer a non-league striker. I was a Premier League forward. The unthinkable had actually happened.

You didn't have long to think, though, because everyone was bouncing. Hundreds of fans on the pitch, the whole staff, Delia and her husband Michael Wynn Jones, Wes with an inflatable ring around his neck, Russ hugging Delia in his pants, bundles, pile-ons, banners, flags. It was brilliant, chaotic fun. Scenes I'll never forget.

***

We got back to the dressing room, and the champagne and beer were flowing. The gaffer announced that they'd booked hotel rooms in Southampton and instead of flying back that night we were going out to celebrate. The boys were buzzing, but I couldn't go.

I wanted to be at the hospital with Fay for the growth scan. Of course I'd have loved to stay, but there was no way I was missing the scan just in case it was bad news. No way in the world.

I got a lift back with some people from the club, and I don't want to sound stupid here, but it was probably actually nicer to go back in the car because I had four hours to really reflect on the achievement and let it sink in. It gave me the chance to speak to my family, read all of the messages coming in from mates, former teammates and managers. Fay had even watched the match!

POMPEY PARTY, PARADES AND UNIBOND PREM TO THE REAL PREM

My car was parked at Norwich airport, so I was dropped off there. It was 3am, and I walked over to my car, knackered but still buzzing. There was a problem, though: my car had been blocked in by one of the lads' cars. There'd been a stream of messages in the group chat all night with photos of them on the piss, and here I was at Norwich airport at 3am, on my own, with my car blocked in. What a way to celebrate becoming a Premier League player.

I grabbed a taxi back, and in the morning the scan went fine. There'd been nothing to worry about. Huge relief. Now I could celebrate properly.

***

Once again we'd all been on the piss in the week leading up to the last game of the season, at home to Coventry. In that state, it was a miracle we got a draw out of it. I picked up the Player of the Season award before the match, which was a huge honour. I'd scored 22 goals, but it was still a surprise when my name was read out. To win it two seasons in a row meant a lot, especially after so many of the lads had had a brilliant campaign and everyone had played their part in such a successful season.

I scored in the match to make it 23 for the season, and I'd known I was coming off early because the gaffer wanted to get people onto the pitch for as much game time as possible. As soon as the final substitution was made, me and Ant McNamee went for a wee. All of the food and beer was already out in the dressing room, so while the game was still going on we cracked open a beer and got a chicken wing down us! We felt like naughty school kids, but that beer tasted bloody good.

I also grabbed a yellow t-shirt and wrote in marker pen on the back, "Unibond Prem to the real Prem. Wow.☺" I slipped the t-shirt on under my shirt, and we walked back out for the end of the game. Sadly you're not allowed to drink while in view of the pitch, or we'd probably have taken a couple of beers out with us!

After the game, we went in for a bit of food and drink, and then came out for a parade around the pitch. We all emerged from the tunnel doing the hokey-cokey – don't ask me why, because I couldn't tell you – and the whole crowd had stayed. It was a real party atmosphere, and we had our families with us on the pitch too, which was a really nice touch. Little Evie and Erica were loving it.

I was in my t-shirt with the message on, and that image became quite famous among the Norwich fans at the time. I didn't think it would get the kind of reaction it did; it was just my way of summing up the euphoria of having somehow worked my way up from nowhere to the Premier League.

The celebrations certainly weren't done that day, though. We had an open-top bus parade around Norwich in the week. We were a bit worried no one would turn up, but there were 40,000 people lining the streets. Everyone was singing and dancing, and I was stood up there telling myself to take it all in.

I'd been part of a phenomenal group that had achieved back-to-back promotions after losing 7-1 at home in the opening game of the League One season. A lot of football is failure, so you're lucky if you have any success in your career and I realised how important it was to soak it all in because moments like that don't come around very often, if at all. Looking out at the sea of yellow was really special, knowing that the next time we saw all of those fans would be when we walked out in the Premier League.

It's fair to say joining Norwich City had worked out all right.

✳✳✳

There was one last thing to do: head to Las Vegas for our end-of-season party. There was a major issue, though. Hattie was due the day after we were supposed to return, so Fay was understandably a little anxious about me going.

I did feel bad about flying out with the boys. If Hattie had been due during that week, there's no way I'd have gone. Both Evie and Erica had been past the due date, so I took the gamble, and I got away with it. We had a brilliant week. Plenty of booze, plenty of relaxing. And, as I'd predicted, we got to watch Swansea in the playoffs while we were having a few beers and some champagne in the sunshine.

The day after I got back, we were in hospital for the birth. I couldn't have timed it better! This was the first time we'd used Carlisle hospital, and I was really pleased Fay had chosen to have the birth there. Every time I went in that hospital it always brought back memories of my dad dying. I used to hate walking in there, because it would just make me think of taking that route to see Dad.

I'd do anything to get out of having to go there, so to come out carrying Hattie changed everything. The weight of that horrible memory had been lifted. It was a lovely feeling walking out of the hospital with a smile on my face knowing we've got this little bundle of joy for the rest of our lives.

CHAPTER 29

PREMIER LEAGUE, MOTD AND PLAYING AGAINST YOUR HEROES

2011-12

It was weird going away for the summer knowing I'd return as a Premier League player. It wasn't something I had ever even dreamed would happen and yet, here I was: Grant Holt, Premier League striker. It definitely had more of a ring to it than Unibond striker.

I couldn't wait to get started, and checking the fixture list was on a different level. You'd scan through it looking for Manchester United, Chelsea, Arsenal. All of the big teams you'd watched every weekend on TV, containing some of the world's best players. I couldn't help but get excited. I was never daunted by it, though; I knew I'd relish it. Who wouldn't look forward to walking onto the pitch at the big stadiums, to look around and soak it all up, to have the chance of shutting up 50,000 fans?

We would get some hidings; that was inevitable. At some point you'd be on the pitch and feel like a boxer getting smacked left, right and centre. But I'd rather be getting the occasional hiding in the Premier League than being in the Championship and winning 1-0. I just knew I was going to love it.

It's fair to say I wasn't prepared for just how different life as a Premier League player would be, though. I thought the biggest difference was simply going to be being on *Match Of The Day*. You think you'll become a bit more well-known, and that your mates will take the piss out of you because you're on the telly every week.

It's when I came back to training that the differences became more noticeable. The Nike balls arrived. The Premier League badge was on the new shirt. Lucozade bottles were everywhere. Not big things; just a drip-feed of little things. Then it gathers pace: you have promos for Premier League TV, you have more photoshoots, you have more national media coming to the training ground. It was much, much bigger than I'd expected it to be. It wasn't just a case of being on *Match Of The Day*; everything felt on a different level.

The reach of your team changes, too. When I was in Dubai ahead of pre-season, I'd pick up a newspaper and most days there'd be a piece on Norwich City. Not only that but we were in the top section of the betting, we were being talked about on Sky Sports News first, our transfer rumours were being written and spoken about in the national media. You were part of something much bigger; it wasn't just football anymore. It was its own universe.

From the coaching team to the players, our ethos was to embrace it. To love every minute of it; to have a good go at each team we faced and to see where it took us. We weren't going to be overawed; if it worked it worked and if it didn't it didn't. Many of us had thought we'd never get the chance to play in the Premier League so we were desperate to make the most of it. We weren't just there as friendly tourists passing through, though; we were going to make it as tough for the opposition as we possibly could. We wanted to set up a home in the Premier League.

The gaffer and the coaching team were relishing the challenge, and they really grew into it throughout the season. They enjoyed mixing up formations, and changing tactics against certain sides. In League One and the Championship we'd played pretty much the same way in each game because we knew we were stronger than most teams. But in the Premier League, we obviously knew we'd be coming up against sides who were better than us, and Lambert, Culverhouse and Karsa showed how good they were in those situations. We were flexible, but they always found ways of getting us to play to our strengths in different set-ups. That, I think, is why we ended up staying up so comfortably.

*** *** ***

Our first match was away at Wigan. Now, with all due respect, that didn't exactly scream 'Premier League'... until you got to their ground. It didn't matter which stadium you were at in the Premier League, they all felt big-time. As soon as you came out of the tunnel, you'd see BBC, you'd see Sky, you'd see Premier League TV. Everyone's there, and everywhere you looked you had a camera following you.

In some ways, it was good to get that first game out of the way. We got a decent 1-1 draw, and I played 90 minutes (which was probably one of the only times I got to play 90 minutes on that pitch!). While I was out there it did feel like the level had gone up. Wigan had guys like Emmerson Boyce, Gary Caldwell, Maynor Figueroa, Ben Watson, Victor Moses, Franco Di Santo. All top players. I felt comfortable, but it was a big jump from the Championship.

It was weird seeing us on *Match Of The Day* that night, especially watching Wes score and all of us run off to celebrate. Obviously we'd been on TV quite a bit the previous season, but to actually be on *Match Of The Day* felt different. You grew up watching it, humming the theme tune, so the first time you see yourself it doesn't quite feel like it's you. It was like watching someone else, and a different team.

Despite all of the media and all of the buzz, I still don't think it quite resonated that I was playing in the Premier League during that game. It was, after all, only Wigan Athletic (with all due respect etc etc). Two weeks later we went to Stamford Bridge, and that's when it really hit home. Now, that felt like a proper Premier League match.

I'd been to Stamford Bridge before in the FA Cup with Nottingham Forest, when I was dragged off at half-time by Calderwood. So this time I just wanted to go there and put on a good show. We knew the likelihood was we'd get spanked, but you wanted to give your all.

It was when we exchanged team-sheets ahead of kick-off that it all hit me. Both captains were there, so it was me and John Terry. That was surreal enough, but then me and Cully looked at their team-sheet and he gave me a look like, 'Shit, just look at the names!' We were both laughing while walking back to the away dressing room, reading the names out. Drogba. Lampard. Torres. Cole. Ivanovic. The bench wasn't too shabby either: Lukaku. Anelka. Mata. Yep, this was the Premier League.

We played well, and were just 1-0 down in the 63rd minute. We weren't overawed at all. It didn't feel like a Cup tie with us being a plucky side from a lower division; it felt like a good match between two teams playing well.

Just after the hour, a cross came in towards the edge of Chelsea's box, and I was thinking, 'Where's their 'keeper going? He's never getting this ball. Never.' I was going to go for the header, but then I saw a defender flying in too, so I decided to let Hilário and the defender both go for it because they looked like they were about to smash into each other. I backed off, they collided, and the ball dropped in front of me. I had my back to goal, so I took the split-second decision to hook the ball over my shoulder and hoped for the best. Luckily, it looped straight in. I couldn't believe it! My first Premier League goal, and it's at Stamford Bridge.

I ran off, and as everyone was jumping on me, I started thinking that it was such a shame my dad didn't get to see it. Those sort of moments were always tinged with sadness because of that. But it was great to get my first top tier goal off my back, especially as it was against one of the big teams. I'd shown a bit of instinct with the goal, and it turned out to be a good finish, so I was pleased with that. I was a Premier League goalscorer.

We ended up losing 3-1 – John Ruddy got sent off when we were level – but I enjoyed a good battle with John Terry. I had a chat with him afterwards, and he told me he'd loved the scrap with me. Branislav Ivanovic was really tough that day too; two old-school centre-halves who knew how to play.

People always ask me who the best defender was I played against. But I couldn't tell you. I could tell you the best attacking players, because I've seen what they've done. But for defenders, I couldn't really say. Against the big teams, I wasn't attacking them enough to judge their defensive abilities; I spent most of the time chasing and hunting down their passes. Against the good sides, it's almost like the roles were reversed: I was defending against their defenders, and their defenders were attacking against me. For 65% to 70% of the game I was closing down and pressing.

I won't lie though. When you're up against the likes of Terry or Vincent Kompany, and you won the ball off them or turned them, it felt really good. You'd seen them on the TV, and in the case of English players I'd probably spent the last five or 10 years slagging them off when they were playing for England! And now I was suddenly playing against them. It was moments like that when I'd just think how bizarre it all was.

I loved testing myself against them. I loved winning headers, or pinching the ball off them, or holding them off, or nipping ahead of them. If I'd been told someone was really strong in the air, for example, I went into the match just wanting to show them how much stronger in the air than them I was. I was relishing it.

There always seemed to be a level of respect between players at that level, so no one ever really chatted shit to me. They didn't have to play mind games or to get under your skin because their ability meant they could let their football do the talking. Either that, or they all thought I was crap and not worth it!

Not everyone was so accommodating, though. In April, we went to White Hart Lane to play Tottenham. I'd gone into a couple of tackles with their centre-back Younes Kaboul, and he told me to stop being so aggressive and swinging my arms around. How did I react to that? I told him to fuck off, of course. Stop being aggressive? Who did he think he was? A bit later, I took a touch and he went in a bit late on me. Caught me. So I looked at him like, 'So that's how you want it to be, yeh?' Next thing, a ball went into the corner and we both steamed in and properly smashed into each other. I was hurt but I bounced straight up, because I wasn't going to show him I was in pain.

He stayed down, and as he was on the floor I told him, "Don't you shit yourself and go off. Don't be a wimp, now, will you?" He was limping around, and I was properly giving him the verbals. He had to go off, and I was calling him all sorts of names. It felt like I'd won a good battle, and even more importantly we won the game.

We had really attacked it, and Elliott Bennett got the winner with a brilliant hit from outside the box. I should have had two penalties in that game. Ledley King brought me down twice, and I was fuming they weren't given. However, King was phenomenal. I couldn't imagine how good he was in his pomp, because he was still amazing despite the fact he couldn't train all week. His reading of the game was unbelievable. The amount of times I thought I had the ball in the channel, and he suddenly nipped in front of me, was astonishing. He timed nearly everything to perfection.

***

Despite some of the defenders being out of this world, in some ways the Premier League actually felt easier to play in.

You get given a bit more room and space, so I was finding little pockets to make runs into more easily. It wasn't as helter-skelter as lower leagues, and defenders let you come off them. In League Two, if I got the ball played into my feet and my first touch was wrong, I'd usually get kicked 10 feet in the air by a defender coming through the back of me. That's just how it was. In the Premier League, if your touch was wrong a defender would never even dream of coming through the back of you. Nine times out of 10, it would be a red card. That meant you could get away with holding the ball up more easily in the Premier League, because you wouldn't get smashed. So you'd get the ball, and move it quicker, which suited our style of play.

While individually it was easier to play in, collectively it was tougher to get results. The sheer quality throughout every team meant you couldn't rest for one second. You had to be on it for the whole 90 minutes. We went to the Emirates towards the end of the season, and we were playing 4-2-2-2. Me and Simeon up top, Wes and Elliott Bennett behind us and Jonny Howson and Bradley Johnson behind them. The game plan was for everyone to defend the middle of the pitch and to let Arsenal go down the wings. We'd let them cross it because they weren't strong in the air.

After just two minutes, Yossi Benayoun picked it up on their left, where we wanted him. Let him cross it in and clear our lines. Instead, he nonchalantly stepped inside and curled a belter into the top corner. That's the sort of quality you were facing; the ability to ruin a clever game plan with one moment of brilliance. We managed to turn it around to go 2-1 up, with me and Wes scoring, and we were holding out with 20 minutes to go. Then Robin van Persie, one of the Premier League's greatest strikers, bangs in two poacher's goals in eight minutes and suddenly we're behind again. How can you deal with that? We did however get a draw, with Steve Morison scoring the equaliser with a fine finish after a brilliant through-ball from Howson; that was us showing our quality too.

Our 2-1 defeat at home to Manchester United in February showed what a tough league it was, too. Of course it did; they're Manchester United. They were in the race for the title (Manchester City would pip them with that incredible Sergio Aguero goal in injury time on the last day of the season), and were motoring under Sir Alex Ferguson.

Paul Scholes put them ahead early, and David de Gea pulled off some sensational saves before I got an equaliser in the 83rd minute. I held off Rio Ferdinand – not bad – and fired it into the top corner from just inside the area. Carrow Road went ballistic, and it was thoroughly deserved because we'd played brilliantly. We thought we'd done enough, but then Ryan Giggs popped up in the 89th minute to win it for them on his 900th appearance. It just showed the strength they had: we'd worked our bollocks off all game to get ourselves back into it, thought we'd got ourselves a fantastic point, and six minutes later a Premier League legend ghosts in to win it.

It was the most surreal match I'd ever played in. I'd loved Man United as a kid and I pretended to be Scholes and Giggs when kicking a ball around in the park. Now, aged 30, I was playing against them, tackling them, and competing for balls with them. I was even marking Scholes for most of the match! In a Premier League game! He was just ridiculous. He'd come back from retirement a month earlier, and he had a fag on. He was unbelievable. It's not often you get starstruck, but he was 36 and I could not imagine how good he would have been at 25. I'm sure he was thinking the same about me; he's probably written the same in his autobiography actually! He was just effortless, and so was Giggsy despite his age.

I was gutted to lose, but to have 'Norwich City 1-2 Manchester United, goalscorers Grant Holt, Paul Scholes, Ryan Giggs' forever in the record books means a lot to me.

The following season when we played them, I went in to do the team-sheets and Sir Alex Ferguson was there. He said, "Hello Grant, how are you?" Sir Alex Ferguson was saying that to me! I acted as cool as I could, and we had a quick conversation. I walked away buzzing. Sir Alex Ferguson knew my name! How had that happened?! I think that was my biggest achievement in football: someone of his calibre, a genuine legend, knowing who the hell I was. Not bad for a fat lad from Carlisle.

Another reminder of how tough the Premier League is came in those inevitable hammerings. We lost 5-1 and 6-1 to Manchester City in that first season. You think you're playing well, and that you're in the game, but you look up and suddenly you're getting torn apart. It takes only a second for everything to go to shit. Someone just has to move a split-second too early, and they're in and score. Then they have their tail up, and they just keep moving the ball around because they don't have to force it, so they're moving it, moving it, moving it, and bang, someone is a yard short of tracking a run and they're in again. 2-0. You feel you're playing really well for 95% of the time, but they absolutely kill you in the 5%.

It's times like that where you just have to hold your hands up and say you've been beaten by a much better side. A big team have played to their potential, and there's nothing you could have done about it. You just have to accept that. I tell you what, though, it's a lot better feeling getting done 6-1 by Manchester City than 7-1 by Colchester United!

***

What makes a top team a top team? For me, the best sides have blokes in every position who can see a game more clearly than most players. I think that's what sets the very best apart. A lot of footballers have great technical ability, or express pace, but they don't always get in the right position, or anticipate the next move, or think two or three passes ahead. To be able to combine ability and a football brain gives you a really top player, and Premier League sides are stuffed with them.

The really great players could set traps, too. Gareth Bale spent a lot of time on the halfway line when we played Spurs in December at Carrow Road. He'd come short and keep passing the ball backwards. I was thinking, 'He's not doing much here. He's not all that'. Next minute, he pretended to go short, one of our boys went short with him as usual, and suddenly he put the brakes on, spun, collected the ball from Modric, and he was away from our player. He went inside, beat a couple of defenders and dinked it over Ruddy. 1-0. He'd laid the groundwork by setting us up, like a bowler in cricket producing five outswingers to the batsman before swinging one back in at the end. Genius.

Playing against that level of quality inevitably made me a better player. It was the same for everyone in our squad. My touch was getting better because I was getting balls whipped into my feet, and I was thinking more clearly about what I needed to do. During games I would map out different scenarios, looking at opposition weaknesses that are occurring during the match and trying to think of ways to exploit them. For example, if I was struggling for room in a certain position and not creating enough space for the likes of Wes to work in, I'd maybe ask Russ to go long for a few minutes in order for me to chase the ball down and stretch the play. That would create more room for Wes to start getting on the ball.

I also had the confidence to attempt things in matches that I'd tried on the training ground. I scored a really good goal against Everton in December, where I held the ball up in the box and sucked a defender onto my back, and then rolled it behind him and spun, before slotting it in. I'd done that in training, and although I hadn't scored, I knew I could use it in a game.

I was training with players who were really good, so I knew if I could get the better of them in training, I could get the better of anyone in the Premier League. Playing alongside real quality gives you that extra confidence. That's why it's such a good league – everyone is constantly making everyone else a better player. You get found out very quickly if you're not good enough and there were a lot of pundits who thought that would happen to us. We proved them wrong, though.

A 12th-placed finish, 11 points above the bottom three, showed we'd taken very easily to playing in one of the best leagues in the world.

CHAPTER 30

ANFIELD GLORY, BUCKING BRONCOS AND JOEY BARTON'S BREATH

2011-12

I certainly didn't have it all my own way in the first Premier League season. I had to get used to not playing every game, which was tough.

We went to Old Trafford in October but I didn't play. I was absolutely fuming that I didn't get onto the pitch. I'd never been there before, and I was sat on the bench. Maybe the gaffer thought I wasn't at it, I don't know. At the time, I thought it might be my last chance to play there and I was pissed off.

After the game, it occurred to me what I'd been moaning about: being sat on the bench at Old Trafford. I told myself to get a grip. To have been sat on the bench at a ground as iconic as Old Trafford in a league game wasn't something I ever thought would be possible, and here I was moaning about it. I should have considered it an achievement to have been there in the first place.

However, we rolled into Anfield a couple of weeks later and I was named on the bench again. I hadn't played at Old Trafford, and now I might not get on at Liverpool. However, I told myself to still soak it all in. It's a special atmosphere at Anfield; a proper stadium where you can feel the history of the place. I touched the famous badge when I walked out of the tunnel, and told myself to remember every moment of being there.

Being on the bench means you have front-row seats, with the legendary Kenny Dalglish just yards away in the Liverpool dugout. It felt amazing, but of course I just wanted to get on. We conceded just before the break and the gaffer told me I'd be on shortly into the second half because he wanted to mix things up. I was buzzing, and on the 57th minute I got the call. I ran onto that pitch and just thought, 'Wow'. How have I done this? From Workington in the ninth tier to coming on at Anfield in the Premier League.

As soon as I got involved in the game, it just felt like any other match at any level in football. Do your basics right, win your individual battles and help your team out. Simple.

Straight away I got the ball, rolled someone and got a shot off that Pepe Reina saved. Right in front of the famous Kop. That felt good, because I'd got going immediately. Then three minutes later, Anthony Pilkington sent over a fantastic cross and I powered my way through Jamie Carragher and Glen Johnson and, with Reina flapping at thin air, I smashed in a header. Not a bad impact. As I ran off to celebrate, I thought of Fay's dad, who was in the crowd and would have been swearing at me because he was a Liverpool fan, and then I thought of my dad. He'd have loved it.

Big John Ruddy made some unbelievable saves that night, including one out-of-this-world diving stop in injury time to deny Luis Suarez. I always got the sense John never got the credit for how great he was at Norwich. He was phenomenal for us. His saves that night were a bigger contribution than my goal, and we were buzzing to get a point.

It felt great to have come off the bench to show people what I could do. It felt like I'd proved a point to the gaffer, too, but I quickly came to realise that Lambert was right to rotate me. He told me that at my age, and with all of the work I put in off the ball, I just couldn't play every single game. I'd be running 10k each match, which is a lot for a forward, so rotating me helped keep me fresh, both physically and mentally.

Although it was hard to take, it was the right call. It also made me even more proud of being able to score 15 Premier League goals that season.

✳✳✳

One of the side effects of scoring at Anfield and Stamford Bridge is you start getting noticed more. There's more attention on you, and my ugly mug became more recognisable when I was out and about.

I remember going to London and there was a group of Chinese tourists on a guided tour, and when I walked past they all looked at me. The next minute I was getting chased down the road! "Mr Holt, Mr Holt! Can we get a picture!" It's so bizarre when that happens, but you have to embrace it.

Doing all of the media stuff with different TV and radio shows was good fun, as was doing photo shoots. I really liked it, probably because I never thought I'd ever play in the Premier League. So I knew I had to make the most of it, and not moan about it, and just enjoy it all. Why wouldn't you?

The downside of being recognised is that you end up in the papers more easily. A big example of that was after our 2-1 win against QPR at Loftus Road in January. Joey Barton got sent off for pushing his head into Bradley Johnson's face. I was a bit surprised Brad went down, because there wasn't really much in it, but you would do anything to get three points away from home. Afterwards the gaffer said Brad wasn't doing any press, and we couldn't say anything about the sending off. He didn't want the focus to be on that rather than on our win.

We'd planned a night out after the game at Alexandra Palace for the darts. The gaffer was fine with that, and I think it might have been because he'd refused to let us have a Christmas do that year. That was the first time he'd pissed the boys off, actually, because those sort of nights were important for that squad. But Paul had felt we needed to concentrate on one thing only, and that was staying up. He didn't want any distractions, he didn't want any photos in the press of us pissed on a night out to curtail our good start to the season. But the boys didn't agree with the decision, and neither did I. So maybe him letting us have a night out for the darts was his way of admitting he might have been too harsh at Christmas, but who knows.

There was quite a few of us out that night, and we were right at the front at Ally Pally. Eight crates of lager, eight crates of cider. Done. We'd been in the Premier League for a few months now, so were more known than we'd ever been. That meant a lot of people were taking our pictures, which was fine. We were having a few beers but everyone was behaved and just having a good time. Enjoying the darts.

We were given a lot of signs to write on, and someone wrote 'Holt for England'. A bloke on our table wrote 'Barton your breath stinks', in reference to how close he'd got to Brad earlier that day. It definitely wasn't one of the players who wrote it, but Brad picked it up and got someone to take a picture of him with it. He sent it to a pal of his for a joke, but it turned out his mate sent it to someone else who then put it straight on Twitter. While we were drinking away we didn't really realise it was getting momentum on social media.

We got back in around 2am and went to bed. Put my phone on silent. Woke up in the morning and had a load of missed calls, mostly from our head of media and from the gaffer. Voicemail from Lambert: "You better call me, ASAP". Uh oh. I checked twitter and suddenly knew exactly what all of those missed calls were about. I walked down to breakfast, and Brad just said, "Oh my god, the gaffer's going to kill me!"

I thought it was probably time to bite the bullet and call Paul.

"What the fuck, Holty!"

"What do you mean, boss?" I asked, innocently.

"That stupid sign!"

I explained it wasn't Brad's fault, that he'd sent a private photo to one of his mates and it had got out, so it was nothing to do with him.

"Nothing to do with Brad? Nothing to do with Brad?! He's in the bloody photo holding the sign!"

That was a fair point, well made. The gaffer asked if Brad was with me. "Oh no, he's not here. He must still be in bed." That was a lie, of course.

Brad was sat five yards from me.

He was shitting himself all of the way back to Norwich. But by the time we got to the training ground, the gaffer was laughing about it. He'd obviously calmed down and seen the funny side, and Brad just had to put a few quid into the fines pot. It also probably helped Brad that Joey Barton had tweeted to say, "Don't worry people I've seen Boris Johnson from Norwich with his sign at the darts. He's irrelevant really, absolute no mark.....".

Brad was brilliant around the dressing room, and his will to win was unbelievable. If you needed a tackle, he'd do that tackle, if you needed a goal he'd get you that goal. A real leader in the group, and all of the boys loved him.

We still knew how to let off steam as a group, even in the Premier League. We knew how important it was; the desire to play for each other is what kept us going. We had a good bonding session during a week of warm-weather training in Spain. Played a bit of golf, did some really tough training, had a few beers.

One night we went to a bar, which just happened to have a bucking bronco. Because it was early in the year, the place was deserted, so the staff were delighted that we all turned up. We asked them to put the bucking bronco on, and Simon Lappin took over the controls. Beers + footballers + bucking broncos + Lapps = trouble.

Elliott Ward had had a few bevvies, so decided to be the first to get on. Lapps started it off slow, but you could see him whispering to the staff to find out how to make it faster. Lapps gradually made it quicker, the bronco started bouncing more, and Wardy was flying around everywhere, but somehow clinging on. Lapps was chuckling away to himself, and suddenly he whizzed the speed right up. The bronco started going mad and Wardy flew off. He looped up and over the crash mat and landed on the concrete! He'd scraped his arm and went ballistic, Lapps was crying with laughter and all of the boys were pissing themselves. The next minute, Wardy was sat at the bar with a towel of ice on one arm, and a huge glass of beer in his other hand!

* * *

It was also easier to wind up opposition fans in the Premier League. For a start, there were usually more of them. Also, your antics would often get reported nationally, which would make things much bigger. That happened when I was winding up the Swansea supporters ahead of our game at their place in February.

It started off with someone on twitter asking what I thought of Swansea, and I said something like, "Good team, nice ground, shame they're Welsh." It was completely light-hearted, and totally in jest. It was during the Six Nations tournament, so there was a bit of English-Welsh rivalry going on. But some Swansea fans took it completely the wrong way and it got picked up by the media in the build-up to the game, so I started using the hashtag GodSaveTheQueen. That didn't seem to go down too well.

At our hotel in Swansea a few of us had gone for a walk to a nearby car showroom, and on the way back we were trying to cross a busy main road. We took a punt and ran across, and this one car, which was nowhere near us, screeched its brakes and slowed down. A bloke wound down the window, stuck his head out, and shouted, "You're going to get beaten today!" And then he pointed at me, "As for you, you fat bastard, I can't wait until we fucking do you!" I laughed and said, "Well, enjoy the game mate anyway. Have a good day, pal!" He drove off swearing, with his mate in the passenger seat shouting, "Up the Swans!"

I took one step off the bus when we arrived at the ground and got absolutely hammered. Massive boos, getting called a fat bastard and a fat fuck, and lots of other things to do with being fat, as well as getting called an English c*nt and things like that. I wasn't bothered at all; could not have given two shits. It was funny. I just walked past politely saying hello to everyone, and that wound them up even more.

The booing continued when I walked out onto the pitch. Lovely stuff. They read the teams over the PA, and it was quiet until they got to my name. "Number 9, Grant Holt." Boooooo!

Every time I touched the ball, I'd get another chorus of boos. At one point I went to pick the ball up on the sidelines during an injury break and the abuse I got was ridiculous. The word fat kept being mentioned a lot again, and I was being called a disgrace and a fraud. I was just laughing, and pointed out to one of the blokes calling me fat that he was wearing a shirt that must have been size 5XL.

Danny Graham put Swansea 1-0 up with a penalty and their fans were loving it. That just ramped up the abuse. In the second half we were outstanding and I equalised with a header, Pilks put us ahead and then I got another. I took my top off to celebrate to show everyone that maybe I wasn't so fat, but I shot myself in the foot because I couldn't get it back on! All of the under-armour had twisted up, so it took me ages to unravel it and get it back on. That gave their fans something new to abuse me for.

We won the game, which took us to eighth in the league, and I absolutely milked walking off to even more boos. I did the press afterwards, telling everyone I'd loved the abuse and it had fired me up. It had become a bit of a pantomime, and I got a lot of tweets from Swans fans saying they loved the rivalry and would have loved it if I'd played for them. It's a shame I didn't have any Welsh blood, actually. At least I'd probably have been called up by Wales!

I got a load of messages that night taking the piss out of me for having my top off on *Match Of The Day*, but luckily I was in decent nick. I hadn't even been sucking in! A lot of tensing up, of course, but no sucking in.

I would say that win over Swansea was my favourite moment of the season. It had been the first Premier League game where all of the focus had been on me: people were saying that for Norwich to win at Swansea, Grant Holt would have to do well. So I took all of that pressure and told myself I had to stand up and be counted. I worked my arse off, brought the ball up the pitch, scored two goals, held it up and linked well. It was brilliant to be bossing a Premier League match, and feeling completely at home while doing it.

✱✱✱

To finish that season with 15 Premier League goals, and to have notched up 12 wins, was unbelievable. We'd all enjoyed every single moment of it, and proved you could get promoted and stay up playing good football. We were occasionally accused of being direct, but that was only in a few games when the gaffer felt that's what would work best. We didn't want to become predictable.

In the vast majority of games we played some terrific one-touch attacking football. We were a mix of silky skills and proper grit and determination. Most importantly, though, we were absolutely loving it, and that came across on the pitch.

Despite my goals, it was a real shock to be voted Player of the Season by the fans again. It was a big surprise when my name was called out, because we'd had some brilliant performers. It was the first time a Norwich player had won it in three successive seasons, and that was a huge honour. To have done it in three different divisions also made it an even more amazing feeling, because it showed the journey I'd been on. To have won it more times than the likes of Martin Peters, a World Cup winner, Chris Sutton, Bryan Gunn, Robert Fleck and Steve Bruce was very special.

I'd more than shown I could succeed in the Premier League, but it also came with regrets about it taking so long to get there. If I'd got there at 26 or 27, I think I'd have ended up with far more Premier League appearances and goals, and maybe a better shot at playing for England. But how can I have proper regrets when the fact I got there in the first place was barely believable?

MY TOP 5...
MOTORWAY SERVICE STATIONS

1. TEBAY, M6

It's got a proper farmshop, and because it's in Cumbria
it feels like being home.

2. CORLEY, M6

You need a good coffee shop, you need fast food and, if you
want the option of something a bit healthier, you need the
option of an M&S or a Waitrose. Corley has all of that.

3. WETHERBY, M1

That was my halfway point between Norwich and Carlisle.
I knew I'd broken the back of the journey when I got
out there.

4. CAMBRIDGE, M11

The best one near Norwich. Good to stop off at with an
hour to go until you're home.

5. WARWICK, M40

Ticks all of the boxes. Can't go wrong at Warwick.

CHAPTER 31

ENGLAND REJECTION, A BATTLE OF WILLS AND A TRANSFER REQUEST

2011-12

You'd probably think that after a season like that, I wouldn't be doing something silly like handing in a transfer request. Well, you'd be wrong.

It had been an amazing year, but it was soured a little by something else I never dreamed of being involved in: an England selection debate. Whether or not I should play up front for my country felt a long way from being binned out on the left by Colin Calderwood.

The talk of an international call-up had started around January. I'd got eight or nine Premier League goals by then and had played well in big games. With Euro 2012 coming up that summer and only really Wayne Rooney also doing well out of the English strikers, there was a lot of debate about who the manager Fabio Capello would take on the plane.

It was mad hearing pundits talking or writing about me being associated with England. Just the concept of me being spoken about in those terms was hard to get my head around. Me, and England? How do you begin to compute that?

Capello had watched a few Norwich games, and I'd heard he was interested in taking a proper look at me and John Ruddy. But to be honest, I firmly believed it wouldn't happen. Why gamble on a 30-year-old in his first season in the Premier League? Of course I really hoped I'd get called up – it would have meant so much to me to represent my country – but I didn't think it was a realistic prospect.

In hindsight I might have spoken to important football journalists to get the bandwagon rolling, as I do think that has an influence. But the thing that really killed me was when Capello resigned in early February. I remember saying to my mum that was bad news for me.

England had a friendly game coming up against the Netherlands at the end of February, and there'd been talk that I would get a call-up by Capello. Stuart Pearce was given the role on a caretaker basis, and I wasn't selected. That killed me. There were five strikers called up: Rooney, Darren Bent, Danny Welbeck, Daniel Sturridge and, unexpectedly, Fraizer Campbell. Now, fair play to Campbell, it's a massive honour to get that call. But he had scored one Premier League goal that season. One.

That was the last friendly before England's squad for the Euros would be announced in May, so I knew that was pretty much my chance gone. I'd been scoring goals and bullying the best defenders in the Premier League, so it did piss me off not to have even been offered the opportunity to show what I could do in training.

As soon as Roy Hodgson was given the job, I knew there was very little chance of me getting called up. I do think if Harry Redknapp had been given the role instead of Roy Hodgson, as had been widely expected, I'd have been given an opportunity. I've never spoken to Redknapp about it, but I really believe he'd have picked me. I think he'd have selected on form, and other than Rooney there was no Englishman in better goalscoring form than me in the Premier League.

However, heading into the end of the season I must have at least been on England's radar because they asked for mine and Ruddy's medical records. That gave me a glimmer of hope that maybe I could be on the plane. But just before the season finished, I got a call from my agent. It was bad news. He'd been told I wouldn't be in the squad.

I wasn't happy, even though I hadn't expected anything. I'd scored 15 Premier League goals, the second most by an Englishman, and had scored against Chelsea, Arsenal, Liverpool and Manchester United. In fact, eight of my 15 goals had come against the top eight. I couldn't have really done much more and felt I'd deserved a shot. I'd just turned 31, but was really fit and this was a one-off tournament. England could build for the future afterwards.

Rooney, Andy Carroll, Danny Welbeck and Jermain Defoe earned the spots. All good players, so fair enough, although Carroll had scored only four Premier League goals that season. What most annoyed me was that I wasn't even on the standby list. The only striker on standby was Peter Crouch and I thought having only one was a bit disrespectful to me, because I'd scored all of those goals. But I wasn't the only one to get left out, so of course it wasn't all about me. A lot of good players would have been feeling the same disappointment.

I didn't think Roy Hodgson had been the right appointment and didn't think England would do that well, but I still supported them in the tournament as an England fan. We were in Cyprus for David Fox's stag do that summer, and we were watching one of England's games in a bar. There were St George's flags everywhere, with huge TVs showing the game. I was thinking, 'It could have been me on that telly.'

I clearly wasn't the only one thinking that, either. England fans in the bar had clocked me and started singing, "You could have been there, you could have been there, you're sat drinking beer, when you could have been there!" They were doing it in a jokey way, and I just had to laugh and drink my beer. Some of them even bought me a few bottles and told me I should have been on the plane, so it was all good-natured.

As disappointed as I was, that moment helped me realise it was incredible how I'd even been in the conversation for a call-up. To have people singing that song to me, how on earth had that even happened? I'd had a great year, scored 17 goals in all competitions, Norwich had stayed up comfortably, I had three beautiful kids and I was a Premier League striker.

By this time, however, I'd handed in my transfer request.

***

I put it in two days after the England squad announcement. My disappointment had contributed to my decision, but it was a mixture of a few things.

Rumours had been going around that the gaffer might be leaving and that he wasn't happy with certain aspects at the club, and I'd also been waiting to hear back on a new deal for two or three months. I was 31 so had wanted a new contract to help the family feel more settled, and I wanted to be rewarded for having a really good first season in the Premier League.

I was told that nothing would be done until the end of the season, but my agent had told them I'd wanted it sorted before leaving for my family holiday. There was also a testimonial match lined up against Celtic for Adam Drury on May 22, and I wanted everything signed before then so it didn't distract from the game.

I arranged a meeting with the chairman and chief executive ahead of the testimonial to talk about my deal, but it kept getting pushed back. That was pissing me off, especially when I was told they'd cancelled one meeting because they were having another one at Lord's cricket ground during an England Test match. Cheers, guys. They were telling me they wanted to offer me a new contract and that there was nothing to worry about, but I thought I was being messed around. Why couldn't we just get it sorted? I was feeling disrespected.

I was happy at Norwich but the longer I was made to wait, the more I started to think that maybe playing for a fashionable, bigger club would have got me an England call-up. The rumours about the gaffer weren't going away either, so I started to take that into consideration too. After I'd heard they'd gone to the cricket, something snapped in me that day. I wrote out a transfer request and handed it to someone at the club who had the unfortunate task of passing it on to the chief executive, David McNally.

An hour later I got a call from a number I didn't recognise. It was McNally. He wasn't happy, funnily enough. Unsurprisingly, the club rejected my request. There was a meeting ahead of the testimonial, and the atmosphere was a bit hostile on both sides.

We eventually agreed on a deal, and the plan was to sign the next morning ahead of the testimonial. But I heard nothing from anyone, and my agent couldn't get through to them. So nothing got signed, which meant I went into the testimonial with all of the media talking about mine and the gaffer's future. I felt bad it was hanging over what should have been a brilliant day for Ads. I wasn't sure how the fans would react to me, so it was a massive relief when the crowd erupted when I came out. They started singing 'Don't sell Grant Holt', which was amazing to hear. I didn't want to leave; I just wanted everything sorted and a certain level of respect that I felt I'd earned.

Lambert left to join Aston Villa at the start of June, and Cully and Karsa went with him. My contract still wasn't signed. I was gutted when they left, but I could understand it. I don't think he was enjoying off-the-pitch stuff at the club anymore, and the lads weren't happy he'd gone. There was no feeling amongst us that he'd taken us far as he could. Instead, we thought we could go on to even bigger things the following season, so it felt like a real blow when he went. It was sad to see him go. We'd had a brilliant ride with him, Cully and Karsa.

Chris Hughton was appointed a few days later, and my contract still wasn't signed. West Ham, who'd just come back up to the Premier League under Sam Allardyce, then launched a series of bids for me towards the end of June, which Norwich turned down. That was tempting, of course. They were a big club, and it would have been a good opportunity to join a side who had top 10 ambitions.

My working relationship with McNally wasn't great during that time. We had a few heated meetings, and I enjoyed telling him he wasn't bigger than the club, and that he was no more important than a cleaner; none of us apart from Delia were more important than the club. I don't think he liked that.

It took until the beginning of July for everything to finally be signed and announced. I was relieved in the end, because it had become a battle of wills between me and the club. I can argue with anyone until I get my way, but that doesn't mean I don't like the person; it's just business.

In hindsight, I think I probably should have left at the end of that season. You just don't know how it's going to go with a new manager. It's no secret I didn't enjoy playing under Chris Hughton as much as I had under Lambert. Chris's training sessions were fantastic and I really enjoyed those, and he's a fantastic guy, but his defensive approach to games wasn't fun to be a part of.

The dynamic at the club had changed. Paul, Ian and Gary had been such a massive part of my journey up the leagues with Norwich, that I look back and think I probably should have left at the same time as they did. That would have kept it to those three amazing years.

Maybe if I'd gone to West Ham and scored goals for them I'd have forced my way into the England team. Who knows. I still had another good year at Norwich, and still scored goals in the Premier League and enjoyed my time with the lads who were there. But it just wasn't the same.

CHAPTER 32

DEFENSIVE FOOTBALL, YOUNG HARRY KANE AND AN END OF AN ERA

2012-13

I was happy with the Chris Hughton appointment when it was announced. Everyone said he was a good guy and you couldn't argue with what he'd done at Newcastle United and Birmingham City. You knew he had calibre.

One member of his coaching staff did raise an eyebrow though: my old friend Colin Calderwood was Hughton's No.2. I had to laugh. Football is such a small world that it didn't surprise me our paths would be crossing again, but it didn't worry me at all. Me and Colin had parted on good terms, and, despite our disagreements, I knew his training sessions were excellent. He was a good coach, so I was actually looking forward to working with him again. We had no problems at all with each other and got on great during that season.

Once my contract had been sorted I was looking forward to the year ahead. I didn't want people to think I was a one-season wonder, so I worked really hard to get fit to give myself the best possible chance. I was positive about the season, and the opportunity to carry on proving myself in the Premier League.

It was pretty early on in pre-season that the boys realised we wouldn't be playing the same sort of attacking football we'd been used to under Lambert. It was clear we'd be sitting in, getting men behind the ball and counter-attacking.

Most of the signings Hughton made were to strengthen the defensive areas of the pitch. We brought in Alex Tettey, a holding midfielder, two strong centre-backs in Seb Bassong and Michael Turner, and a left-back in Javier Garrido. They were all really good lads and great players, but you could see the direction we were going in.

I think the players who'd been there under Lambert found it a bit weird to have gone from a very attacking manager to a very defensive manager. Why hadn't we looked to continue with the same ethos that had proved so successful? Why change direction completely? But the gaffer had a good track record, and we trusted him to get it right.

I had a feeling it was going to be a tough grind of a year. I wouldn't be getting as many chances and I'd be playing a more defensive role for the team. That was fine, of course, because I was always a team player first. Even if I wasn't happy with my role, when I went out onto the pitch I would always give 100%. I might grumble about it off the pitch, or put my opinion across to the manager, but I'd never go out there and not try my hardest.

However, you won't be shocked to hear I didn't enjoy having to go and defend for 90 minutes. Ask most players and they will tell you they want to get on the ball as much as possible; to attack teams and score goals. Spending the majority of matches working off the ball with little hope of keeping possession not only isn't as fun, it is also mentally and physically tiring.

Chris's job was keep us in the Premier League, though, and he believed the best way to do that was to defend deep and look for clean sheets. It was his philosophy, and we had to respect it. There isn't just one way of being successful in football, and it's no secret a lot of teams have done really well playing defensively.

The start of the season went as I'd expected. We were struggling for goals, trying to sit deep, and I wasn't getting involved as much. That meant some people started to question my desire, especially on top of my transfer request in the summer. In October I was even asked in an interview on local radio whether I'd lost my hunger to play for Norwich. My answer was typical of me: "I've given up this year, I've decided to bin it off. I've signed my three-year deal and I thought I'd leave it this year, have a few cans and cigarettes and chill with the kids.

"It's a ridiculous question, of course I haven't lost my hunger."

Maybe I looked grumpier out on the pitch because I wasn't getting as many touches, but I was still giving my all for the team. The hunger was very much still there. However, I think it was obvious I wasn't enjoying it as much, and to be fair I don't think the fans were either.

I was never a bad egg, though; I had a good relationship with all of the coaching staff and I was always myself around the training ground. I didn't cause any trouble or just work my ticket. I was in the Premier League, and I wanted to make the most of it while I still could.

***

Norwich signed only one striker at the start of that season, a 19-year-old lad who came in on loan from Tottenham. His name was Harry Kane.

I'd seen he'd been on loan at a couple of clubs but I didn't know a great deal about him. There wasn't a big hype about him, and it's not like he was coming in with a massive reputation. He was quiet, but a great guy. A nice kid.

We played with one forward up top with very little support, and that was a big ask for a 19-year-old. My goodness he could finish, though. Wow. Right foot, left foot, bang, bang. You could see in small-sided games in training just how good his finishing was. He'd stay out and practice his shooting when a lot of people had gone home, too, so you could tell he was really dedicated and had been brought up well through the Spurs academy.

I was 12 years older than him, but I didn't feel I needed to pass on advice. We were different sorts of strikers, and I was always rubbish in training anyway so I couldn't give him any words of wisdom there. He often showed me up during sessions, but then nearly everyone could show me up in training because I'd get bored so easily!

Despite missing a really good chance in the last minute, he looked decent when he came on for his Norwich debut against West Ham in the Premier League. He also played well in the League Cup against Doncaster but unfortunately he did his metatarsal in the second half and that put him out for three months. We never got to see how good he could be.

You couldn't say he was going to be a world-class striker who'd lead the line for England, but you could tell he was going to be a good forward. And he was just a nice guy. What you see is what you get with him. He's humble, and appreciates playing football. There are no airs and graces, just a dedication to be the best he possibly can be.

***

One of the highlights of that season was our 10-game unbeaten run from October, which was kicked off with a 1-0 win over Arsenal when I grabbed the winner at Carrow Road. I think it was more enjoyable for the fans in the stands than it was for us, though. It was great not to get beaten, and we got loads of plaudits for it in the national media. In all honesty, though, we got draws against some poor teams during that run. It wasn't like we were turning up and playing good football and dominating teams around us.

We defended and defended against Arsenal and I tapped in a winner, and it was also great to win 1-0 against Manchester United at Carrow Road. The game plan worked: sit in and hit them on the counter. The problem was, that game plan never changed. We set up in the same way against Southampton, Stoke and Reading as we did against Arsenal and Manchester United. Regardless of the opposition, we would play exactly the same way. The thing that frustrated me the most that year was when we were behind in a game, we wouldn't change.

I remember having a big ding-dong at half-time at Old Trafford in March.

We were 1-0 down and we'd been battered. We'd won only once since December – in the previous match against Everton, when I'd got a 90th-minute winner – and we were getting sucked into a relegation fight. There was pressure on us, the press were turning a bit and the fans were giving us stick, so I thought it was a good chance to use that win over Everton, which was our first in 10 games, to get some momentum. I just couldn't believe we weren't mixing things up at half-time to try and get back into the game, and I spoke my mind to the manager. But we didn't change a thing, continued to sit in and got beaten 4-0.

After that we got properly dragged into the relegation scrap, but still we'd sit back and defend deep. Nothing changed. Teams had found us out, and that 10-game unbeaten run felt like a long time ago. I was getting frustrated, and started picking up yellow cards with silly fouls and niggles.

I was often saying to the gaffer we should be more proactive and attacking teams, because we had the players to be able to do that. But it wasn't his philosophy, and that's fine. He was probably sick to the back teeth of me coming to him, and we did have arguments, but we never fell out.

With three games to go we lost at home to Aston Villa, and suddenly we were in real trouble. We'd won only twice since the turn of the year, and now we needed to beat West Brom at Carrow Road in the penultimate match of the season to secure our safety. Lose, and we would have the daunting task of going to Manchester City on the last day of the season to get a result.

The shackles finally came off. Hughton told us to have a go at West Brom, and we tore into them. They didn't know what had hit them. I put us 2-0 up in the second half and we ended up winning 4-0, and the relief was immense. It kept us up. It just showed how good we could be when we attacked sides, and then the week after we beat Manchester City 3-2 at their place. They were massively on the beach, but Jonny Howson scored an incredible solo goal, and we jumped up a load of places to finish 11th.

It looked like we'd had a better year than the previous season, which wasn't true, but it was still nice to be up there.

Don't get me wrong, it was a great achievement to have stayed up. That was always the goal for any promoted side in only their second season in the Premier League, no matter how the first year had gone. Despite my disagreements with Hughton about the way we played, I'll never have a bad word to say about him as a person. He's an absolute gentleman. He carried himself brilliantly, his training sessions were fantastic, and, at the end of the day, his philosophy worked that season. His mandate was to keep us up, and he did.

I didn't have a great year – although I was still pleased to get eight goals – but guys like Michael Turner, Seb Bassong, and Alex Tettey had phenomenal seasons, and that was down to Hughton.

I knew in those last few matches of the season that they would be my last games for Norwich City.

In the back of my mind I thought I was just a stop-gap for that season, and the club had already agreed to sign Ricky van Wolfswinkel from Sporting Lisbon in the summer for quite a lot of money. That meant I would no longer be the main guy up top. I didn't want to be the person who did 10 or 15 minutes here and there, especially at my age. I wanted to play.

Melbourne Heart came in for me to take me to Australia. I quite fancied that, as did Fay, but I don't think they could get the deal right with Norwich. I went away for the summer, and was reading stuff in the newspapers about Norwich being keen to sell and that clubs were coming in for me.

I came back in for pre-season for a couple of weeks, and was told by my agent that I'd been touted around for a transfer. I hadn't been told that by the club, but at the age of 32 I could understand it.

While I was at a local match watching a friend of mine play, the club called to say they'd accepted a bid from Wigan Athletic. I was told the offer was good, and at that point I had nowhere to go really. I couldn't turn it down because van Wolfswinkel was in the building, and Norwich obviously thought it made sense to move me on.

Wigan had just been relegated from the Premier League but had won the FA Cup so would be in the Europa League. I was very tempted. I hadn't wanted to drop down to the Championship, really, but the opportunity to play in Europe and join a team with a decent chance of bouncing straight back up was a good one. It was closer to Carlisle, too, so it felt like a good fit.

I went up there, met and liked the manager Owen Coyle, and signed. That was that. My Norwich City adventure was over.

Leaving Norwich for the last time was sad in one way, because I was saying goodbye to a really good group, but a relief in another way because I'd had a frustrating year. But what a ride it had been. I left with a smile on my face knowing that the guy who had walked through the door at Norwich as a League One footballer, had left as a Premier League footballer. What I achieved, and what we achieved as a team, is very rare in football, and that will never change. It's something I'm massively proud of.

I got amazing messages from Norwich fans, and it just felt like the right time to move on. It had been a brilliant adventure that had given me the biggest highs of my career, but it was time for a new challenge.

CHAPTER 33

MANAGER PROBLEMS AT WIGAN, THE LEPER AND A PRANK CALL

2013-2016

There aren't many moves in my career that turned out to be a waste of time, but joining Wigan Athletic was a wrong turn. There was a really good group of lads there, but injuries and properly falling out with a manager meant I never got the chance to get going. Their fans didn't get to see what I was all about, and never really took to me.

I'd started with a bang, scoring on my debut in a 4-0 win at Barnsley. I was really fit and playing well, and got another goal against Middlesbrough in August. But that was as good as it got for me at Wigan. Five matches in, and I'd already peaked. It was all downhill from there.

My fall started in the second half of that Boro game, when I got smashed on my knee and had to be taken off. The bruising was so black that I had to wait for around a week until I could get it scanned, and I was out until October with severe bone bruising.

A couple of months on the sidelines isn't ideal when you're trying to make an impression at a new club. But even when I came back my knee was still hurting. Something just didn't feel right, and it was niggling away at me. The injury just wouldn't disappear.

Because of the constant pain, and with the mood around the club poor after a bad start to the season, I didn't really have time to take in my first European experience. It was against Rubin Kazan of Russia, and although I'm glad I got to play in Europe – even though we lost – it felt like a distraction at the time. It's funny how something as big as that can quickly become a nuisance, but that's what pressure does to a club.

Things had quickly turned sour at Wigan. Owen Coyle got sacked in early December and was replaced by Uwe Rösler.

This did not go well for me.

I've been told that Rösler thought I was chucking the knee injury because it was just bruising. Whether that's true or not, I don't know, but it would explain a lot of what was to come. I started in Rösler's first few matches, but the knee was still really hurting me, and meant I could play at barely more than 75%.

Out of the blue, I got a call from my agent saying Aston Villa wanted to take me on loan in January. Even more unexpectedly, Wigan were happy to let me go there.

Uwe said I didn't look happy at Wigan, but that wasn't the case at all. It was just that my knee was hurting. I spoke to Paul Lambert at Villa and warned him about my knee, but he wanted me in and said their physio team would help with managing my injury. In the back of my mind I was concerned that Rösler didn't think I fancied it at Wigan, but I hadn't pushed for the move at all. It felt like I was in limbo. Wigan clearly weren't going to play me if they were willing to get me out on loan, so I decided to go to Villa, enjoy it and get my knee right.

I knew I wasn't going to play all of the time at Villa – they had Christian Benteke, Gabby Agbonlahor and Andreas Weimann as options up top – but Paul wanted more bodies in and a bit of experience around the group. It was good to be working with the gaffer again, and it was great to be back in the Premier League. The physios were brilliant, and looked after my knee.

I had a good four months there. One of the oddest matches was when

Norwich came to Villa Park. We were already 4-1 up at half-time, and every time I warmed up you could hear the Norwich fans singing my name. When I came on with 10 minutes to go the away section erupted. I couldn't believe it. It was almost embarrassing, in truth, because Norwich were getting hammered. They were in a real relegation scrap, and the fans were belting out my name. That made it a weird atmosphere to play in for the Norwich lads, I think.

I didn't get a chance to score, but I definitely wouldn't have celebrated. I'd already made my mind up. I'd have been lynched if I'd done that!

There was an added element of drama to the match because Wes had opened the scoring for Norwich, but didn't celebrate. He'd been linked with a move to Villa during the transfer window, and I think he was in the same position as me when I'd left; he just wasn't enjoying his football as much as he had in the previous seasons.

Paul, Cully and Karsa hadn't changed at all in their few months at Villa. Their training sessions were the same, and they went about everything in the same way. There was one difference, though: there was definitely more pressure on them; more of an expectation to do well. At Norwich everything had basically been a win-win situation for them, but at Villa their fans expected top-half football at the very least. Paul had barely been given any money to make signings with, though, so it seemed like a lot of fans might have had ideas above their station that season. It was always going to be a relegation scrap.

The worst thing to happen while I was at Villa was Benteke snapping his Achilles in training. We heard a pop in training, and everyone looked at each other and thought, 'Oh shit.' We were devastated for him because he was going to miss the chance to play at the World Cup. That's the pinnacle for any footballer; it's what you dream about most as a kid. You just didn't know what to say to him in the physio room; he knew he was done. It was so sad to see, especially for such a young lad.

MANAGER PROBLEMS AT WIGAN, THE LEPER AND A PRANK CALL

✳ ✳ ✳

It was a good effort to keep Villa up in the end, and I enjoyed being in and around it. But again I was in limbo at the end of the season, because Wigan said I could leave. That was a bit of a shock, despite what had happened in January. To this day, I still don't know why Rösler didn't want me. He never told me. Whether it's because he thought I was feigning an injury, I'll never know.

I wasn't going to just take their decision and piss off, though. I had two years left on my contract, and we'd moved back to the area and bought a house. A few clubs came in for me who weren't offering me anywhere near what I was being paid at Wigan, so why would I leave for less money when I was a third of the way through a three-year contract?

Some might say that's greedy, but look at it like this: you move to a different city to work for a new company. Your wages are sorted for the next three years. You buy a house and put the kids into a new school. Then, all of a sudden, that company tells you to leave because they don't want you there anymore. How would you react? Not only that, but you have to go to a different company on less money and move 200 miles away from where you've just bought a house. You wouldn't want to leave, would you?

So my thinking was if no one came in for me and offered me similar money to Wigan, I'd stay – especially as they'd not told me why they wanted to sell me. Prove myself, and force my way into the team.

I got myself as fit as I possibly could for pre-season, and went in early with the fitness guys. I was really trim; the slimmest I'd been in years. I was even winning running sessions with the lads, which wasn't bad for a 33-year-old.

We were supposed to be going to Germany for a training week at the start of July. The day before the trip I got pulled into the office with Rösler and his assistant Graham Barrow, and they told me I wasn't going to Germany. Not only that but I wasn't going to play for the first team, and I had to train with the Under-21s. Oh, and they wouldn't be giving me a squad number. Plus I had to be in at 8am and leave at 3pm every day. Basically, they wanted me out of the building.

I told them I was the fittest I'd ever been and I was better than the other options they had. They wouldn't have it, though. They wouldn't say why they didn't want me there, but instead of getting angry I told them I was happy coming in at 8am and training with the U21s. Doing that didn't bother me. After all, if I'd been told when I was a tyre-fitter that I would one day be working from 8am to 3pm as a footballer, I'd have been ecstatic. I was on the management committee of the Professional Footballers' Association, so I knew my rights and reminded them of that. It always helped in that sort of situation.

I found out that a lot of people had been telling the boss to let me prove my worth, especially as I'd come back to pre-season really fit and showing my desire to get into the team. So I don't know why Rösler didn't take me to Germany to at least see what I could do; I just didn't get it. Fair enough if he thought I wasn't good enough or wouldn't fit into the way he wanted Wigan to play, but I was never told that. I would have debated it, of course, but at least I'd have been given an answer.

* * *

When I got back to Wigan, I wasn't allowed to eat with the first team. That meant I had to be out of the canteen by 9.30am, which is when they had their breakfast. I used to get in at 7.30am, half an hour before I was due in. All of the staff, including the coaching staff, would be having breakfast and I'd walk through and cheerily say, "Morning everyone!" I wanted to make sure I was still full of energy and positivity, so Rösler couldn't use that against me. I was trying to conduct myself in the right way and making the best of a bad situation.

I'd known a lot of the boys at Wigan for a long time through playing against them, and they knew I'd done nothing wrong. Some of them would jokingly call me the leper. Then I had a couple of more lepers join me in the same situation, who'd also been binned off from the first team.

Things got weirder when, out of nowhere, I was told I was in the first-team squad for a friendly at Rochdale. I couldn't believe it. Due to not being allowed to train with the first team I didn't have a clue how Wigan played. I hadn't done any formation work with them, and I didn't know about game plans or set ups. But I was thrown into the squad.

I turned up at the game expecting to be on the bench, but Rösler started me. Banned from first-team training for a month, and now he was starting me. Was he trying to humiliate me at my old club by throwing me in at the deep end and thinking I'd sink? Or was he just testing my character? Who knows. But I played really well, gave 100% and stayed on for the whole 90 minutes.

The next morning, I was back with the U21s. It was like the match had never happened. No one said a word to me about the game, or if it had changed my situation at all. I went back to coming in from 8am until 3pm and when the first team went to Germany again to play some friendlies, I was left behind.

For three more weeks I was with the U21s, and then, once again out of nowhere, I was told I was playing for the first team in a League Cup game away at Burton Albion in August. I still hadn't trained with the first team at all, and yet here I was being chucked in at the deep end again.

I got on the bus to the game, and was greeted with the most ironic cheers you've ever heard from the boys. "Here he is!" "Who's this lad?" "Nice of you to join us!" "Who's the new signing?". Everyone was laughing, because they couldn't believe what was happening to me. I had to shrug my shoulders and laugh.

I was on the bench for the game, and didn't think I'd get on. I didn't even have my boots on, but Graham Barrow told me to get them on and warm up. I did one little jog, and was told I was going on. We were 2-1 down, but I did well and got us higher up the pitch. Another decent performance, despite being in the bizarre situation of not knowing how the team I played for actually played.

I believe this was Rösler's chance to bring me back into the fold. I'd done well, I hadn't kicked up a fuss and I'd got my head down. Instead, the next morning I was back in with the U21s.

It was coming to the end of the transfer window and I was getting desperate for a move. I just wanted to play.

Huddersfield were on the phone and I had Neil Adams, the new Norwich manager, asking if I wanted to go back on loan. That was massively tempting, but I don't think everyone at Norwich wanted me back, so nothing happened.

I was left in limbo. I thought I'd have to stay fit, play with the U21s and then hope for a move in January. Although I was happy to go about my daily business, it was coming to the stage where something had to snap. It wasn't fair I was being treated like that, and there's only so long you can walk around like everything's OK.

It all came to the fore in the canteen when I was having breakfast. A few of the first-team lads were in early, so they came and sat with me. It was before 9.30am so I was fine to be in there. It was before my curfew.

However, Joe Parkinson, the U21s manager, gave me a wave and said I had to leave the canteen because the first-teamers were there. Me and Joe got on great so he'd obviously been told to tell me, so I pointed out I still had until 9.30 to sit there. We were kind of having a laugh about it, and I jokingly said the first-team pricks were to blame because they weren't leaving me alone to have my breakfast in peace. I told Joe that if Rösler wanted me out of the canteen, he had to tell me himself. They were his rules, so if he wanted to change them then it was up to him to tell me.

Rösler came down and, as he did every morning, he shook everyone's hands on the tables. Everyone's, that is, apart from mine. Unbelievable. What a prick. I started laughing out loud, and everyone looked at me.

This was the moment. Those months of being disrespected and messed around had bubbled up. I looked across at Rösler and said, "I knew you'd hang yourself at some point."

He asked what I was going on about. I told him that not shaking my hand was bullying and a disgrace. To purposefully shake everyone's hands apart from mine was deliberately excluding me in front of my peers and friends. I told him I'd be taking it further with HR.

I'd had enough. I'd been in limbo with no explanation ever since Rösler had come in, and it was getting worse. I wrote a formal complaint and handed it to HR to take further. Some might think him not shaking my hand wasn't a big deal, but it was the culmination of a series of incidents where I was left feeling like an idiot. As I said before, if he'd just been open and honest with me about why I was being left out of the first team then that would have been fine. All I'd wanted was an honest conversation.

Shortly after that, Chris Powell, the manager at Huddersfield, got in contact. He wanted me in full-time, but could only get me on an emergency loan until the end of October. Huddersfield were under a bit of pressure, but they had a decent side and I fancied it. Anything to get away from Rösler.

It was great to be playing again. We didn't lose for my first seven games, which included a 2-2 draw away at Ipswich. They were giving me dog's abuse. It was so hostile, but I loved it. It was good to feel like a footballer again.

***

In the middle of November, Wigan sacked Rösler. I'll be honest, I was absolutely gutted I wasn't there to see him walk out of the building, carrying all of his stuff with him. I was told he'd pulled his calf as well, so he had to limp his way out of the building. I really hope that's true, because that's a brilliant image to have in my mind.

There's not many people I don't like in football, but he's one of them. I'm sure he had very good reasons to do what he did, but he never told me them. If he'd given his explanations, I'd have taken it. But he didn't have the bollocks to actually tell me why he binned me off, and that's why I have no respect for him. If I'd been a prick, I could have taken it. But I always tried my hardest, despite the crap that was thrown at me. Him getting sacked also closed my complaint against him.

Just before his dismissal I'd signed a contract extension with Huddersfield that took me up until the end of December, so I had to see that out before heading back to Wigan. In December we travelled to Norwich, which was the first time I'd been back to Carrow Road since leaving. I started the game, and the fans were singing my name from the start. It was really surreal, especially when you're 5-0 down – as we were – and the fans were singing, 'Holty give us a wave'. You don't really feel it's right to do that when you're being hammered!

I thought I'd get a good welcome, but I never expected everyone to stay and cheer for me at the end of the game, so I ended up doing a lap of honour. It was nice to be able to say goodbye properly, and it felt special.

***

Wigan had appointed Malky Mackay as their new manager and he wanted me back when my loan at Huddersfield came to an end. I had one more game left, against Rotherham at their place on Boxing Day. Just after half-time I jumped with my left foot to try and dink the keeper, and I felt a slip. I landed badly, and my knee really hurt. The physios came on, and I tried to run it off. Bad idea. I turned on the pitch and collapsed. My knee was swelling like a balloon, and I had to come off.

I went back to Wigan the next day on crutches. Not the way I'd wanted to return. Mackay had been desperate to play me, and then this injury had happened. I couldn't believe my luck. I was in bed when I got a call from the physio, and he told me the bad news. "It's nine, Holty." I thought nine weeks wasn't too bad; I'd be back around March, so it could have been worse. It wasn't weeks, though, it was months. Nine months. I'd snapped my ACL.

I cried when I heard that. At my age, 33, I thought that was my career done. I was sat there, on my bed, crying. Fay was with me and was a bit taken aback because I hardly ever cried. I'd had 18 months of frustration since leaving Norwich, and just as I thought I might be back on track, I'd got my first serious injury. I told myself to get a grip, and braced myself for a long bout of rehab. There was one plus point, though: I could finally eat with the first team again!

* * *

The two things I most associate my time at Wigan with are injuries and Rösler, but I bet if you asked Wigan fans what they remember me for, they'll mention one thing: a prank call.

In May I was going through my rehab, when my agent told me that Burnley manager Sean Dyche had been in touch and was interested in me. Burnley had been relegated to the Championship and we'd been relegated to League One. Mackay had been sacked in April and Gary Caldwell had stepped up from being a player and moved into the dugout. It had been a nightmare couple of years at Wigan, so I was keen to hear what Dyche had to say. Plus, you don't say no to taking a call from a manager because you'd just come across as rude.

There was a problem, though. Sean Dyche was actually a teenager called Ben. He'd pranked my agent with a gravelly voice that sounded like Dyche's, and then he pranked me. About three minutes into the call

I started to have an inkling it wasn't Sean; it wasn't a bad impression, but maybe not quite gravelly enough! I actually thought it was funny. I told Fay about it and we both thought it was great.

I'd done a few pranks calls with Robert Snodgrass when we were at Norwich, so I thought it was hilarious. It wasn't so hilarious, though, when it turned out the kid had recorded the call and it was suddenly all over social media! Some Wigan fans thought I was a snake, but to be honest who wouldn't have been interested in moving to a club in a higher division.

It was an amusing distraction from rehab, especially as I was still about five months from my return. I finally came back in October, aged 34. It was good to get back, but it quickly became obvious that I'd returned too early. I wasn't right. I'd worked so hard to get myself fit, but my knee never felt in a good place. I was desperate to play, but I probably should have given it another couple of months. I had a spell on loan at Wolves – a fantastic club – but when I came back to Wigan in January they said I could leave. This time, though, I could understand their decision. It was almost like they were putting me out of my misery.

It had just never worked out at Wigan for me. I'd got injured early, had to deal with a manager I had zero respect for, and then got injured again. I was lucky in my career to suffer very few bad injuries, so to get two in two years at Wigan was just really bad luck. I wish I'd been able to show the Wigan fans what I was capable of, but it never panned out that way.

I'd already been thinking about retirement since the knee injury, so me and Fay had sat down for a chat about where we'd most like to live in the country. It was time to set up a base. The girls had only really known Norwich and we loved it in the city, so we made the decision to move back there. I'd been offered an ambassador role at the club, and I would commute to wherever I was playing.

I thought I probably had two or three seasons left in me, so I spoke to Keith Hill at Rochdale. He'd been the youth team manager when I'd been there the first time 10 years earlier, and now he was manager. He wanted an experienced head, and was OK giving me days off when I wanted to. That was perfect for me. I went there in February on a free, and we went on a great run but missed out on the playoffs.

I really enjoyed being back there, although my knee still felt uncomfortable. It was good fun being back in League One, especially as I was playing for a club I really liked.

The three seasons since I'd left Norwich had flashed by, and although I knew I was on my way down in my career, I was in a good place. I'd had my time in the Premier League, and although I wish I'd got there sooner, it was still something I thought I'd never do. So I didn't mind dropping back down the leagues; a game of football is a game of football whatever level you're playing at. I was just relieved that Rochdale helped put a smile back on my face after my time at Wigan.

MY TOP 5...
MOST IMPORTANT MANAGERS

1. PAUL LAMBERT

He knew how to make me better, and gave me the captain's armband to turn me into a leader at Norwich. He gave me the extra pressure to get the most out of me.

2. STEVE PARKIN

He gave me a kick up the backside at Rochdale when I needed one. He knew when he had to hammer me and he knew when he had to put an arm around me.

3. KENNY LOWE

He took me to Barrow and made me believe in myself again. He wouldn't let my standards slip at all.

4. PAUL SIMPSON

He changed my game at Shrewsbury. He gave me a bit more responsibility and got me back to believing I could go out and score goals.

5. EDDIE JARDINE

Without him I would never have been a centre-forward. He's the one who saw a striker in me at Harraby. Who knows what career I'd have had as a defender or a midfielder.

CHAPTER 34

SUNSHINE ON LEITH, FORWARD ROLLS AND ANOTHER LEAGUE TITLE

2016-17

At the age of 35, and with a dodgy knee, I wanted one last new challenge as a footballer. Something a bit different. I'd played in most tiers of football in England, I'd done Singapore and Australia, and now I was on the look-out for something else.

I got a phone call from Neil Lennon out of the blue. He had just been appointed manager of Hibernian, who were in the Scottish Championship. He wanted some experience and leadership in his squad, and asked if I fancied it. I'd never played in Scotland, so it gave me the chance for a new challenge.

I'd watched a film about Hibs winning the Scottish Cup the previous season, which was the first time they'd won it in 114 years. It was a brilliant film, and I remembered their fans singing The Proclaimers' song *Sunshine on Leith* at Hampden Park. It sounded amazing. I thought it would be awesome to hear the song in person; to be on the pitch when it was sung by 20,000 fans.

I went up to Edinburgh and I couldn't believe how good it was at Hibs. The training ground was fantastic, the lads were brilliant, and Easter Road was a great stadium. I got a flat on the Royal Mile, which was a lovely area. I'd lived in over 10 places in Britain, and Edinburgh was definitely one of my favourites. Really chilled, with plenty to do.

Despite being really happy with everything, it did take a little while to get settled. Fay and the kids were in Norwich, and, let me tell you, Edinburgh to Norfolk is a properly long drive. It would take almost six hours after games, which wasn't so bad because I took ages to wind down after matches anyway. It was driving back on the Monday morning for training that was killing me. We had Wednesdays off so I'd also fly to Norwich on the Tuesday evening and fly back Thursday morning.

All of the travelling was becoming exhausting, so around October Lenny let me change it so I could have Mondays off. That meant I could have a longer weekend with Fay and the kids, and then I'd stay in Edinburgh from Tuesday until Saturday.

That's when the Hibs fans started to see the best of me. My knee was finally feeling comfortable, and I was in good shape. I wasn't scoring many goals but I was playing well and forged a good partnership with Jason Cummings up top.

The standard was decent in the Championship, although some of the grounds did feel like Conference standard. One week you'd be at a tiny stadium playing in front of 1,000 people, the next week you'd be at home in front of 20,000 people at Easter Road. I embraced it, though. I'd been looking for a new challenge, and that's exactly what it was.

***

We got drawn against our Edinburgh rivals Hearts in the Scottish Cup, which I was thrilled with. I'd seen the derby on TV before and it looked really tasty. I couldn't wait for it. We were playing them at their place, and the build-up to it was ridiculous. I would walk out of my door in Edinburgh and within a couple of minutes I'd have a Hearts fan coming up to me and telling me they hoped we'd get smashed, and then a Hibs fan telling me to make sure we beat those Jambos. It was intense.

Outside of Scotland not too many people talk about the Edinburgh derby. It's all about Celtic v Rangers, but let me tell you that Hibs v Hearts is a proper battle. Both sets of fans love telling you it's one of the oldest rivalries in the world, and having seen it up close, it's fierce. There's no love lost between the two sets of fans.

Early on in my time in Edinburgh, I ended up in a Hearts pub and was told in no uncertain terms by the landlord to drink up quickly and move on. In half an hour it would be full of Hearts fans, and me being there would not have been OK. He didn't have to go into details about what might happen if we stayed, so me and my mates downed the pints and legged it out of there.

On the way to Tynecastle for the match, Hearts fans were banging our bus as we drove past them. The noise when we came out onto the pitch was deafening; you could barely hear anything out there. The atmosphere was amazing; totally different to anything I'd played in before. It was brilliant to be involved in a match like that after three years of frustration.

Tackles flew in, people were pushed and shoved. Hearts, who were in the Scottish Premiership, were horrific. They played so badly and we passed them to death, but the game ended 0-0. We rolled into the replay at Easter Road under lights. What an occasion. Really special.

We tore into them from the start and Cummings put us 1-0 up. On 37 minutes I doubled our lead. We'd broken swiftly, Cummings played me in, I took a touch to get it out of my feet and used the outside of my right foot to knock it past the 'keeper. The roar was deafening. It felt amazing to score in a derby on such a big occasion, and I took off on a run with all of the lads. I finished my celebration with a roly-poly, to mark little Erica's ninth birthday.

We won 3-1, and with all of the Hearts fans leaving the ground, they put on *Sunshine on Leith* over the PA. You had 20,000 Hibs fans belting it out, and it sounded phenomenal. Spine-tingling. It got louder and louder as we walked around clapping everyone and I remember thinking to myself,

'My god this is a big club.' We were progressing in the Cup, and leading the Championship. Things were going brilliantly, and my goal in that match meant I'd be remembered fondly by such a brilliant set of fans.

* * *

We beat Ayr United 3-1 in the quarter finals, which got us a semi-final draw with Aberdeen at Hampden Park. I'd always wanted to play at that famous old ground, and now was my chance. I was a bit frustrated to be on the bench because Lenny had wanted to go with something a bit different.

We were 2-0 down in no time and, fair play to Lenny, he changed things up straight away and got me on after half an hour. Martin Boyle put in a brilliant cross from the right and, bang, I crashed home a header with my first touch.

It was fantastic to score at Hampden, one of the most iconic football grounds in the world. Then I set up Dylan McGeouch for an equaliser with a neat one-two and we were back level. It was an amazing comeback against a side second in the Premiership, and we were full of belief.

With half an hour to go the game became really end-to-end, but Aberdeen scored five minutes from time off a cruel deflection. Gutted. There was nearly an amazing ending for us, with our goalkeeper Ofir Marciano coming up for an injury time corner and planting a brilliant header at goal, but their 'keeper dived to save it. He managed to cling on to the ball right at my feet; that was the final chance, gone. I had my head in my hands.

That was a massive disappointment, but we were proud of our efforts. We also knew we'd be joining Aberdeen the following season, because the week before that semi-final we'd won the league with a 3-0 win over Queen of the South. That was a brilliant achievement, and it returned Hibs to where they belonged after three years in the Championship.

SUNSHINE ON LEITH, FORWARD ROLLSAND ANOTHER LEAGUE TITLE

After the difficult few seasons I'd had it was fantastic to get a winners' medal and another title under my belt.

* * *

I'd loved my year there, and was keen to stay on for another 12 months. The fans were great, the Hibs half of the city was buzzing and I felt my body could last another season. I also fancied testing myself in the Scottish Premiership.

I'd been asking the club for ages whether they wanted to keep me on, but I wasn't getting an answer. I'd scored in a 1-1 draw in the last game of the season at home to St Mirren, and it was a real party atmosphere. I loved the celebrations, but I also just wanted to get everything sorted.

I headed back to Norwich with my future up in the air, and a week later I read on my phone that I'd been released. No one had called to tell me, which was really disappointing. I'd helped them achieve promotion, and we'd all been really close, so that left a bit of a sour taste.

I really enjoyed the season, though, and I was glad I'd chosen to go to Scotland for a new challenge. I felt they should have kept me on, as I know I could have done a good job for them, but it wasn't to be. That's football. I'll still always remember my time there really fondly.

When I was released I was pretty certain that was me done with football. At the age of 36, and without the offer of a new deal, that season felt like it would be a brilliant full-stop to my career.

CHAPTER 35

ONE FINAL YEAR, FAMILY MATTERS AND A JOURNEY'S END

2017-18

For the last season of my career, I returned to my roots. Non-league.

I knew I wanted to get into coaching – I'd done my badges – but I wasn't ready to give up playing just yet. There were a few league sides who asked me to come on trial, but to be honest I couldn't be bothered with that. At my age I didn't need to go through having to prove myself.

There was also an offer from India to go out there and play, but there was no coaching involved and I wouldn't be able to take my family. It was tempting, as I was always looking for new challenges, but it was at the wrong stage of my career for that.

Out of the blue, Ian Culverhouse called. He was manager at King's Lynn Town in Norfolk, and they played in the Southern League Premier Division, which was the seventh tier. He wanted me to come in and play as well as doing some coaching, which sounded perfect for me. Exactly what I was after, especially as it was close to home. My former Norwich teammate Simon Lappin was also joining, so it sounded like a really good opportunity. I got to work alongside Cully, who was a coach I really respected and knew I could learn from.

It was going really well, but a month later my old club Barrow asked if I wanted to be a player/coach there. They were in the National League, the fifth tier of English football and just one below League Two. It would be a step up from King's Lynn, but I was torn because I was grateful for the opportunity they'd given me. I phoned Cully and he told me to go for it.

He said I should try and coach at the higher level, and he was more than happy for me to go.

Seventeen years after I'd first gone to play for Barrow as a 19-year-old when it wasn't working out at Halifax, I headed back there. The plan was to be a coach first and a player second, but things didn't pan out like that. Our squad didn't have enough depth and we were struggling, so I ended up playing more than coaching because the manager Ady Pennock really needed me out on the pitch.

While I still enjoyed playing, I just wasn't able to perform to the standard I wanted. I'd had too many injuries, and my body wasn't always doing what my head was telling it to. Sometimes I could bang out 90 minutes, but most of the time I was feeling like I was done after 60 or 70. That was a killer for me. I wanted to put a proper shift in all of the time, but it would take my body three or four days to be ready again after a match. Every game seemed to make me feel worse.

There was no real recovery time between games because I was setting up sessions at 8am, doing the training, collecting everything in from training, doing a debrief with the gaffer and putting in plans for the next day.

I was playing, coaching, scouting, looking at budgets and plenty more, so it was a case of being dropped in at the deep end and making the most of a difficult situation. I enjoyed scouting and analysing the opposition, and the coaching was good fun. I learned a lot, but it was just a shame I ended up having to play more than I'd hoped, and that me and Ady didn't have the freedom we thought we'd get.

Despite barely having a budget, we managed to stay up on the last day of the season. That felt like a real achievement, and I was really proud of the boys. We knew we had one of the weakest squads, but all of the lads fought for each other out on the pitch. It was nice to finish on a bit of a high.

I had another year on my contract, but I knew my time was up. My body was telling me I couldn't play, and my mind was agreeing. I was ready for the next stage of my career, whatever that might be.

***

Playing football had been all I'd known, but my mind was made up. Twenty years after joining Workington as a 17-year-old, my playing career was over. It just felt like my time to stop.

I didn't know what the reaction would be when I retired. Would anyone be bothered? I hadn't played in the Premier League for four years, which is a long time in football, so would anyone even remember me? I never thought of myself as a well-known footballer, and still don't, so when I tweeted my decision to retire on August 24, 2018, I was amazed by the reaction. I had a brilliant response from people saying they'd enjoyed what I'd brought to football, and wishing me all the best for the future.

When you get someone like Henry Winter, the most respected football journalist in the country, congratulating you on a great career, it really means a lot. Maybe I'd done all right, after all. Maybe people respected me for what I'd achieved. I think I had a reputation where if I was on the team-sheet, opposition fans would think, 'Oh god, not him today.' They knew I'd be a pain in the arse and give their back line hell all game. I was surprised by the number of Swansea fans who got in touch to say they hated me when I played against them, but that they would have loved me if I had played for them. I think that probably summed me up as a footballer.

It's a bizarre thing to realise you've retired. I'd never add to my 157 league goals, I'd never walk out in a professional football match again, I'd never give another post-match interview. Then the enormity of the decision drops on you: hang on a minute, what am I going to do with myself now? Is it the right decision? I have to get a job! What if no one wants me?

I got lucky, though. Everything seemed to fall into my lap, which I was massively grateful for. Stuart Webber, the sporting director at Norwich, asked me to come in and help with coaching their young lads, I got the opportunity to be director of football at Langley School in Norfolk, and then BT Sport offered me punditry work for some of their live games.

It was a huge relief to know people wanted to work with me. It also gave me the chance to do something I'd never thought I'd do: wrestling. It started off as a charity thing, and it went bigger than I ever thought it would. I've always loved wrestling, right from when I was a kid. I model myself on someone like Triple H: a little bit of style, a little bit of aggression, a little bit of everything.

If I hadn't been decent at wrestling straight away, I'd have dropped it after the charity event. But I found myself being quite good at it, and it helps keep me fit (just don't tell my knees and back). I like playing a character, and I like the athleticism involved. It's good fun to play to the crowd, too. I must have learned that from all of the boos I used to get when playing.

Wrestling isn't my future, though. I've not got a specific goal in mind for what I want to end up doing. Whether it's coaching, or TV work or something else entirely, I'm letting it come to me now. I'm not chasing it. I'm just floating down the river and seeing where it takes me, which is a nice place to be; sat on a lily pad watching the world go by.

Some former pros can find retirement really tough, which I can totally understand. You're taken out of an environment you've known for 20 or more years and have to adapt to a new way of filling your days. Luckily, I've not found it difficult. I will always miss the day-to-day stuff of being a footballer, though. The camaraderie, the joking around at the training ground. When you see a group of lads celebrating when they're coming off a pitch having won a game, and what it means to them, that's what you miss; being in a dressing room after a win, sitting there with that feeling of having achieved something with a bunch of mates.

If I'd had to leave football entirely, I think that would have been tough. Maybe I'd have struggled. But I'm still in that football environment through coaching, which has made retirement easier. Plus, I enjoy playing footy at a lower level every Sunday. I don't think that desire to kick a ball around in a competitive match will ever leave me; it's all I've ever really known.

***

The best thing about retirement is being able to spend more time with Fay and the kids. I've even had a proper family Christmas without having to rush off. It reminded me of being little, and my dad making me, Steven and Rachael walk backwards into the living room to see our presents under the tree.

Family has been such a massive part of my life and career. I think they're all proud of what I achieved in football – they wouldn't tell me, of course, they're not soppy – and that's what's most important to me. I'm so lucky that I've basically got two families all rolled into one. My mum, brother and sister, and my uncles, nephews and cousins are all up in Cumbria. They've always been so supportive, and although we've never been a family to have to talk every day on the phone, we're all really close.

Fay's whole family has been such a massive part of my life, too. They've all been there for me when I've needed it. I'm very lucky to have had Fay's dad Paul to help guide me, too. He's been great, especially after I lost my dad so young. He never replaced my dad, he's just always been there if I needed someone to listen or needed help with anything.

When I met him for the first time, back at the turn of the century, he asked me what I wanted to be. I said, "I'm going to be a footballer." Fay always tells me that after I left, her dad had a right good chuckle about that. "He thinks he's going to be a footballer! He's deluded!"

He's been really important for me, and I don't think he realises that. He'll be sat reading this, saying out loud, "Don't be such a softie!"

ONE FINAL YEAR, FAMILY MATTERS AND A JOURNEY'S END

From the ninth tier of English football right through to the Premier League, my family was with me the whole way. It was a brilliant adventure, and one that would have been nothing without them.

* * *

A former professional footballer. That's what I am now, and it took a little while to get used to that. To be honest, though, it also took a while to get used to being a professional footballer. So to even be able to call myself a former pro counts as an achievement in my eyes!

My journey from becoming a pro to becoming a former pro wasn't conventional, and it was full of bumps and bruises along the way, but I don't think I'd change it even if I could. Maybe it would have been nice to have been spotted at a young age and taken into a top academy, but I'd have been a very different footballer. Not necessarily a worse one or a better one, but absolutely a different one. This book would have told a very different story.

I'd never have known what it was like, and what it means, to be a non-league footballer desperate to win matches in order to help get bonuses for your teammates. I'd never have had the incredible experiences of going to Perth or playing football in Singapore. I'd never have learned to grapple and fight for everything. I'd never have had to work while trying to make my way in the game.

That's why I wouldn't change a thing; it made me who I am today. From start to end, my journey was a real football life.

EPILOGUE
A LETTER TO MYSELF

Dear Grant

Hi 21-year-old Grant. This is Grant, aged 38. No, really. It is. Bet you're surprised to hear from me!

I'm writing to you because I remember what it was like at 21. It didn't go well at Halifax, you feel messed around by Carlisle and you're sick of going on trials that end up nowhere. It's become a waste of time, and you've turned your back on professional football. You just can't be bothered with it anymore, can you? It was a nice dream while it lasted, eh?

I'm here to tell you to be patient.

Don't give up. Just follow the journey. Enjoy the adventure. Don't set targets. Let things happen and follow your instinct. Remember that feeling you had when you scored at Wembley in the Smiths Crisps final aged just 11? Well, you'll have that again. Loads of times. Because, and I don't want to spoil all of the surprises for you, you're going to go from sitting on your stacker at the warehouse to walking out at Anfield as captain of Norwich City Football Club in the Premier League. That's right. The Premier League. I'm not even joking. There's a chance you might score in front of the Kop, but that's for you to find out.

You'll play against Rio Ferdinand and Steven Gerrard, and get on the same scoresheet as Paul Scholes and Ryan Giggs. Seriously! Scholes and Giggsy! You'll love winding up the opposition (nothing changes there). You'll have newspapers and TV channels debating whether you should play for England. Honestly!

It'll be a thrilling ride. Just watch out for groups of tourists chasing you down the street, and be careful around offended Swansea fans. Maybe pack some extra shin pads when you play against Carlisle for Norwich City, and stick to just one bottle of red after you've been sent off against Brentford.

Most importantly, just go out there and love absolutely every second of it. You'll be happy at nearly every club you play for (try and avoid Uwe Rösler though), and you'll enjoy the company and camaraderie of your teammates everywhere you go. Especially when they're being attacked by swans on the pitch or stealing your well-earned bath.

There will be disappointments, but don't worry about them. They will lead to better times. Don't put too much pressure on yourself, just go onto the pitch like you're playing Sunday football. Go for every header, make every tackle, never give a defender a moment's peace. Don't stop enjoying it, and when you do, move on.

You won't believe this, but you'll also end up being a wrestler. An actual wrestler. Remember learning the DDT wrestling move on Steven in the bedroom when you were a kid? Well, that'll come in handy.

You're always going to miss Dad. That'll never change. He'll be proud of you, though. He'll be looking down on you and loving every single thing you achieve as a footballer. Apart from scoring against Leeds United. That'll wind him up!

Also, man to younger man, Fay's a keeper. The best thing that ever happened to you. One word of advice, though: maybe stock up on car snacks in December 2006. They'll come in handy when driving Fay to hospital for the birth of your first daughter. You'll thank me later. And, yes, I did say *first* daughter. You'll have your hands full! But you'll be the happiest dad in the world.

Towards the end of your career you'll occasionally wonder if you could have done even better if you'd looked after yourself a little bit more when you were younger. You'll think that maybe you could have not eaten so many battered sausages, chips and curry fried rice before matches. Forget that, though. Don't think that. Keep eating those chips and always remember what you achieved, and how far you climbed, doing it your way.

I bet you're reading this thinking what I'm saying is all bollocks. Trust me, though. You'll have the absolute best of times and, most importantly, you'll do it all with a smile on your face.

All the best,

Grant

ACKNOWLEDGMENTS

I'd like to thank every person in football who I've been involved with. All of the fans who ever cheered, booed, screamed, abused, heckled and loved me, because without you the journey would have been nowhere as fun. I've always said football is and always will be about the fans.

Thank you to everyone I've played football with. From the Sunday morning to the Premier League and up until now, thank you for being a part of my journey and my football career. It doesn't matter what level you are, you all contributed to where I ended up. I hope there's a story about me in the back of your mind that makes you laugh from when we played together. If there isn't, why not?

To all of the managers, coaches and staff at every club I've played at, thank you for your help, guidance and support. All of what I achieved was made a lot easier by the little things you helped me with day in, day out. There's too many to name, but you know who you are. With 17 professional clubs, numerous sides at kids' football, and too many headers in my career, please forgive me if I've forgotten to mention you!

I'd like to thank Dan Brigham for taking the time to sit with me and listen to me bang on about myself for months. As a Norwich fan, I don't think he ever thought he'd be sat there wondering what to do with himself while I was crying about my dad! Thank you for your time and company while putting this book together.

And of course, thanks to all of my family members across the board. Without your help from the day I was born until now, and without your advice, your criticism, your joking and your kicks up the arse, without all of that none of this would have been possible